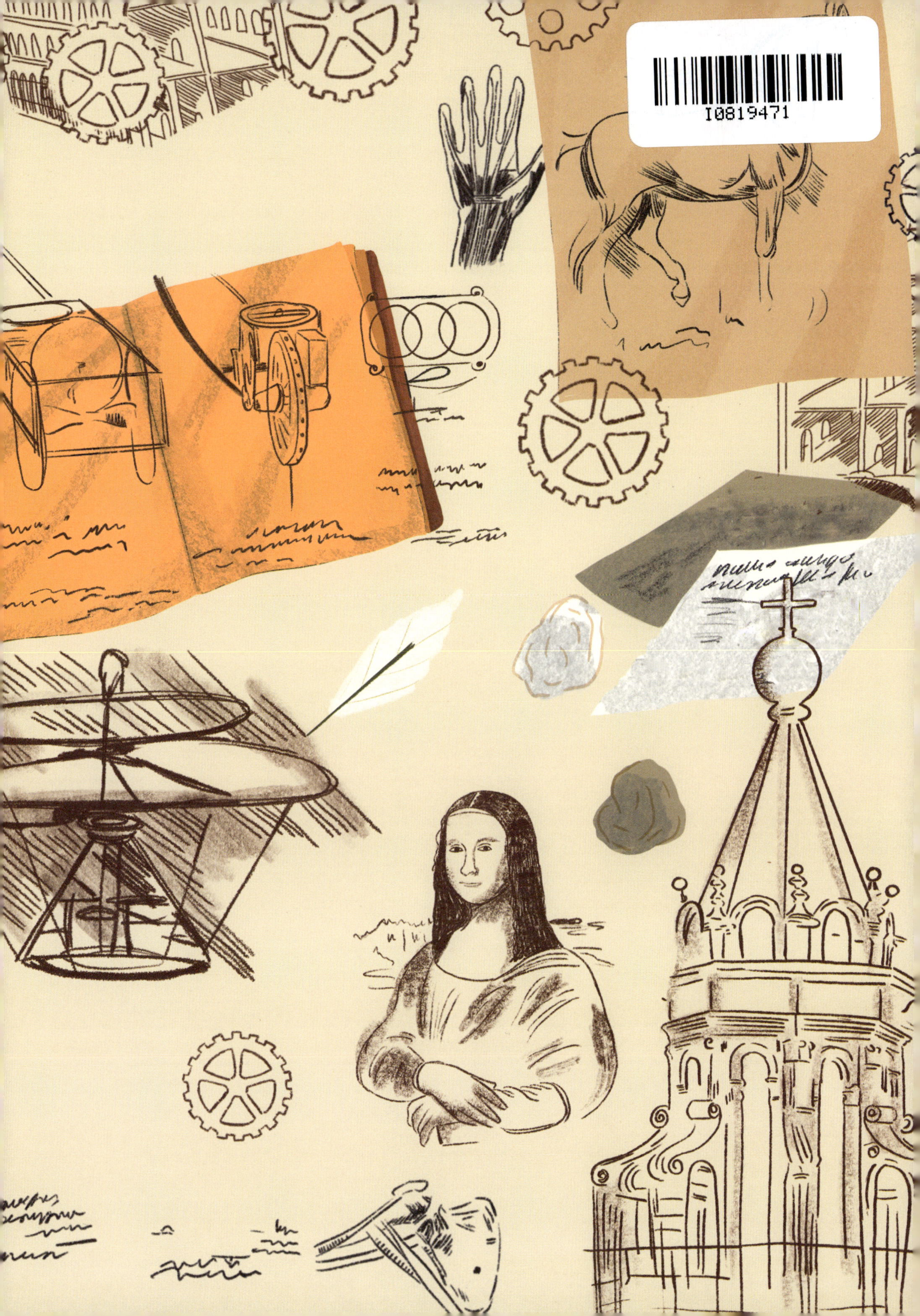
I0819471

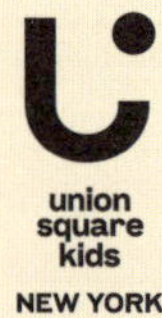

ISBN 978-1-4549-6169-7

Library of Congress Control Number: 2025024755

Union Square Kids books may be purchased in bulk for business, educational, or promotional use. For more information, please contact your local bookseller or the Hachette Book Group's Special Markets department at special.markets@hbgusa.com.

Printed in Guangdong, China

Lot #:
2 4 6 8 10 9 7 5 3 1

08/25

unionsquareandco.com

Text by Wil Mara
Book design by Clarisse Hassan
Edited by Sarah Carpenter

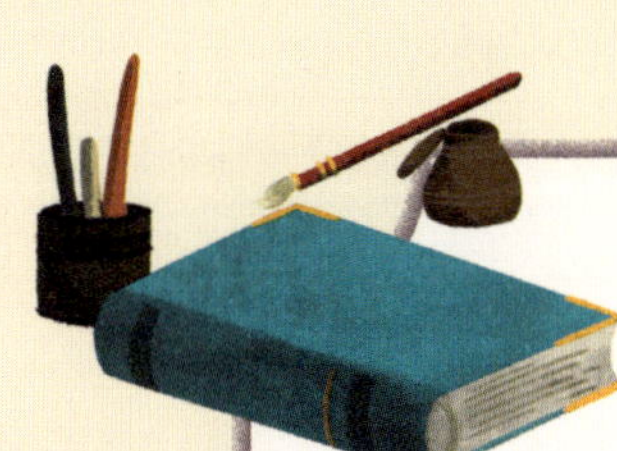

For my girls, who make it all worthwhile.
—W.M.

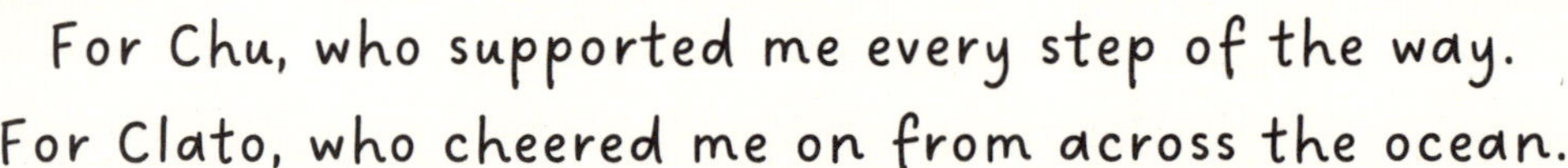

For Chu, who supported me every step of the way.
For Clato, who cheered me on from across the ocean.
—L.M.

5 Minute Genius Stories

LEONARDO DA VINCI

Written by Wil Mara

Illustrated by Laura Martín

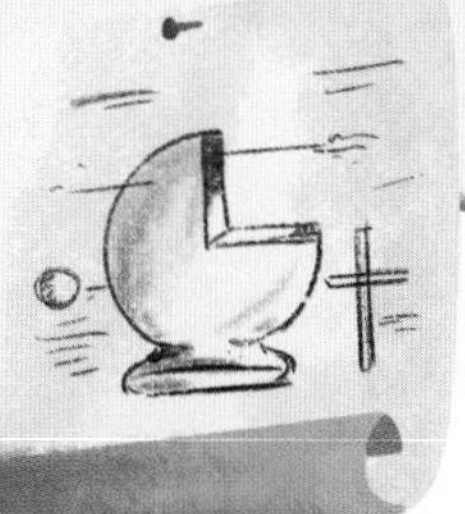

How to use this book

In this book you'll find **ten genius stories** to read, each one just **5 minutes long**.

At the end of each story, explore an informative **"all about"** spread.

Want to learn more? Turn to the back of the book to discover a **timeline of key events**.

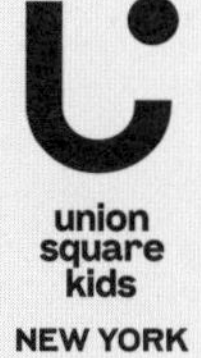

union square kids

NEW YORK

WHO WAS LEONARDO DA VINCI?

Leonardo da Vinci is best known as a world-famous artist. But he was also a successful inventor, musician, architect, engineer, scientist, and mapmaker. Follow his path to becoming a Renaissance icon.

THE GREAT FOSSIL FIND

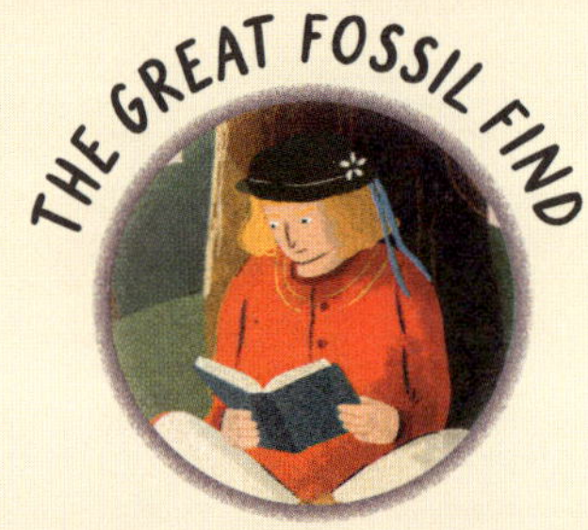

Leonardo is a curious boy who will carefully study anything that interests him.

Page 8

THE PAINTING PIONEER

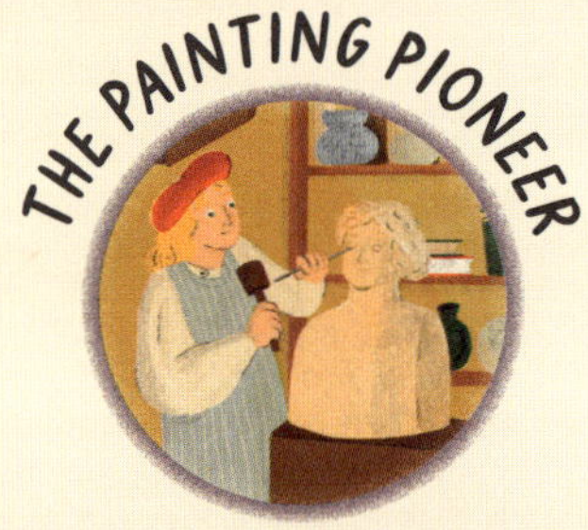

Young Leonardo is accepted as an apprentice by master Andrea del Verrocchio.

Page 18

THE MASTER ON THE HILL

Leonardo sketches a landscape of the Arno River. Pictures of landscapes are fairly rare at the time.

Page 28

THE GREAT INVENTOR

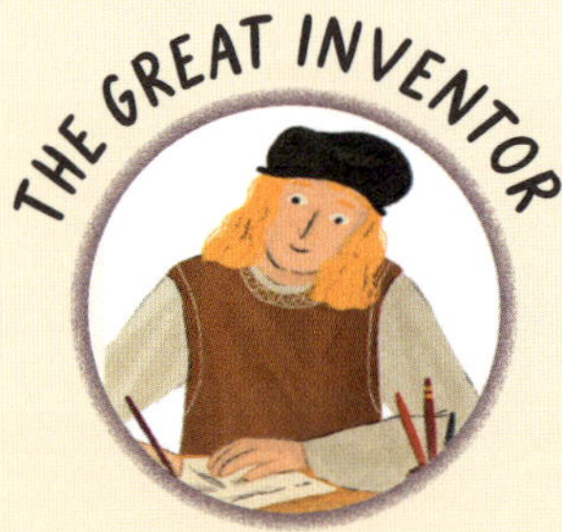

Leonardo makes improvements on a device that measures long distances while traveling.

Page 38

A note to the reader: Leonardo was naturally left-handed, but was taught to write with his right hand. Scholars today believe this made him ambidextrous, which means he was equally capable working with either hand. The illustrations in this book show Leonardo using both his left and right hands to write and create.

WHICH 5-MINUTE GENIUS STORY WILL YOU READ TODAY?

THE GREAT FOSSIL FIND

A Curious Young Boy

One of Leonardo's favorite interests was nature. He would spend time carefully studying animals and plants. One day, this led to an amazing discovery.

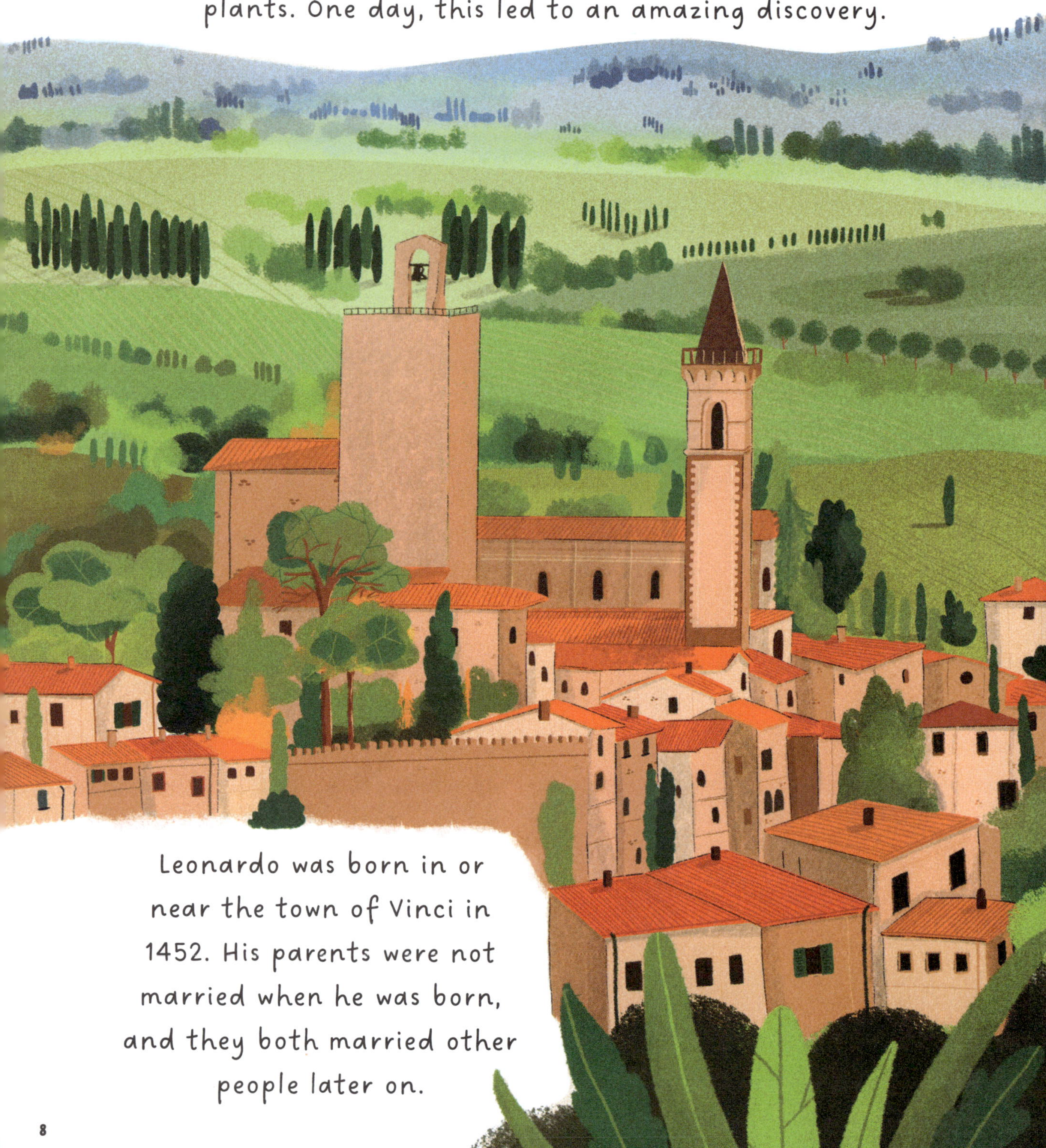

Leonardo was born in or near the town of Vinci in 1452. His parents were not married when he was born, and they both married other people later on.

Growing up, Leonardo spent time with both of his parents. But he never felt like he was fully part of either family.

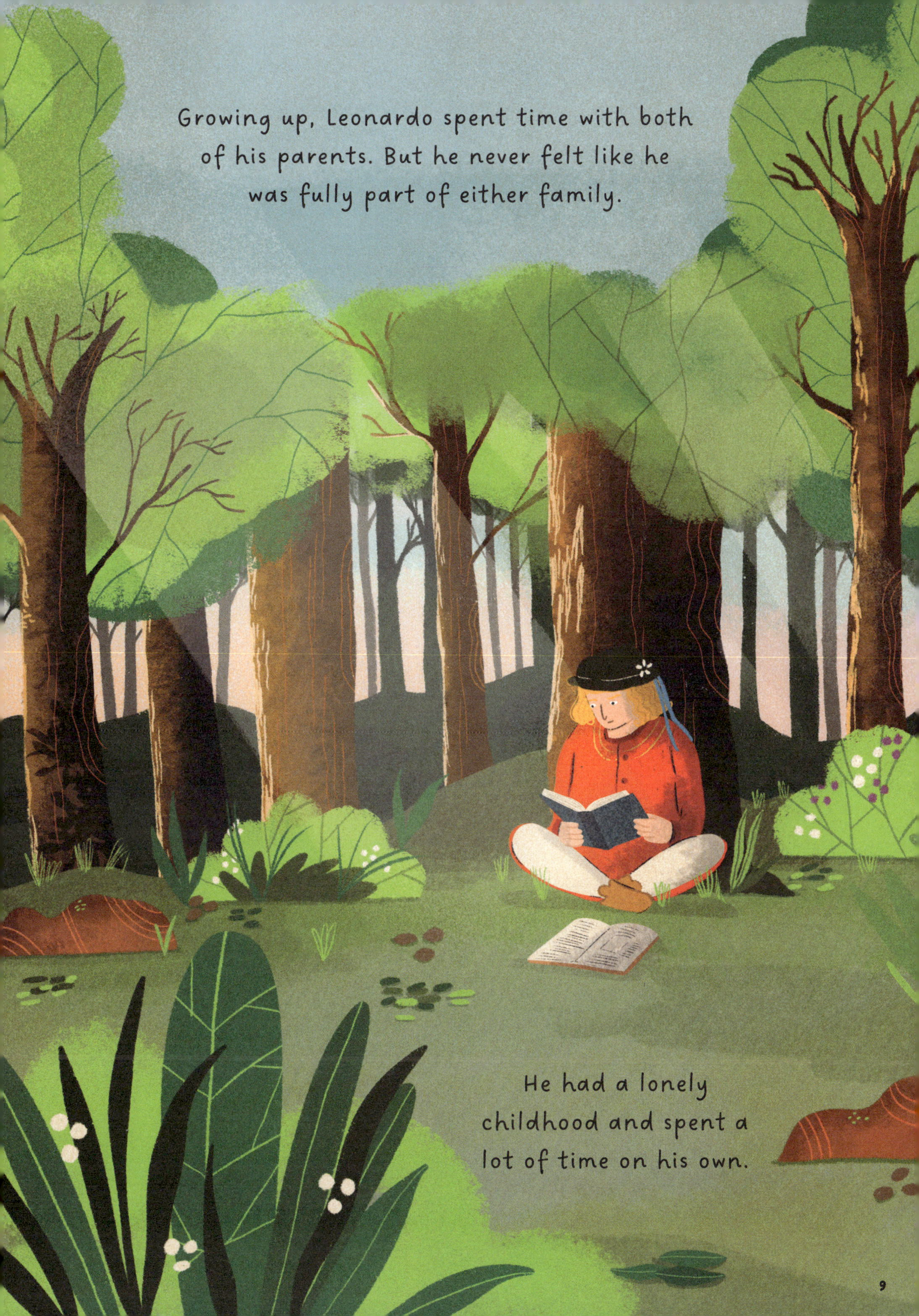

He had a lonely childhood and spent a lot of time on his own.

As Leonardo grew, his intellect began to develop quickly. Leonardo's mind would one day become one of the greatest in history.

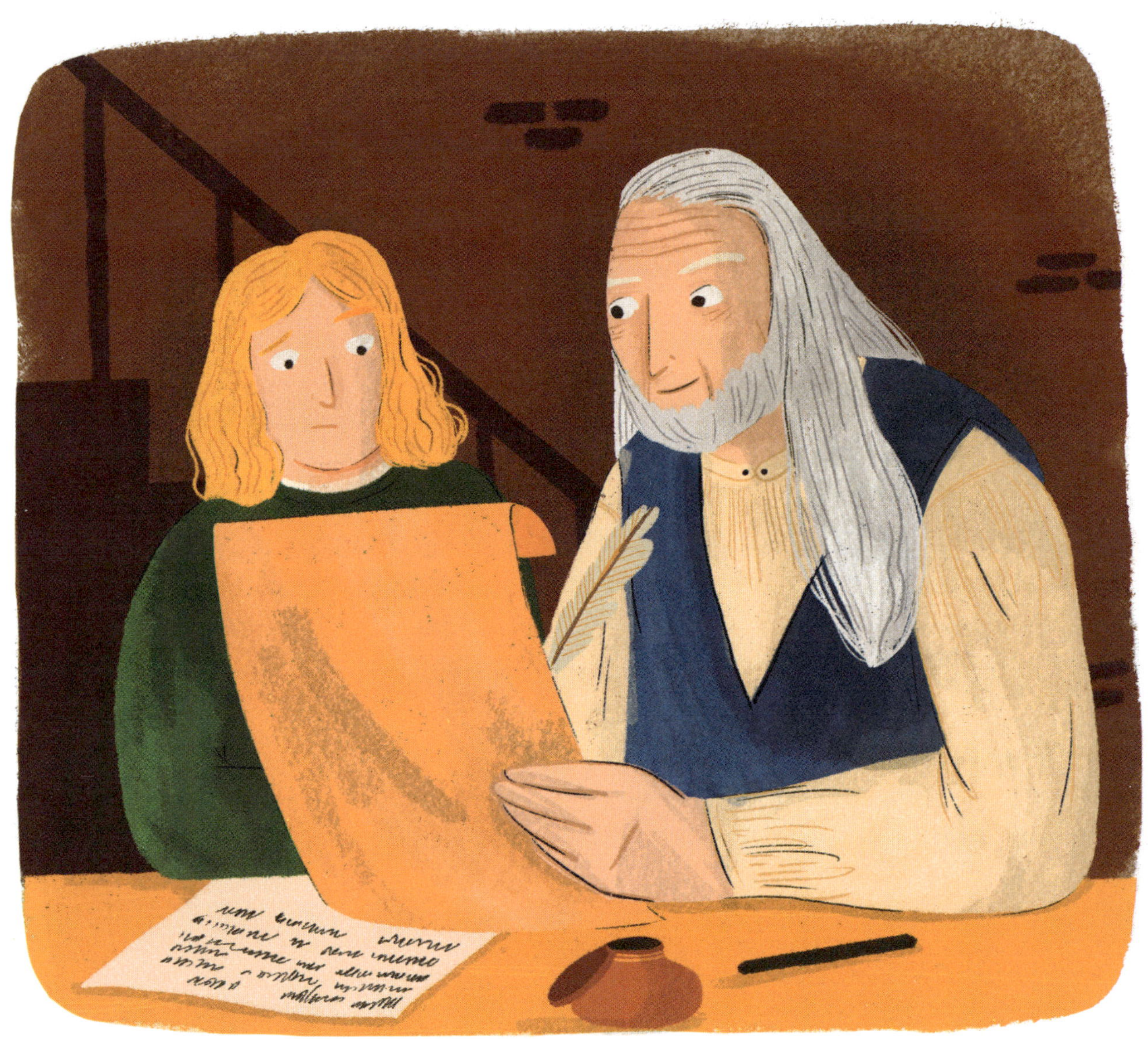

His father was a notary, which is someone who made sure people signed important documents correctly. But young Leonardo had no interest in notary work.

He was fascinated by too many other things. His curiosity was one of the keys to his growing genius. Leonardo learned about the world by watching, thinking about what he saw, and making notes.

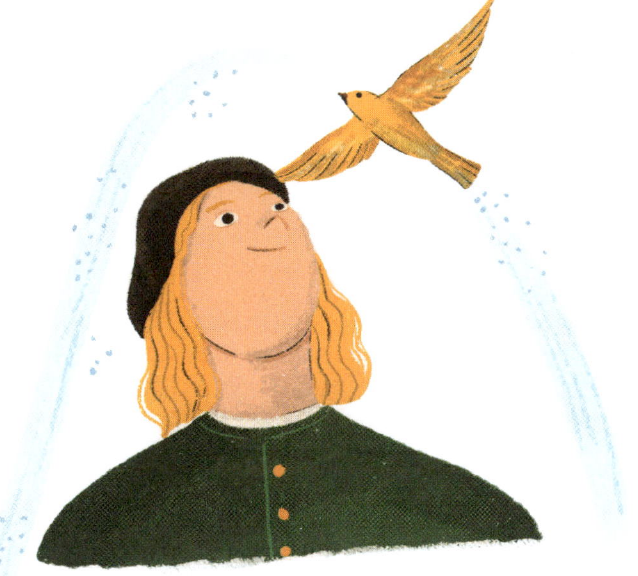

Though he was born left-handed, like most children of the time, Leonardo was taught to write with his right hand, so he could write well with both.

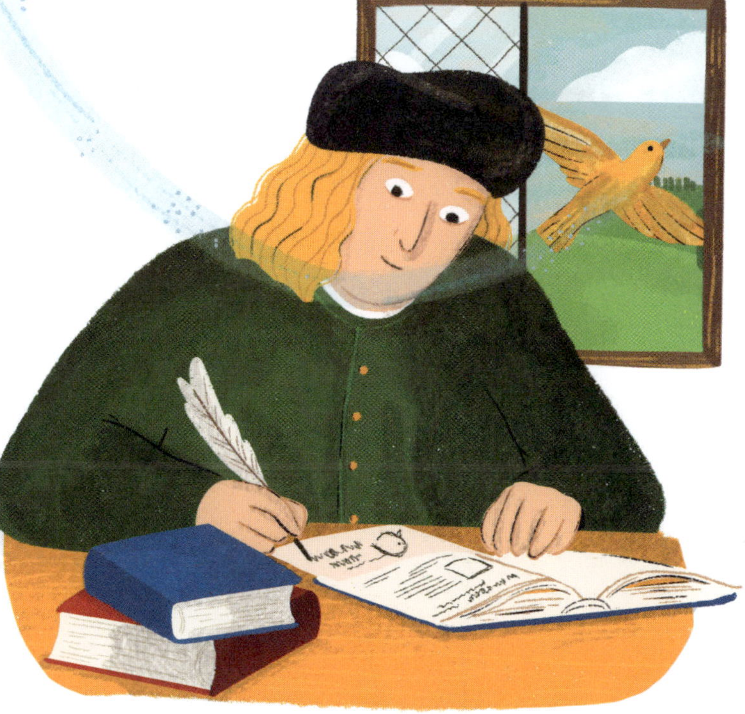

He could sit for hours and study something until he felt he had a better understanding of it.

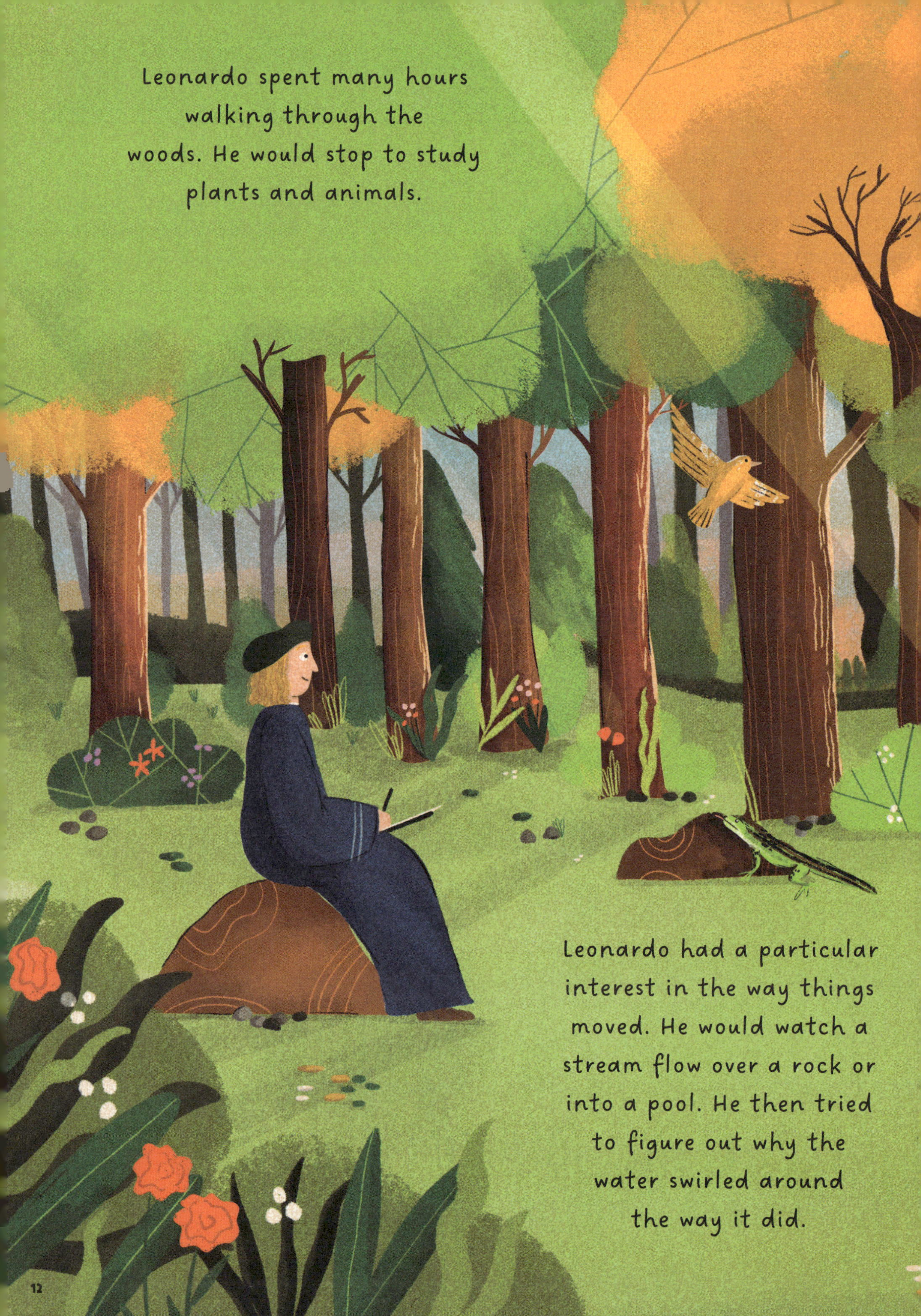

Leonardo spent many hours walking through the woods. He would stop to study plants and animals.

Leonardo had a particular interest in the way things moved. He would watch a stream flow over a rock or into a pool. He then tried to figure out why the water swirled around the way it did.

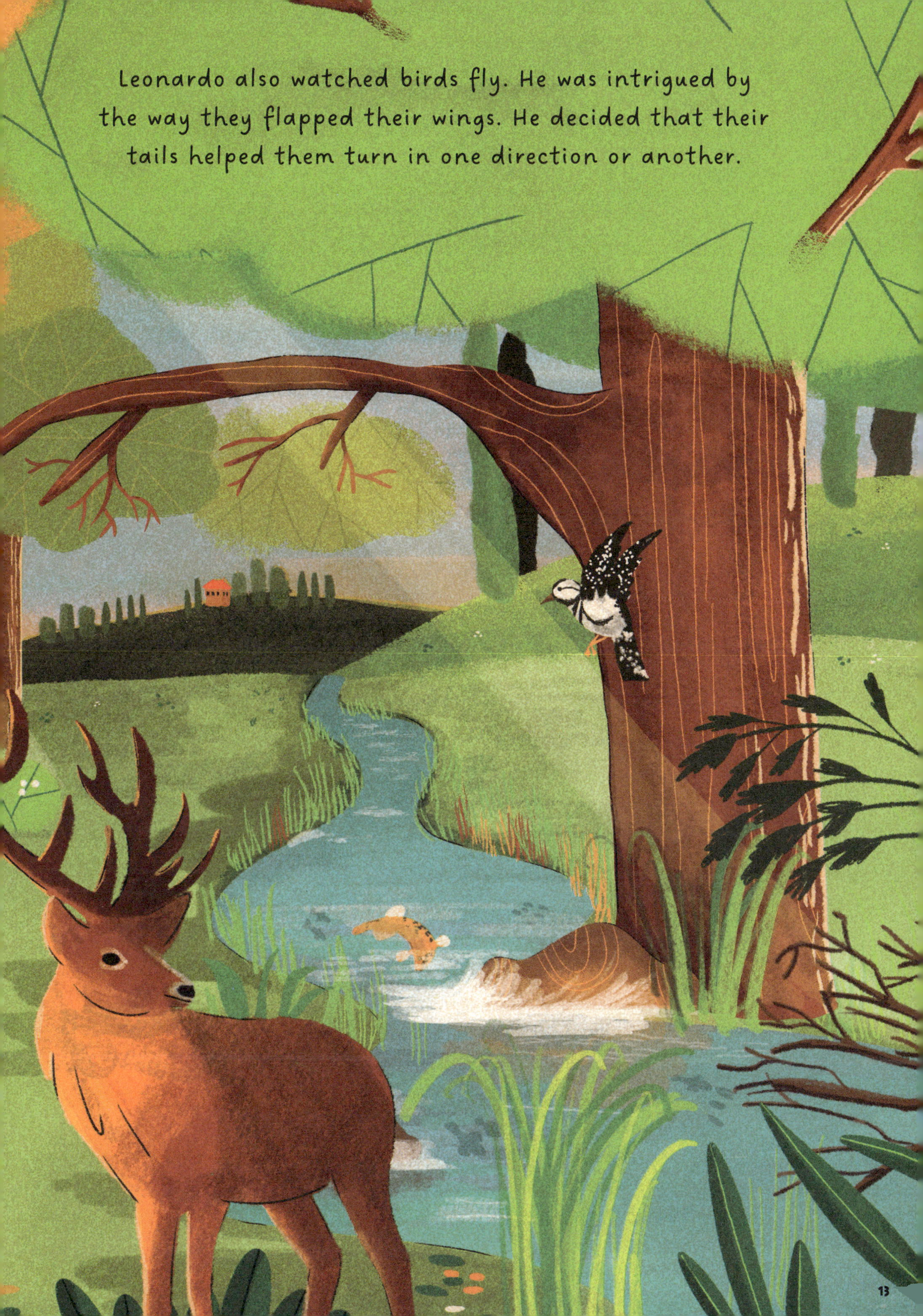

Leonardo also watched birds fly. He was intrigued by the way they flapped their wings. He decided that their tails helped them turn in one direction or another.

While wandering around the hills one day, Leonardo came across a cave. Inside, he discovered something amazing—the fossil of a whale!

Leonardo imagined that the mighty animal used to sink ships with the strength of its tail.

Leonardo figured it must have been thousands of years since the whale died. He realized that a vast ocean must have once been there, but it had since dried up.

Through carefully watching and wondering about nature, Leonardo made leaps of discovery that no one else ever had.

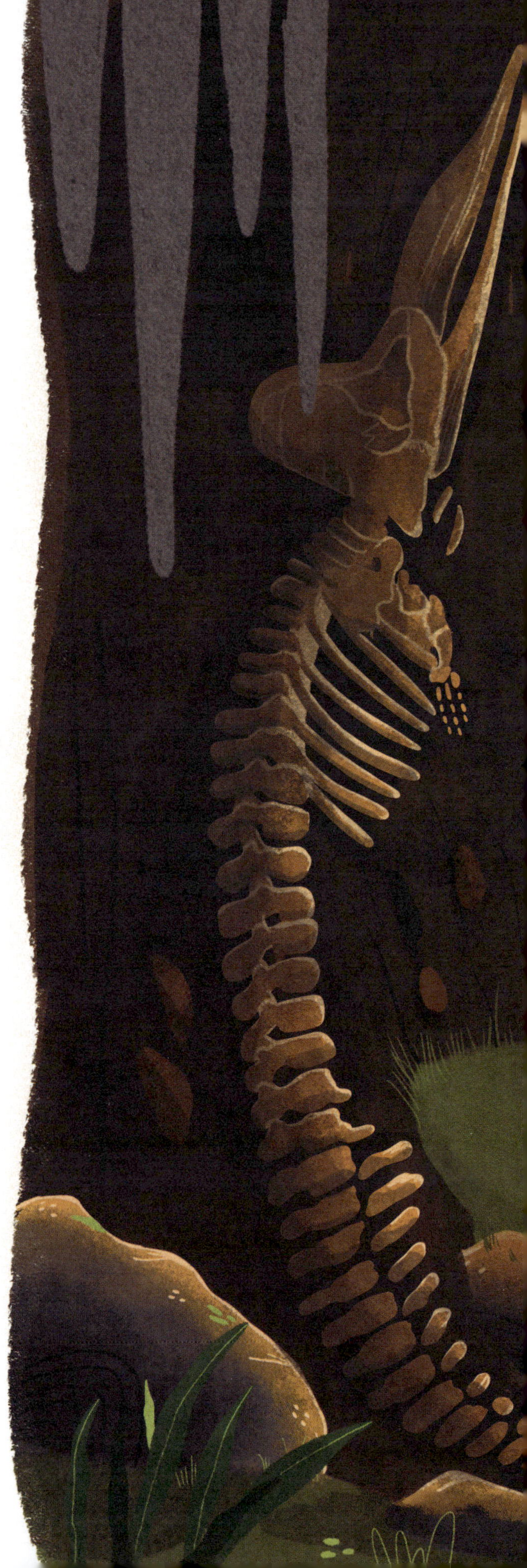

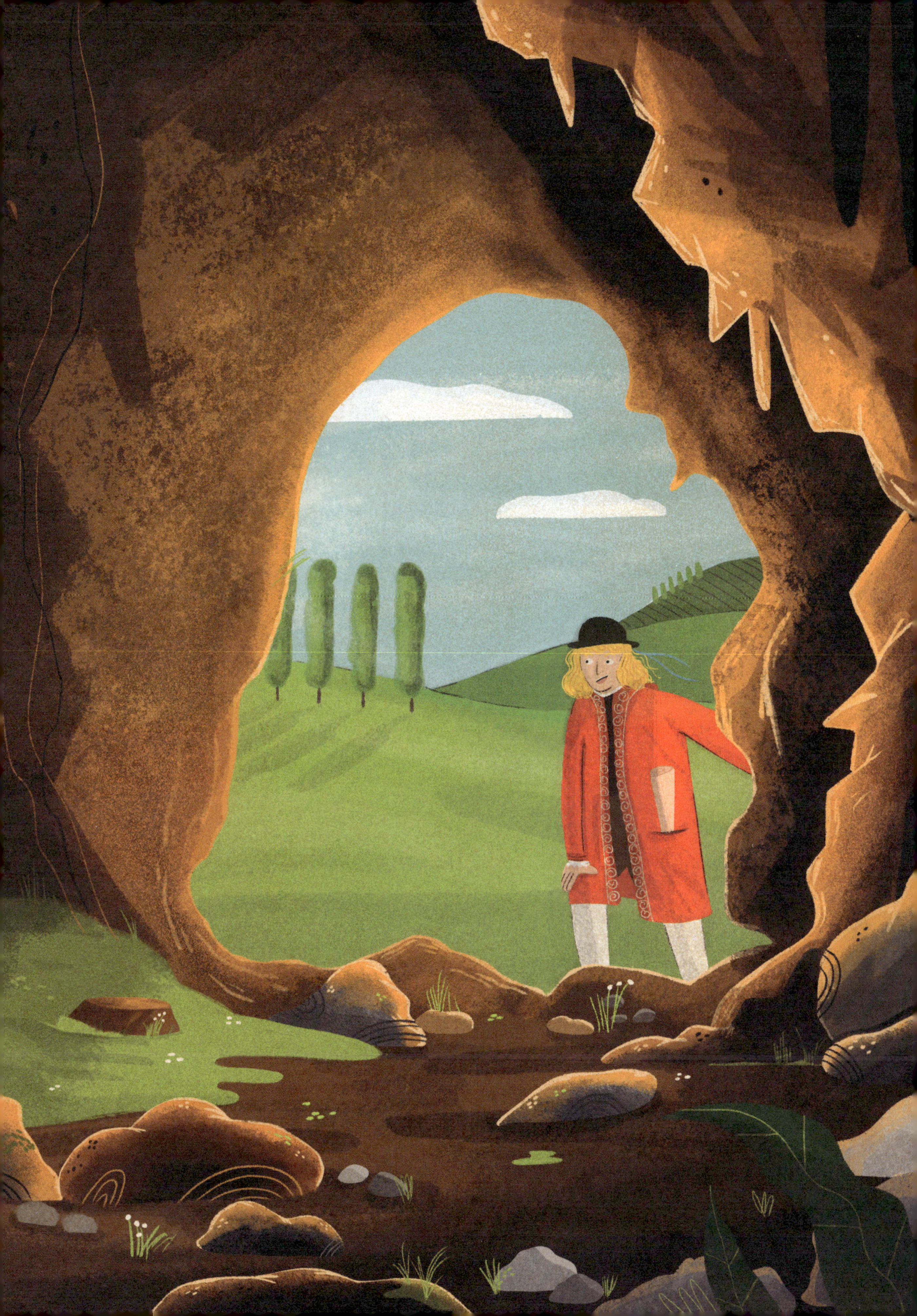

What are FOSSILS?

Leonardo was one of the first people in the world to write about fossils. Fossils are what remains of plants and animals that lived thousands or even billions of years ago.

Fossils can include bones, shells, and even bits of hair. They help scientists better understand what life was like a very long time ago.

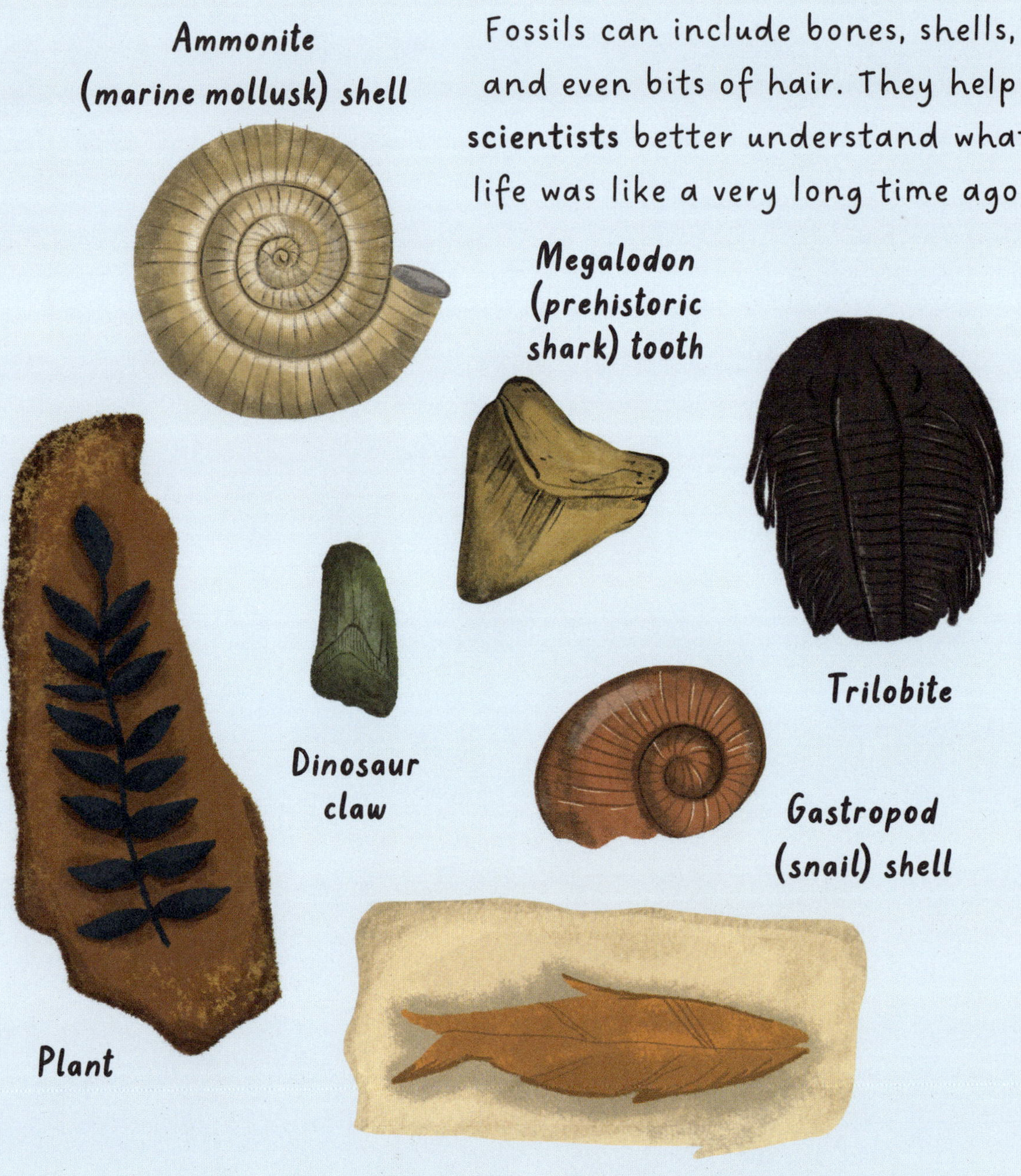

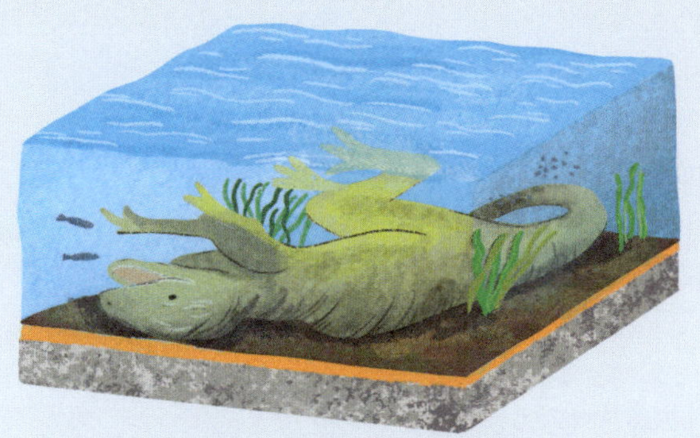

1. The animal dies

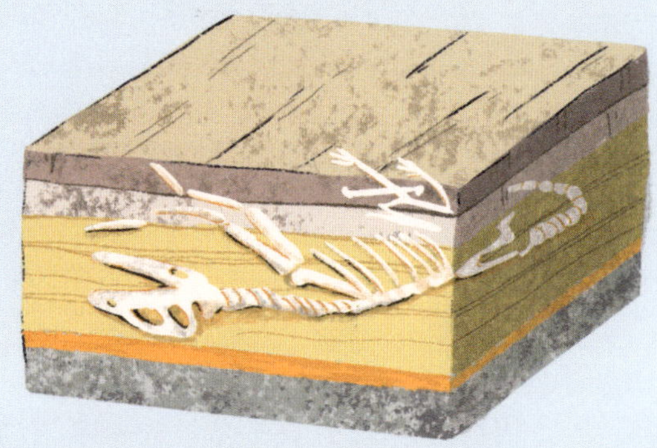

2. The body becomes buried over time

The best fossils are those that are complete or nearly so. Dinosaurs with **complete skeletons**, for example, are very valuable to scientists.

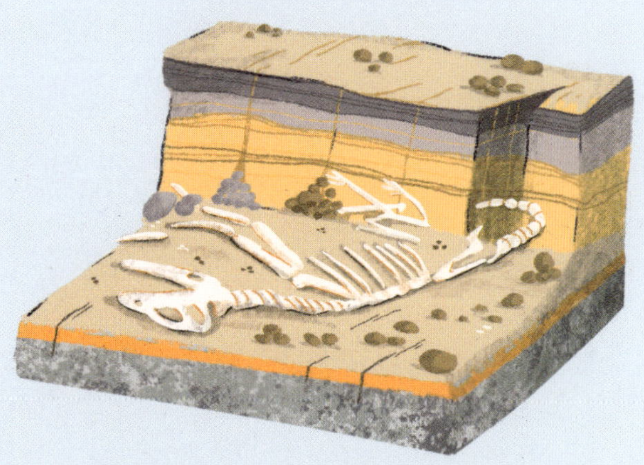

3. A fossil is one day discovered

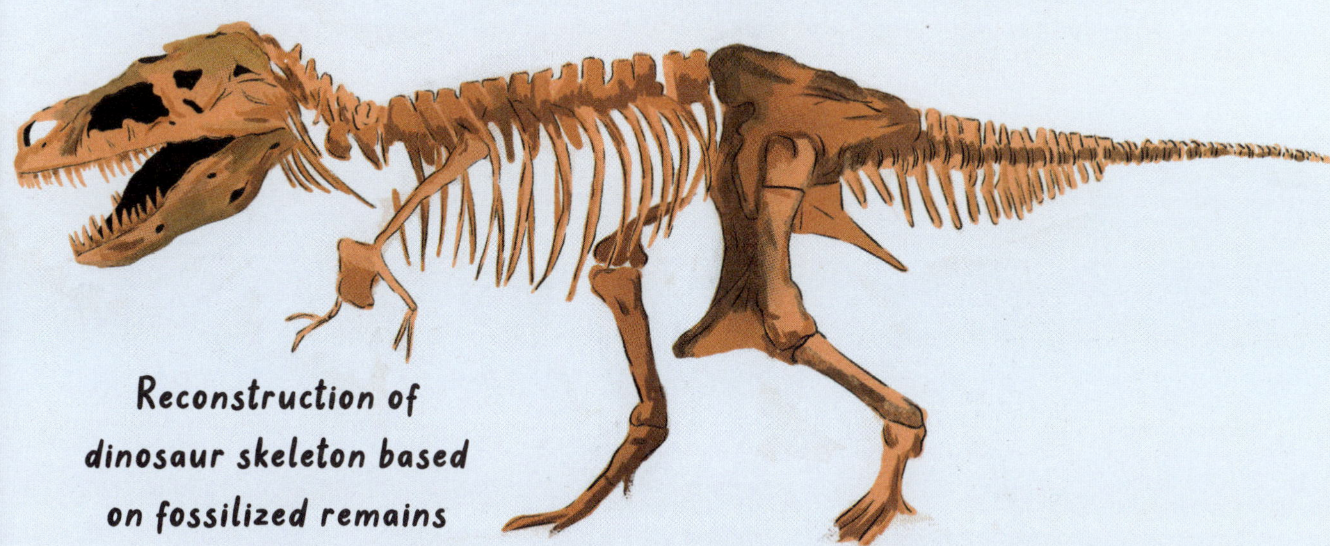

Reconstruction of dinosaur skeleton based on fossilized remains

Fossils also tell **stories**. For example, other whale bones have been found not far from where Leonardo found his. This meant Leonardo's theory was correct, and the area was once covered by an ocean!

THE PAINTING PIONEER

Leonardo Develops a New Method of Painting

Since Leonardo had little formal schooling during his youth, he was able to view the world differently than others and think beyond artistic boundaries.

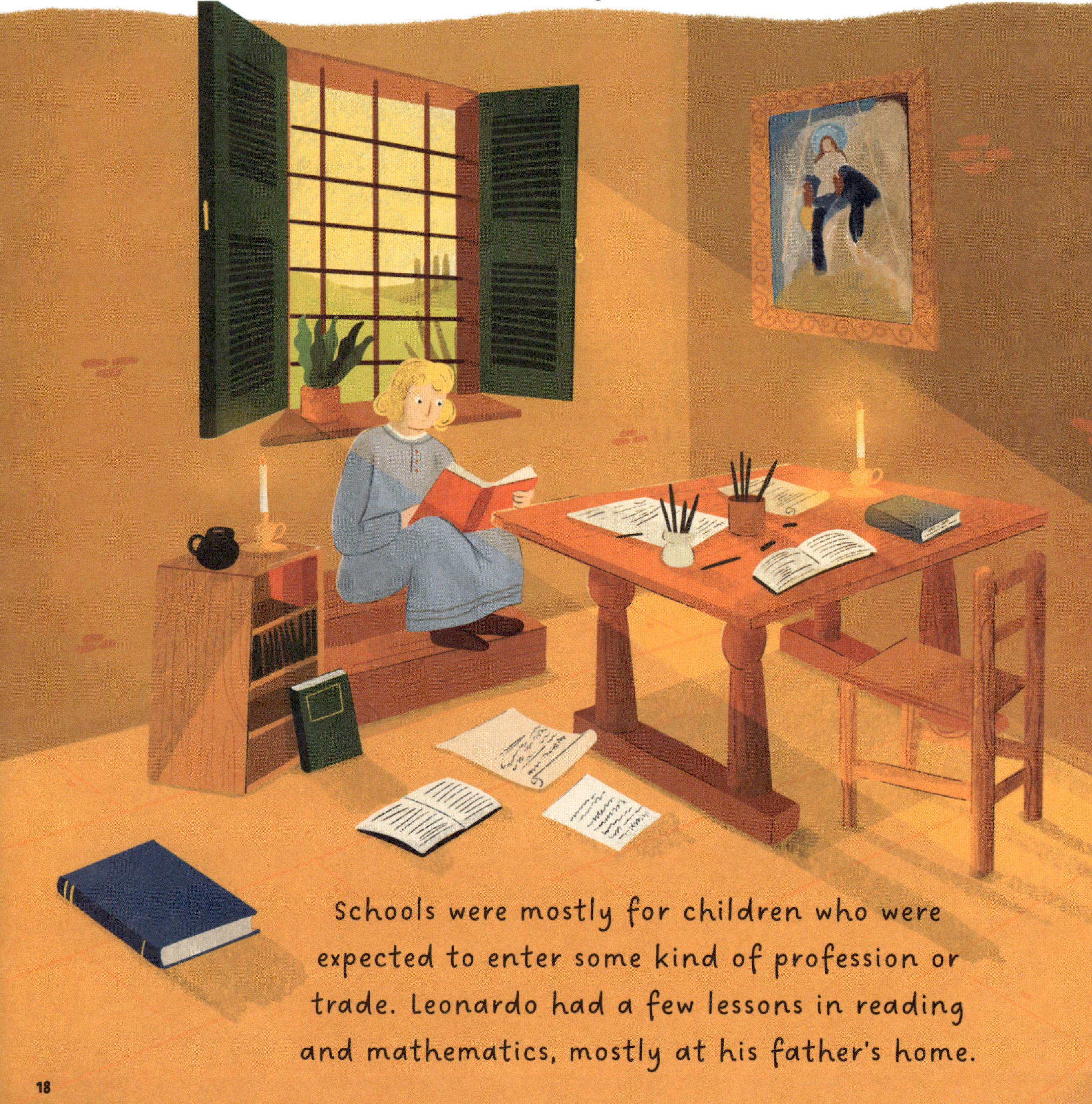

Schools were mostly for children who were expected to enter some kind of profession or trade. Leonardo had a few lessons in reading and mathematics, mostly at his father's home.

As Leonardo grew older, he became angry toward those who had gone to school. He felt they thought too highly of themselves and looked down on him.

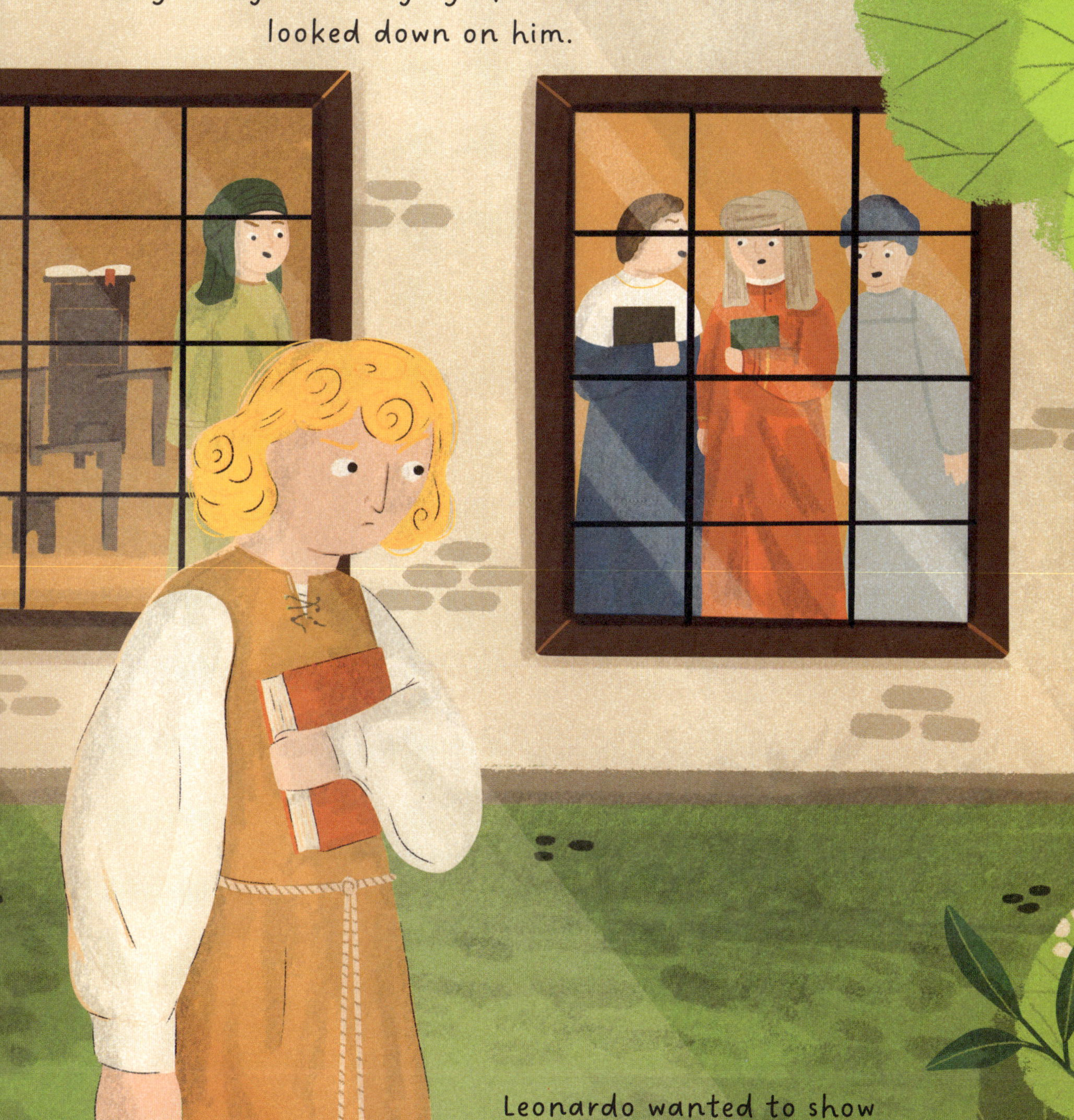

Leonardo wanted to show them he was every bit as smart as they were—maybe even smarter.

Just as Leonardo was about to enter his teen years, he moved in with his father, Piero, in Florence. His father knew Leonardo would not follow in his path as a notary.

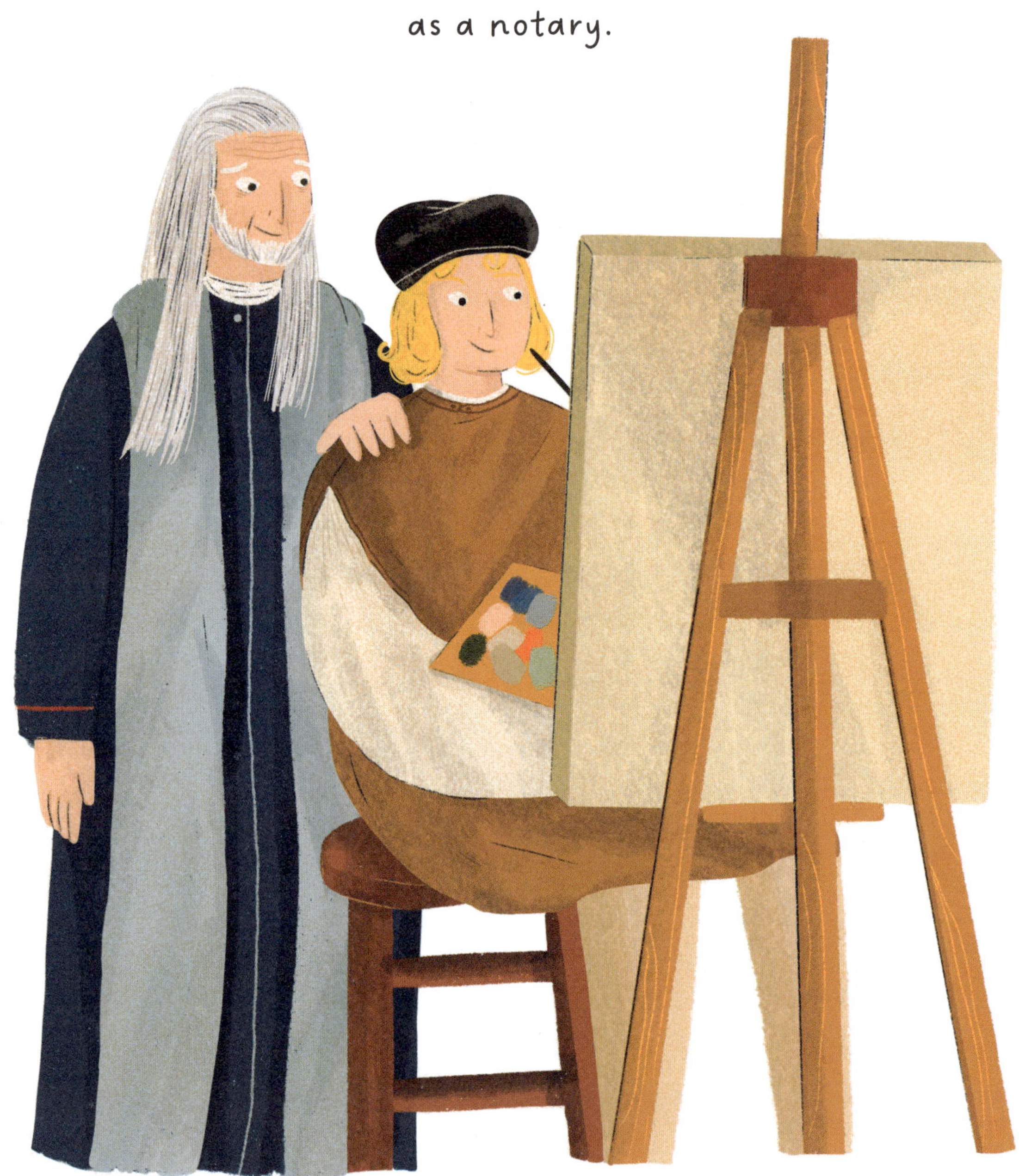

He did realize, however, that Leonardo had a natural talent for art. The boy was always drawing, painting, and sculpting. And he was very good, too!

Florence was a big and busy city. The streets and markets were full of people from diverse classes and backgrounds, including fellow artists. Here, Leonardo's mind was opened to new ideas and possibilities.

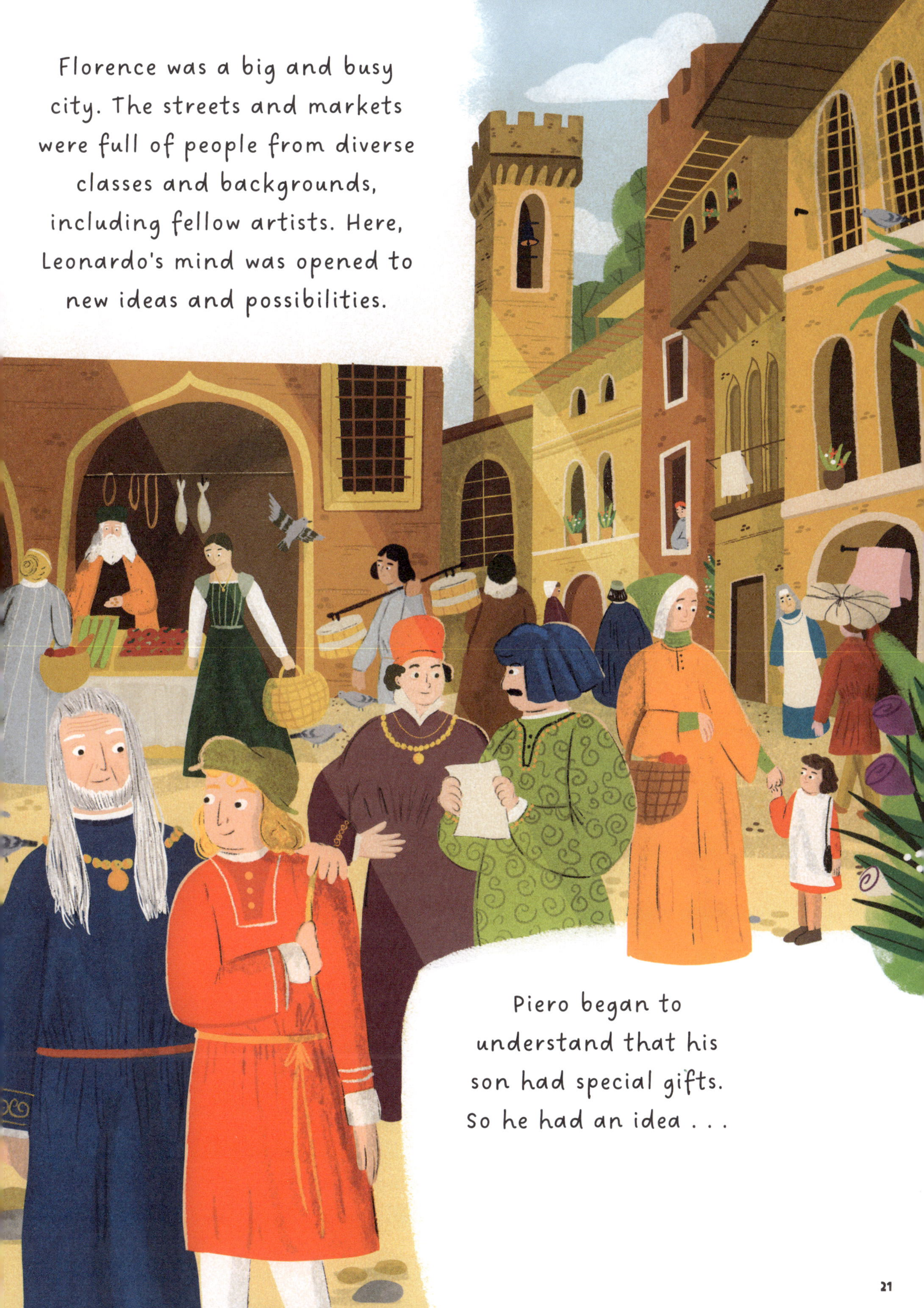

Piero began to understand that his son had special gifts. So he had an idea . . .

One day, Piero gathered some of Leonardo's best work. Then he paid a visit to a friend named Andrea del Verrocchio.

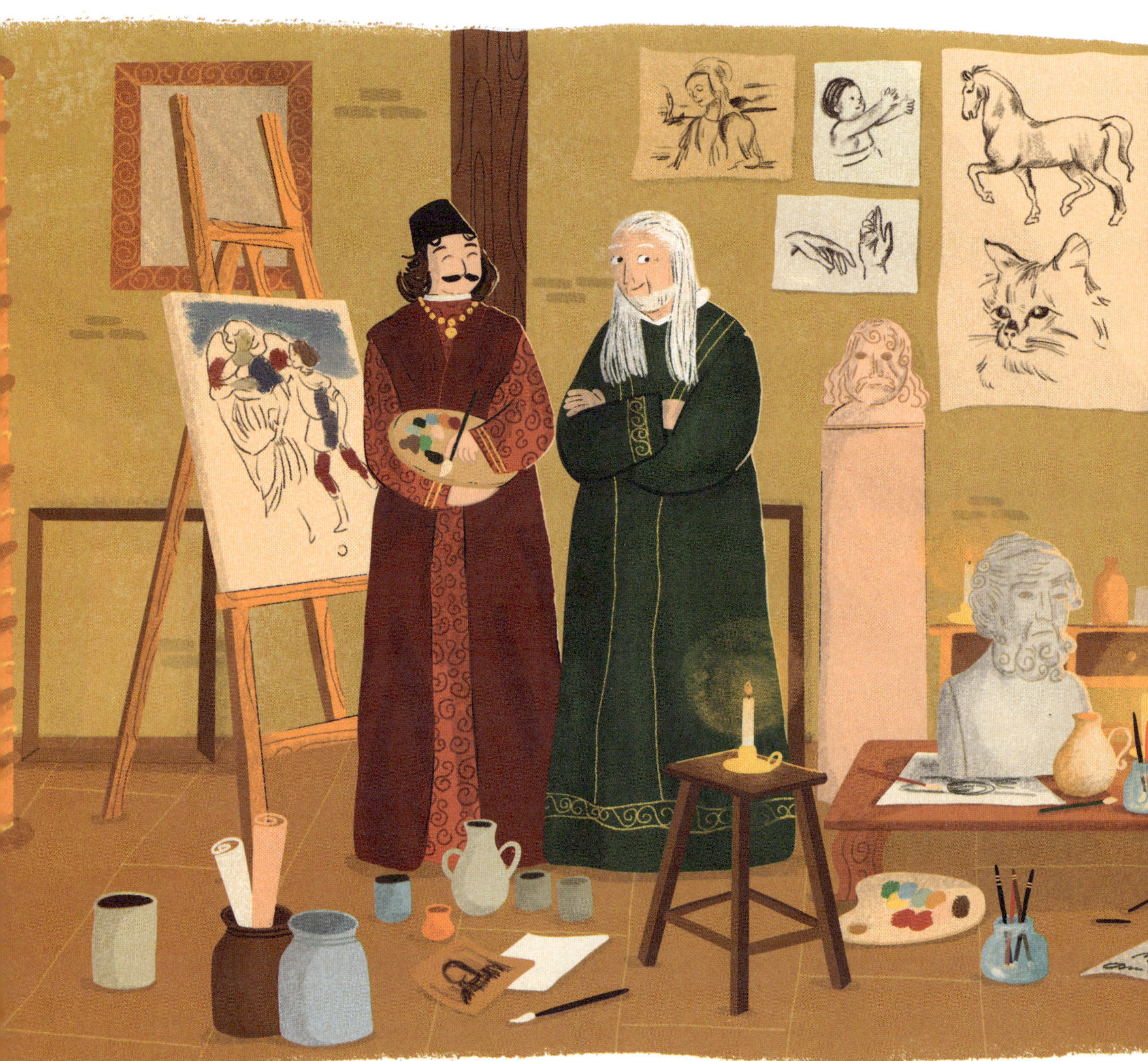

Verrocchio was an engineer by profession. But he was also an excellent artist, and he ran one of the busiest artists' workshops in all of Florence.

Piero hoped that Verrocchio would consider having Leonardo as an apprentice. An apprentice is someone who learns a trade from someone who has already mastered it.

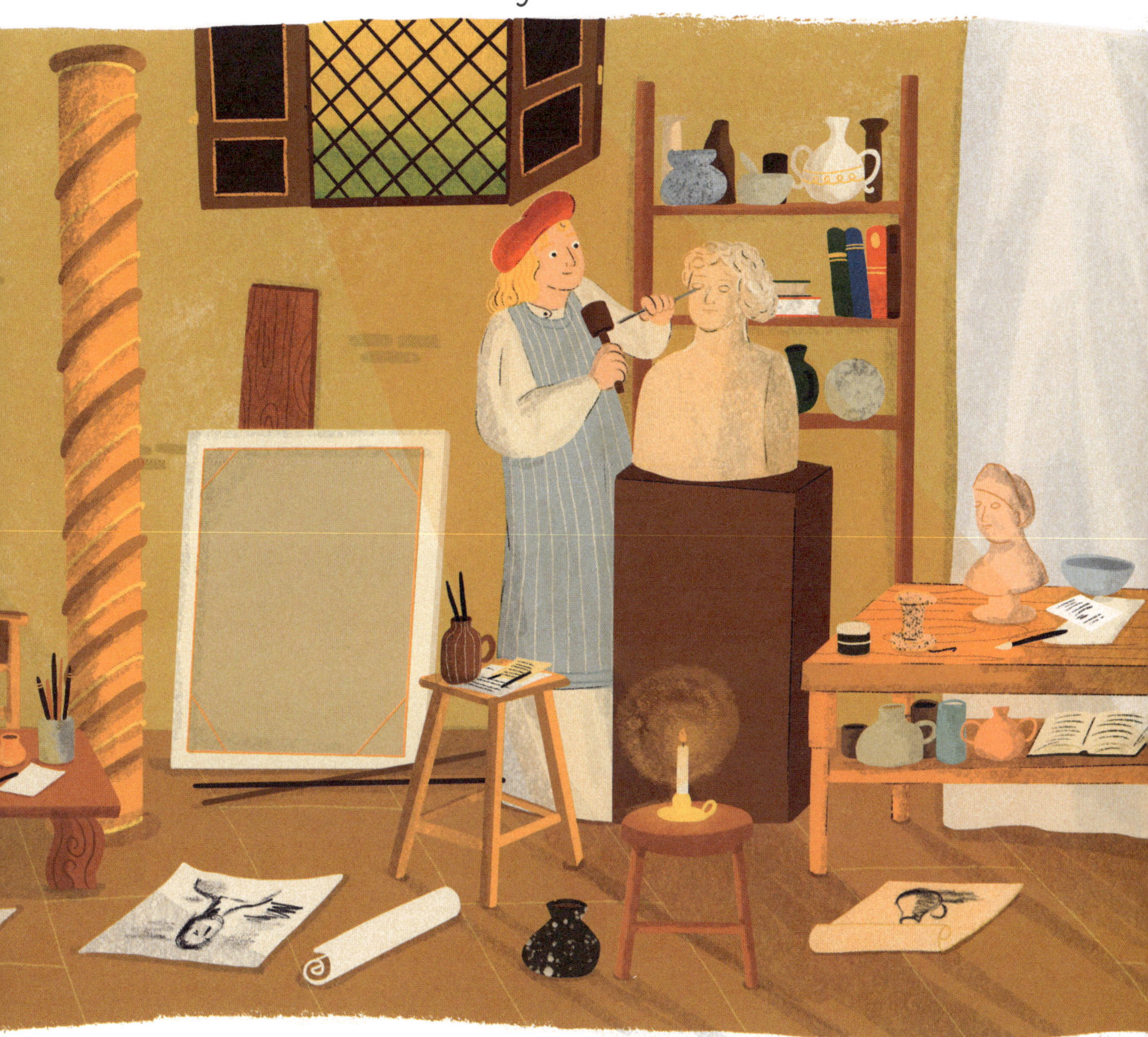

Piero may have thought he was asking a big favor of Verrocchio. But Verrocchio could not believe the quality of Leonardo's work. He thought it was amazing, and he was happy to take Leonardo as an apprentice.

Leonardo was taught different artistic methods as an apprentice, from sketching to sculpting. He had already studied some of the other masters of the time.

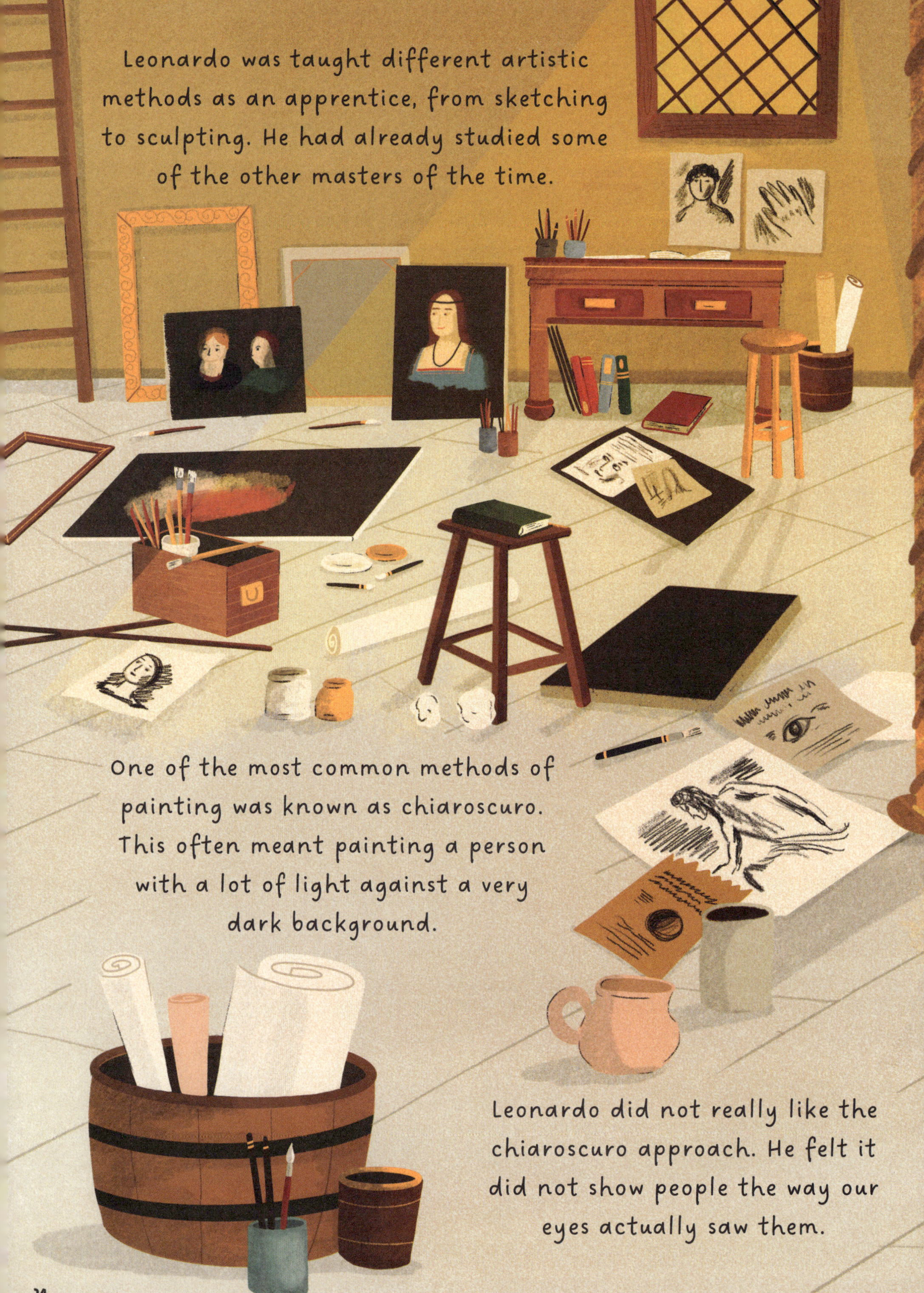

One of the most common methods of painting was known as chiaroscuro. This often meant painting a person with a lot of light against a very dark background.

Leonardo did not really like the chiaroscuro approach. He felt it did not show people the way our eyes actually saw them.

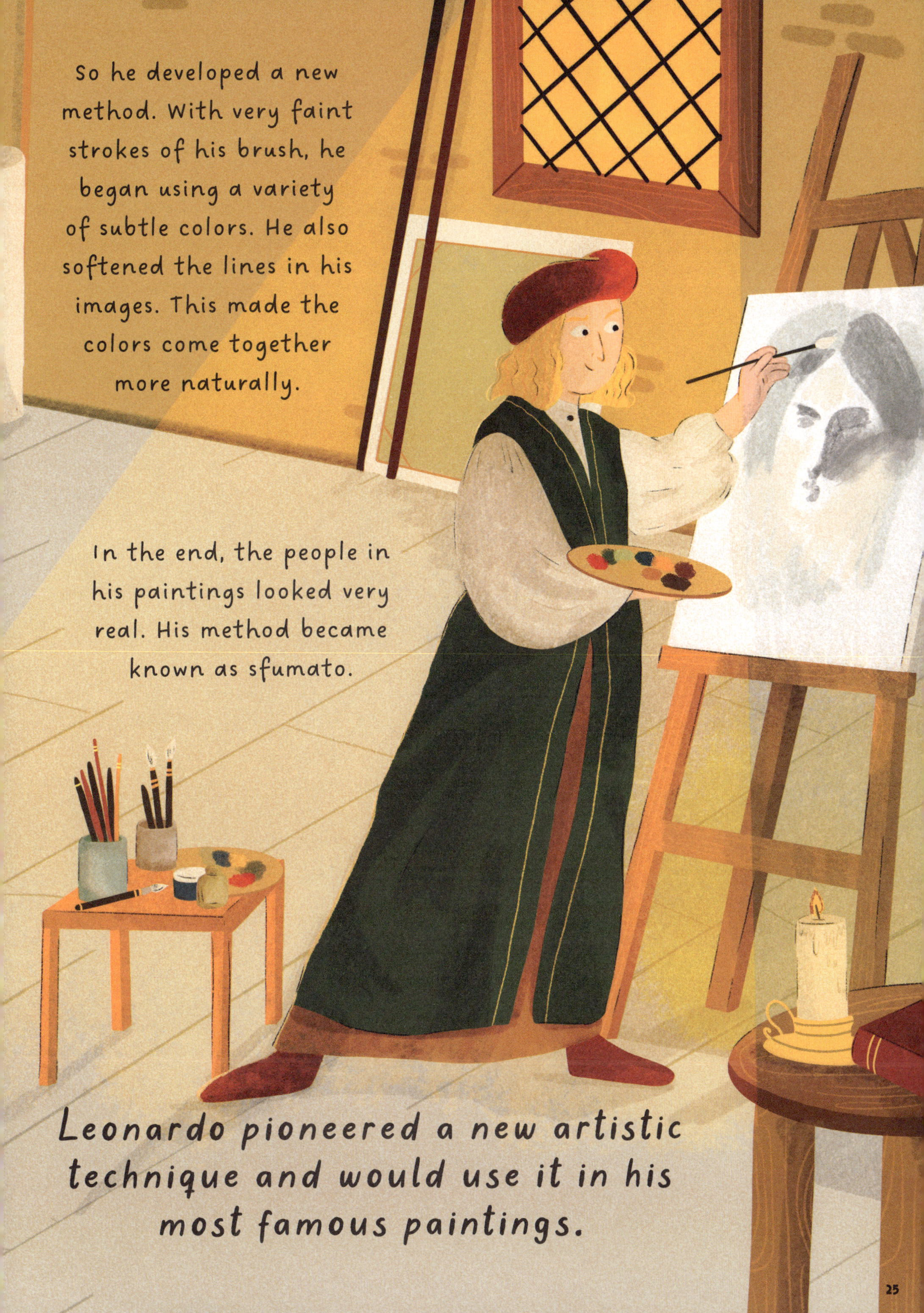

So he developed a new method. With very faint strokes of his brush, he began using a variety of subtle colors. He also softened the lines in his images. This made the colors come together more naturally.

In the end, the people in his paintings looked very real. His method became known as sfumato.

Leonardo pioneered a new artistic technique and would use it in his most famous paintings.

The Sfumato EFFECT

Today, Leonardo's most famous paintings can be recognized by the distinctive sfumato technique. Through the years, many other artists have used sfumato in their own way.

The **sfumato** approach is supposed to make a painting look softer. Shadow and light ease into each other in a gentle and gradual way.

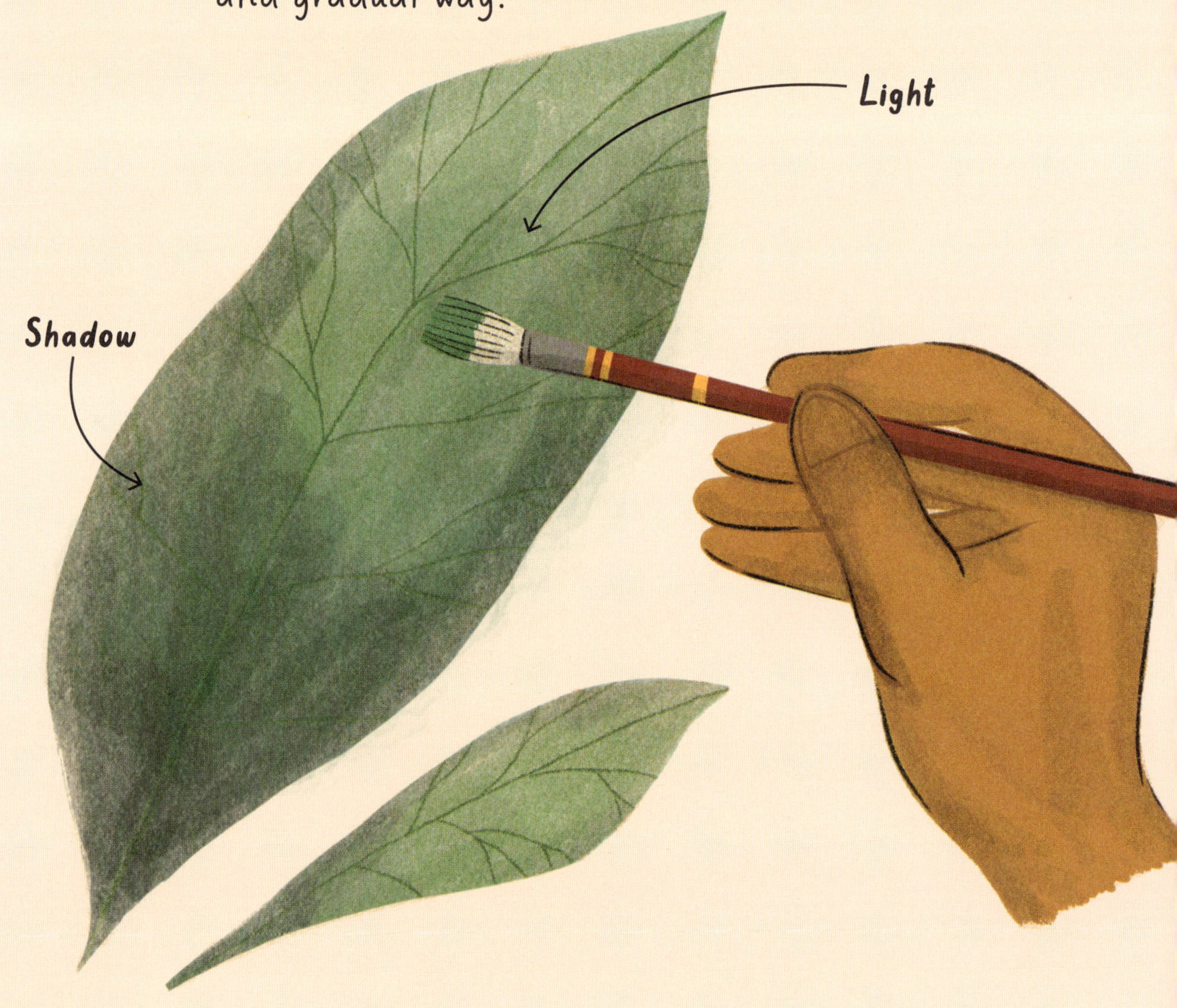

The **brushstrokes** used to create this effect are often very small and delicate. Sometimes an artist will even use their **fingers**! A very light touch is all that's required.

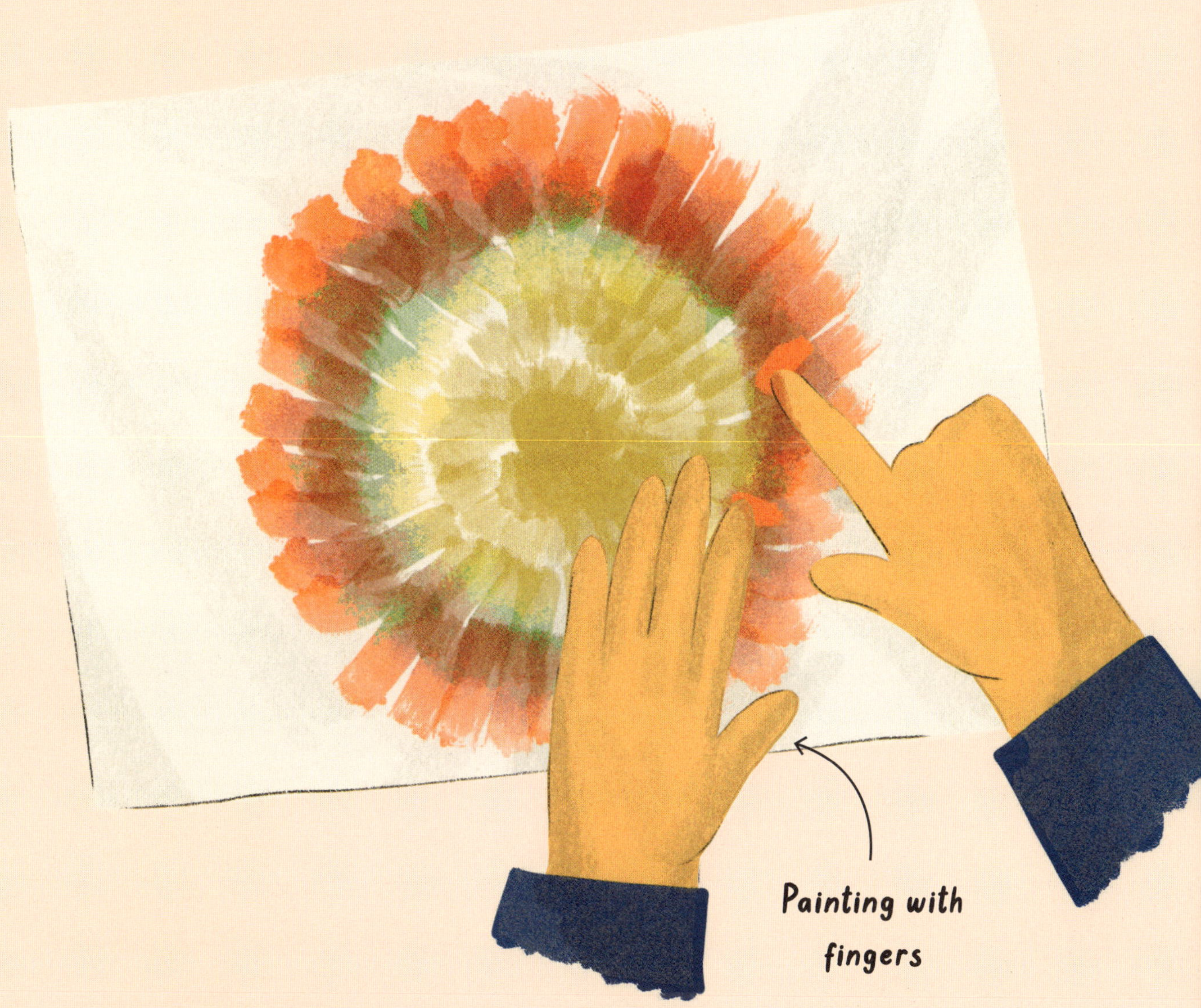

The word sfumato is Italian. It means **"to tone down."** Another meaning is "to evaporate like smoke."

THE MASTER ON THE HILL

Leonardo Sketches a Landscape

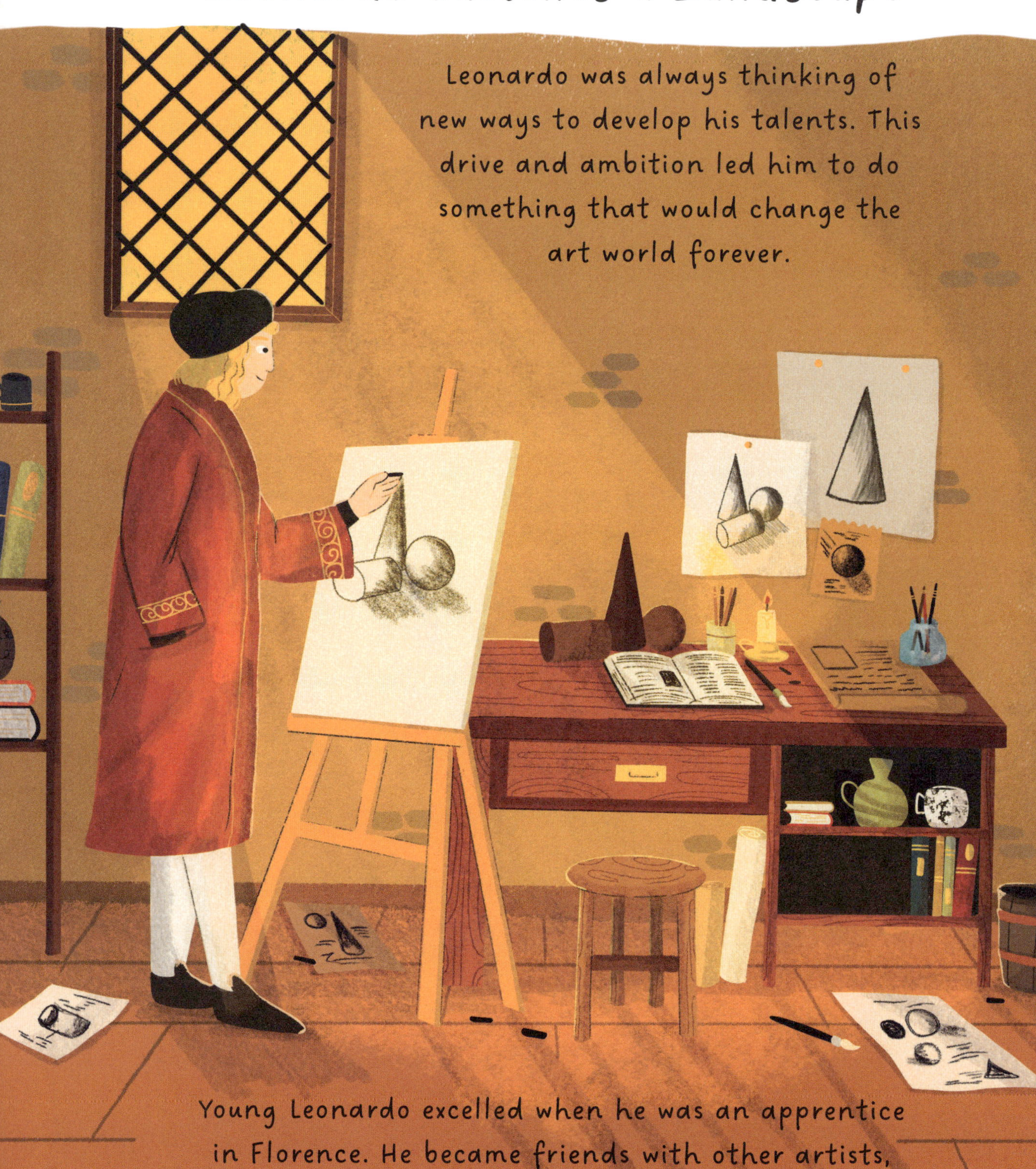

Leonardo was always thinking of new ways to develop his talents. This drive and ambition led him to do something that would change the art world forever.

Young Leonardo excelled when he was an apprentice in Florence. He became friends with other artists, and his artistic skills improved tremendously.

His teacher, Andrea del Verrocchio, wanted his apprentices to feel free to discuss anything. Leonardo would enthusiastically join in these discussions. In many ways, these discussions were like a formal education for him.

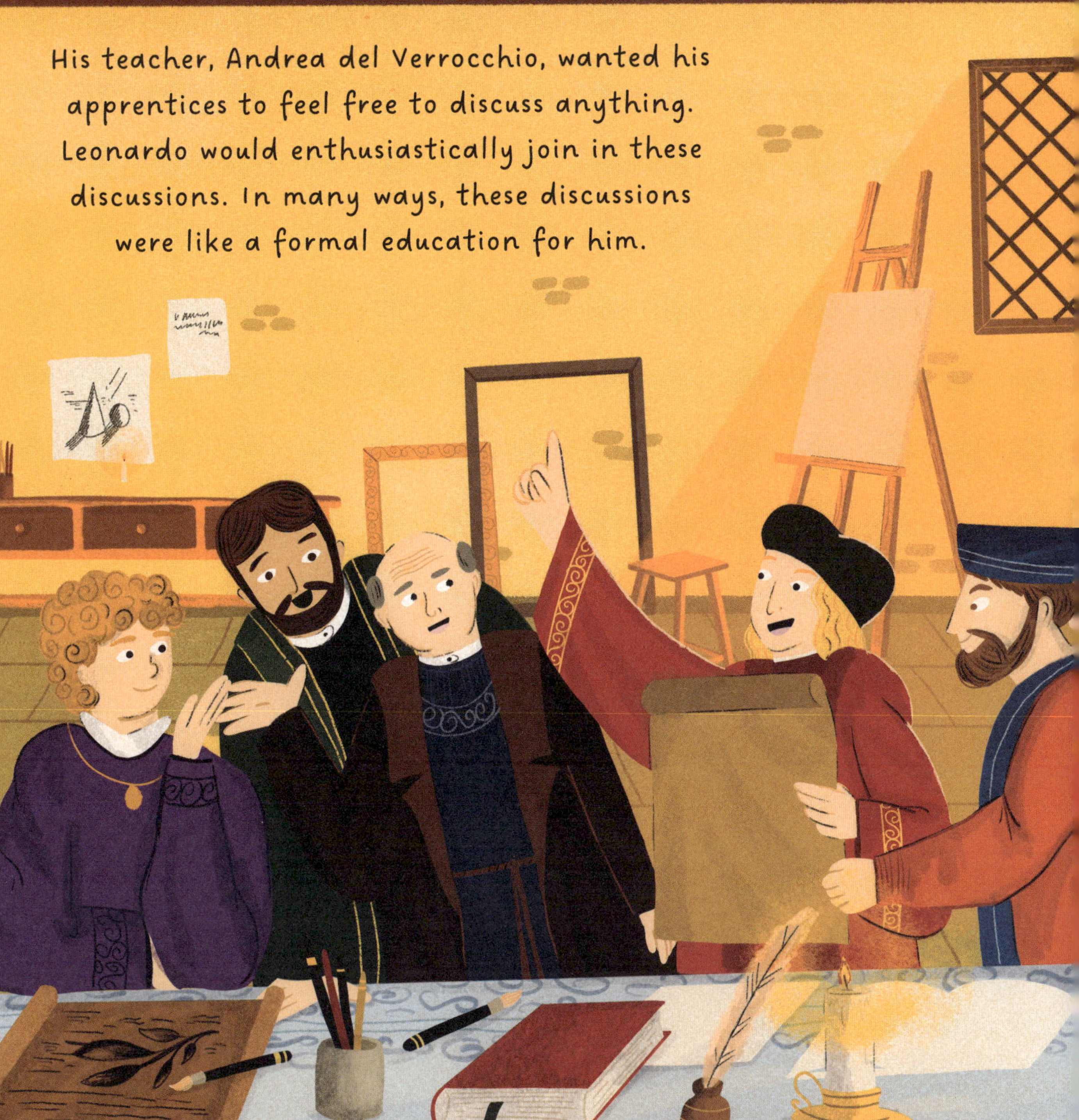

The group would talk about everything from music and philosophy to math and science. Leonardo particularly liked the scientific discussions.

Leonardo enjoyed helping with projects that taught him new skills, such as sculpting. He also made paintings of famous religious figures, and designed banners for celebration events.

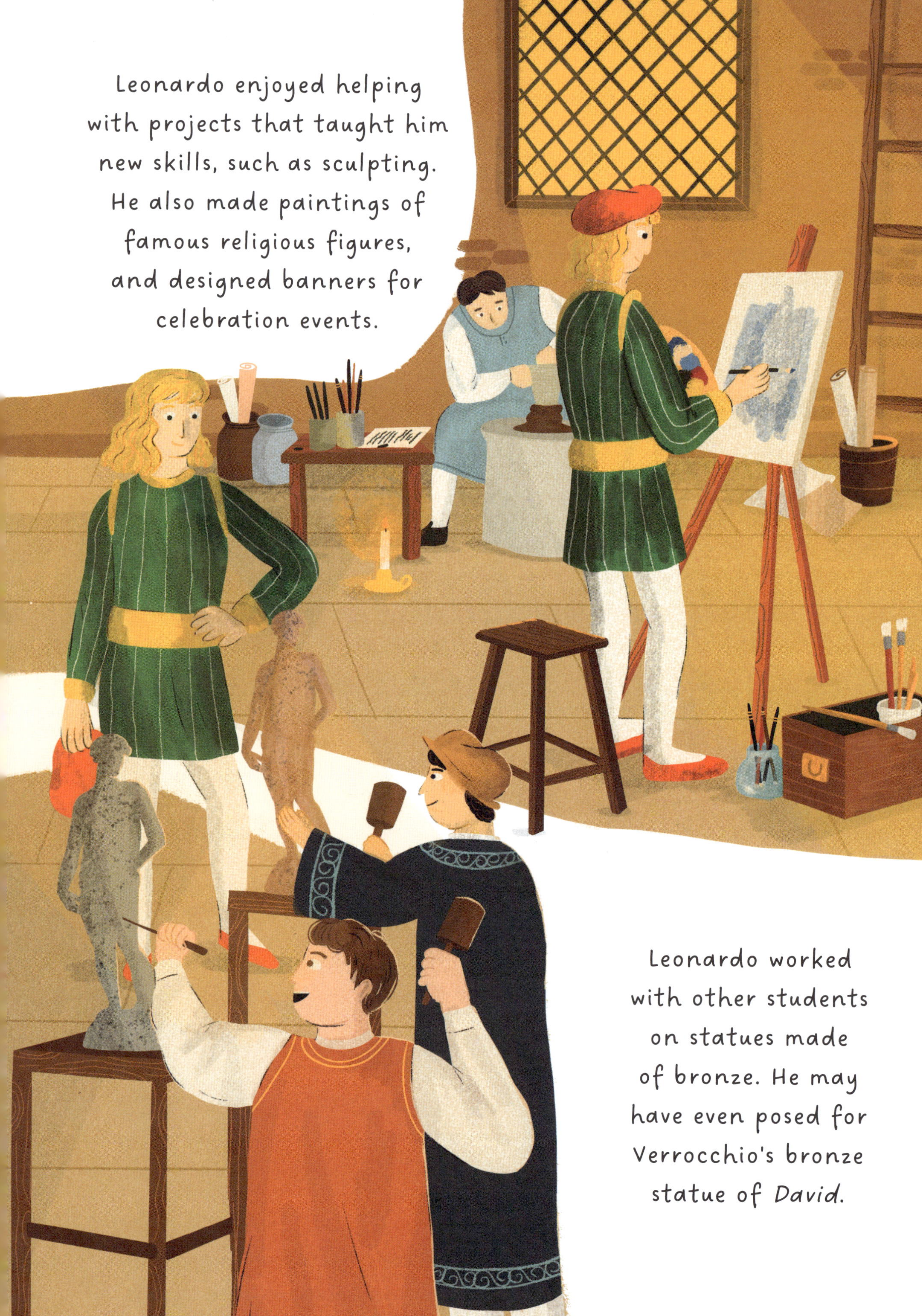

Leonardo worked with other students on statues made of bronze. He may have even posed for Verrocchio's bronze statue of *David*.

When Leonardo was twenty, his apprenticeship came to an end. Verrocchio considered him an equal—he could teach Leonardo nothing more.

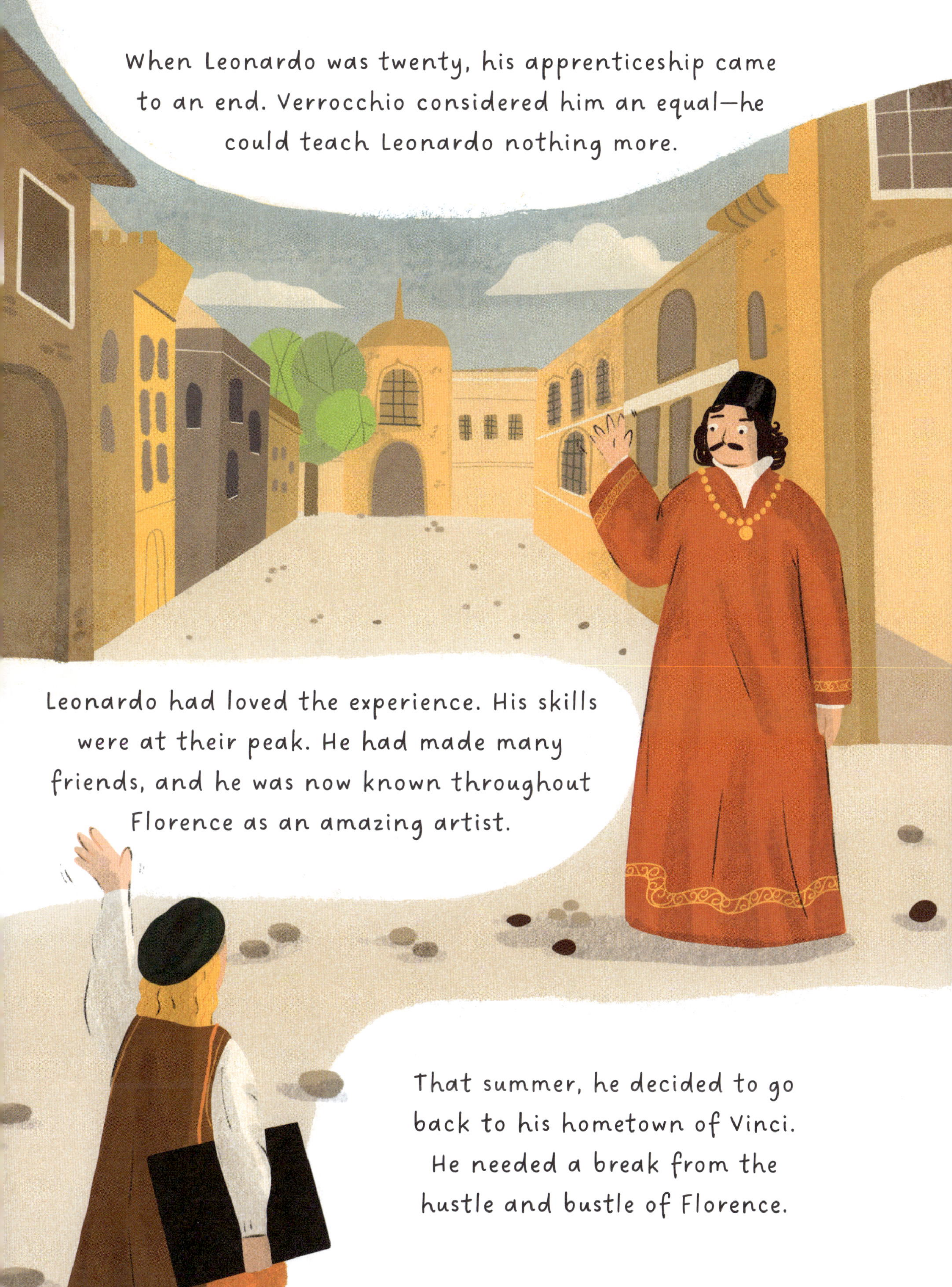

Leonardo had loved the experience. His skills were at their peak. He had made many friends, and he was now known throughout Florence as an amazing artist.

That summer, he decided to go back to his hometown of Vinci. He needed a break from the hustle and bustle of Florence.

Back in his hometown, he was soon wandering the woods, just as he did when he was a boy growing up in Vinci.

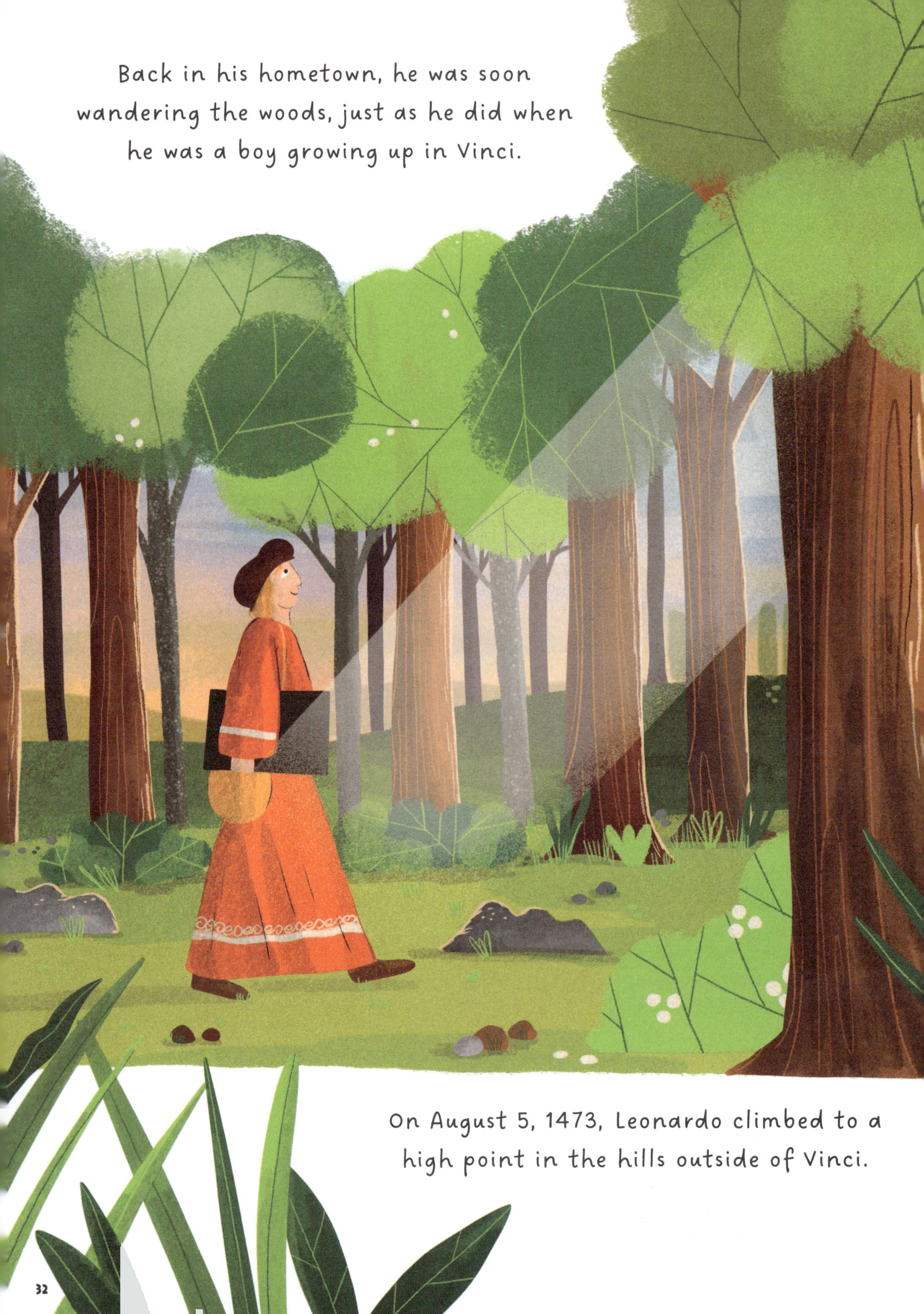

On August 5, 1473, Leonardo climbed to a high point in the hills outside of Vinci.

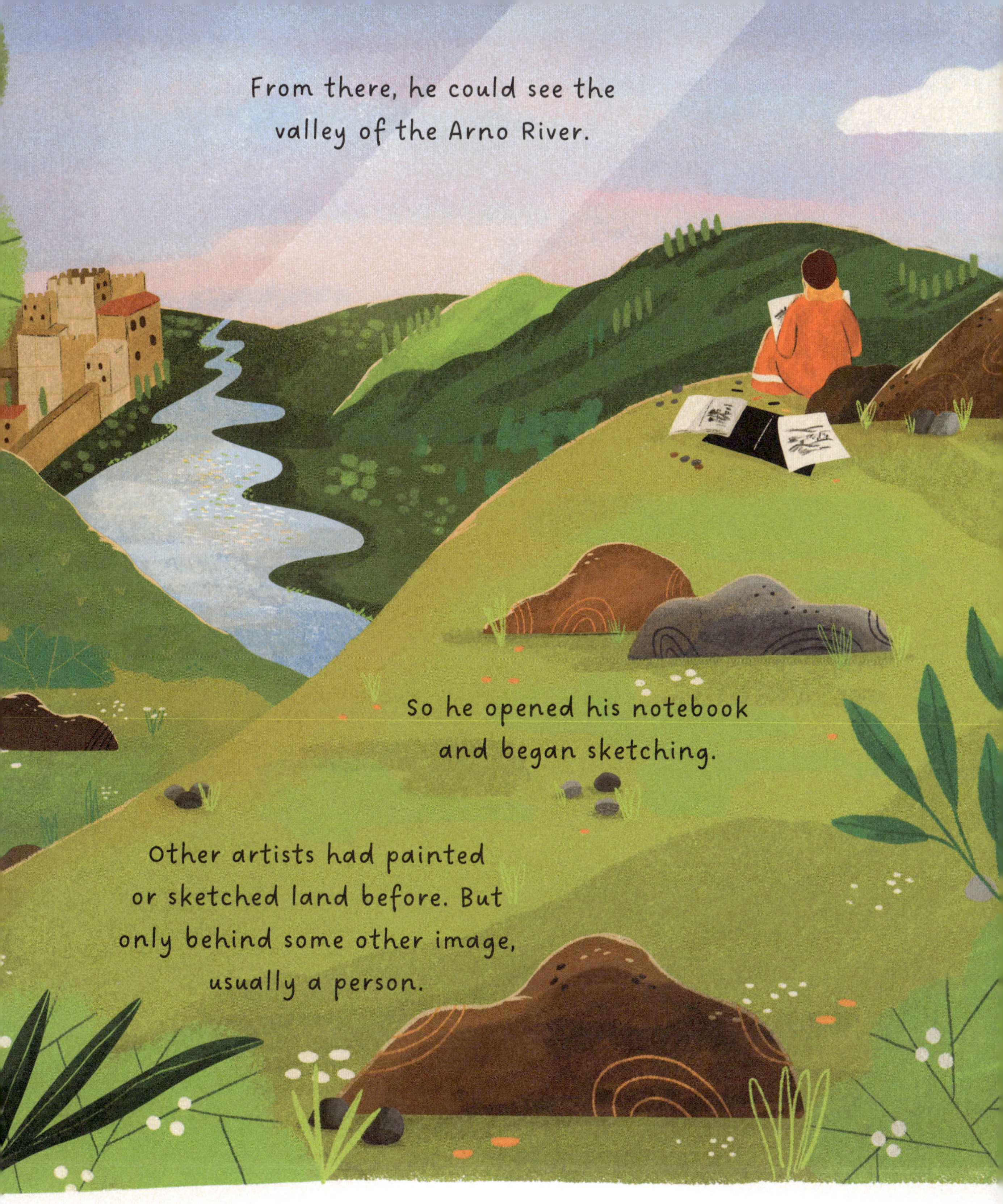

From there, he could see the valley of the Arno River.

So he opened his notebook and began sketching.

Other artists had painted or sketched land before. But only behind some other image, usually a person.

The idea of sketching a landscape by itself was very unusual at the time.

Soon Leonardo had created a picture that showed the valley in all its wonderful beauty. It had mountains and farms in the distance. A castle appeared on the left, and there were trees waving in the breeze.

This was a huge moment in the history of the arts.

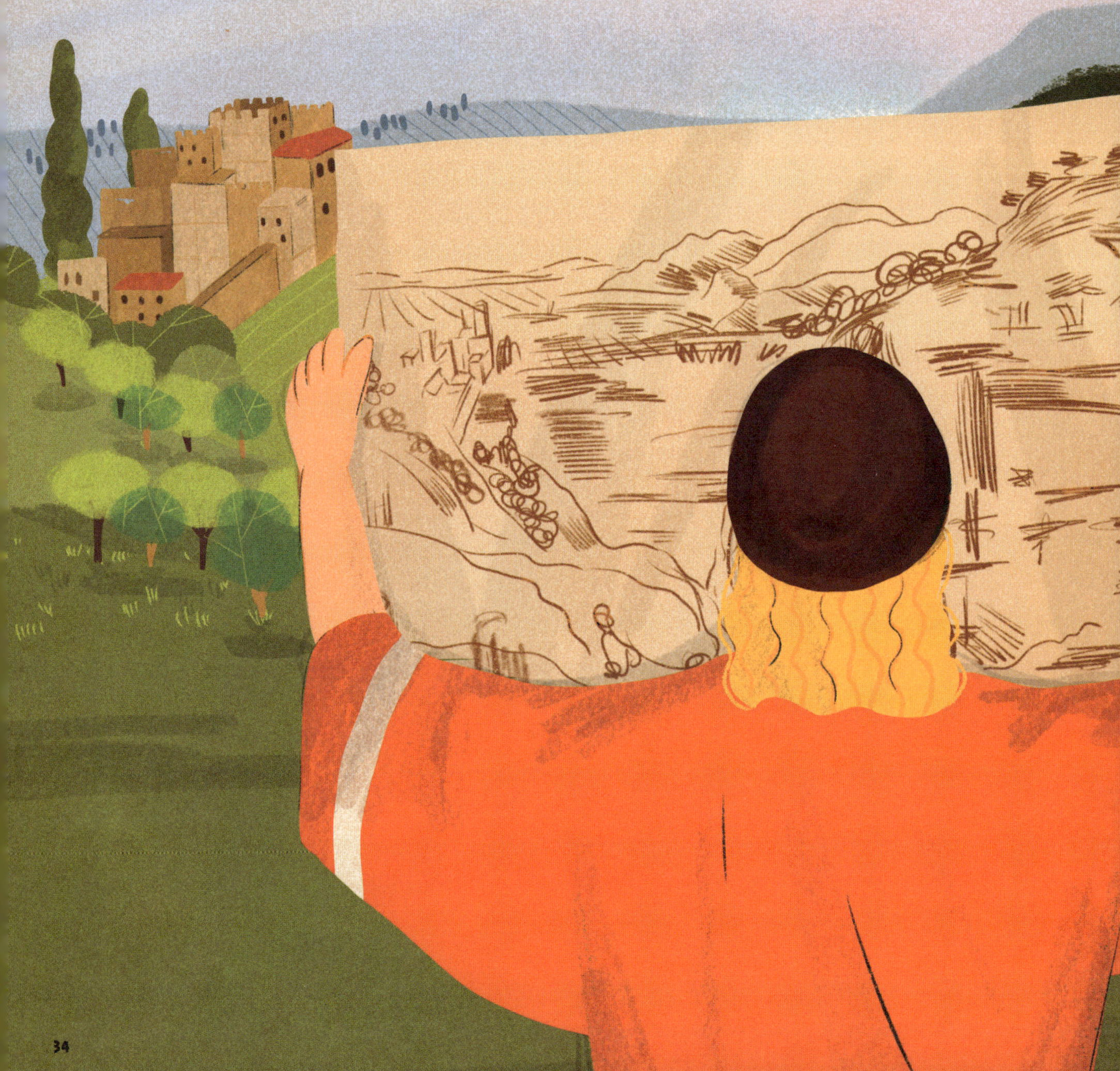

The type of image Leonardo created that day would become known as a landscape. This is because it shows an area of land.

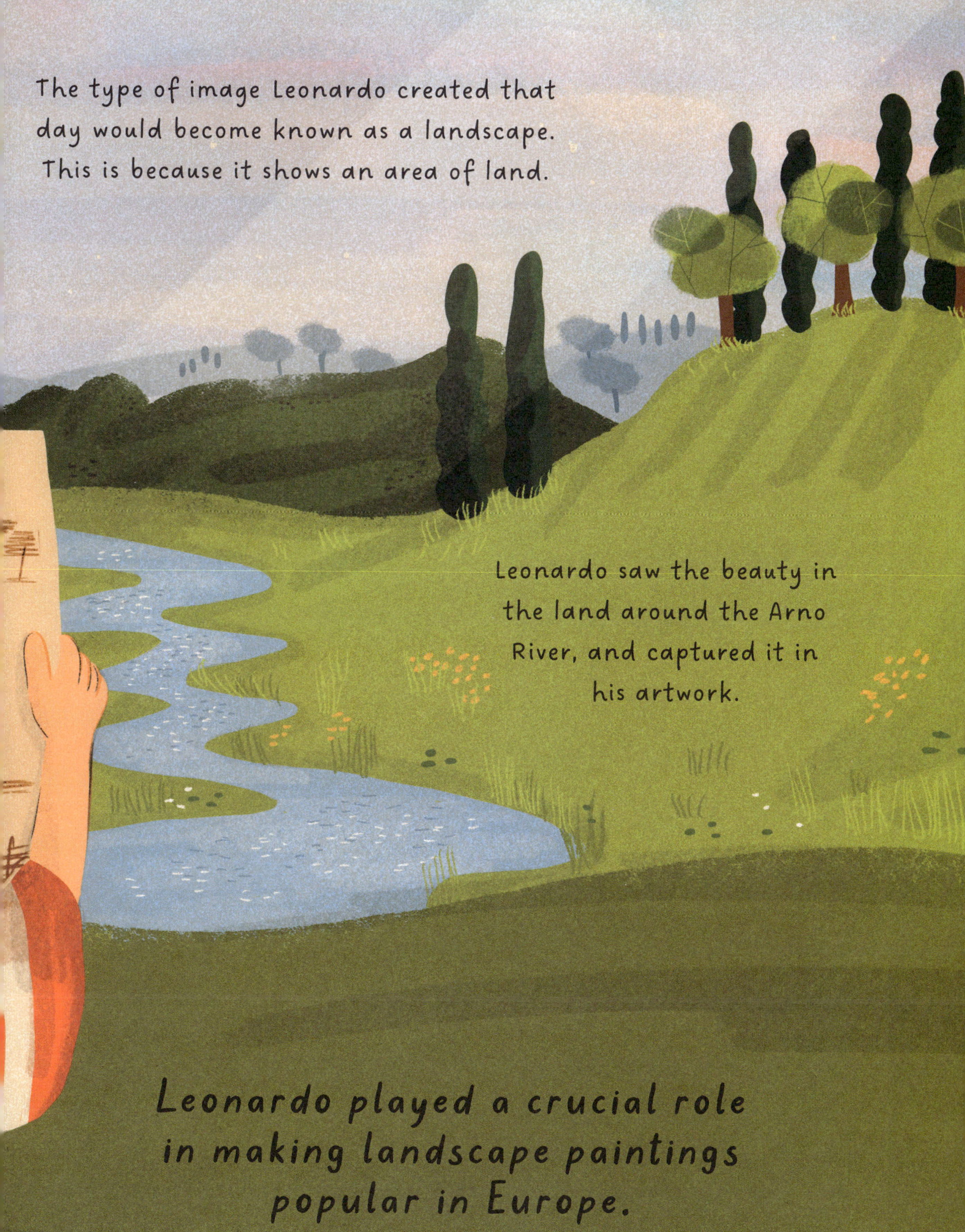

Leonardo saw the beauty in the land around the Arno River, and captured it in his artwork.

Leonardo played a crucial role in making landscape paintings popular in Europe.

Painting LANDSCAPES

Landscape art has become increasingly popular since Leonardo's time.

Most landscapes show a **wide view** of a particular area. Common features of a landscape painting include rivers, oceans, valleys, forests, and villages. The sky is almost always included, too.

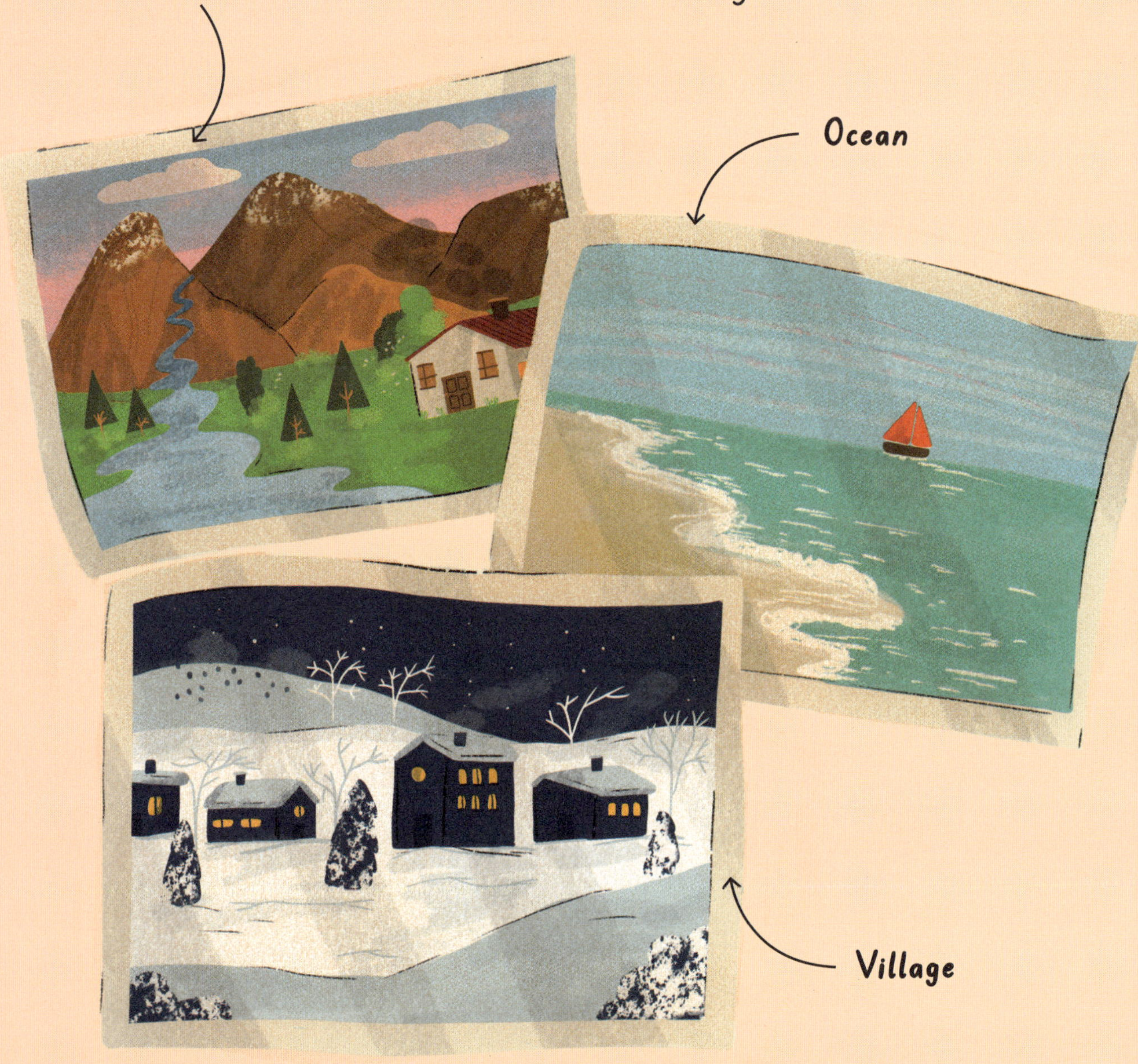

In Leonardo's time, most paintings showed figures from religious or mythological stories. Now, some landscapes are counted among the **greatest paintings** in history.

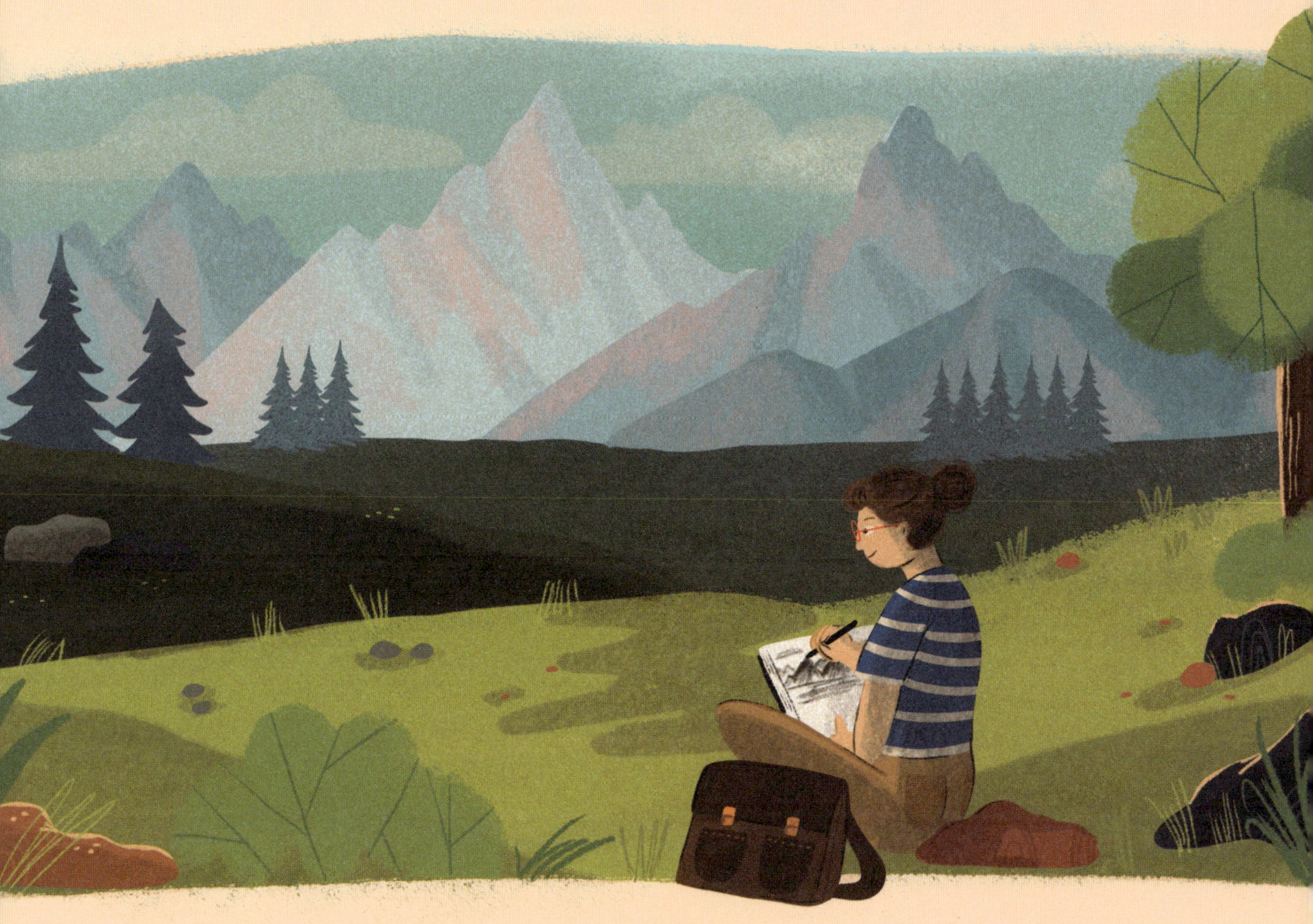

Many landscapes show a place that's real, where the artist has been. Other landscapes show a place that exists only in the artist's **imagination**.

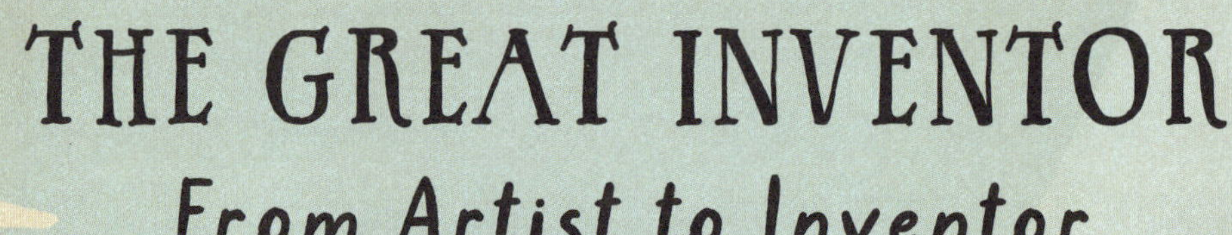

THE GREAT INVENTOR

From Artist to Inventor

By the mid-1470s, Leonardo was in his early twenties and known as one of the most talented artists in Florence. But he had other ambitions.

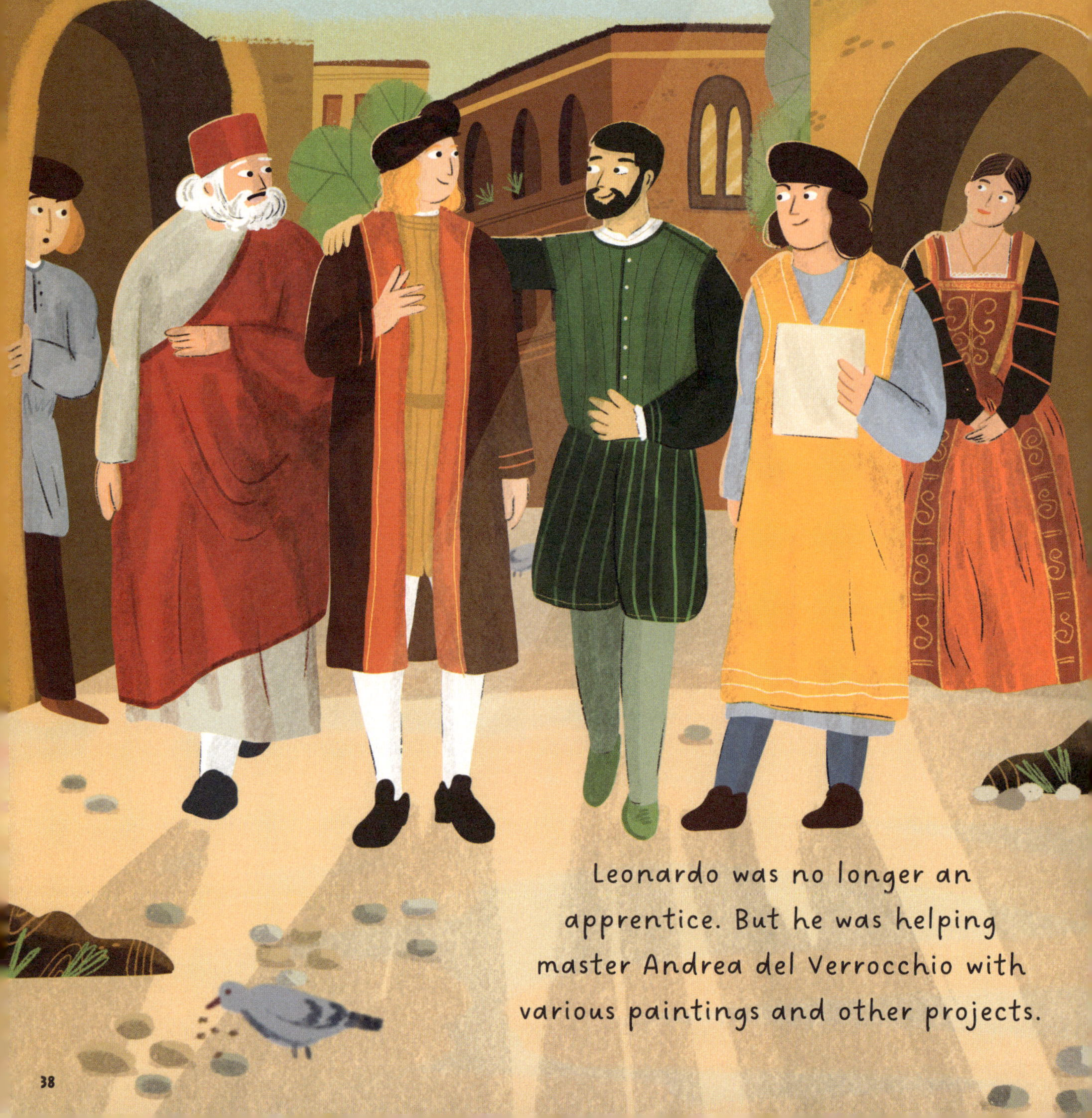

Leonardo was no longer an apprentice. But he was helping master Andrea del Verrocchio with various paintings and other projects.

The work he produced during this time was not his best, however. He was becoming restless and bored.

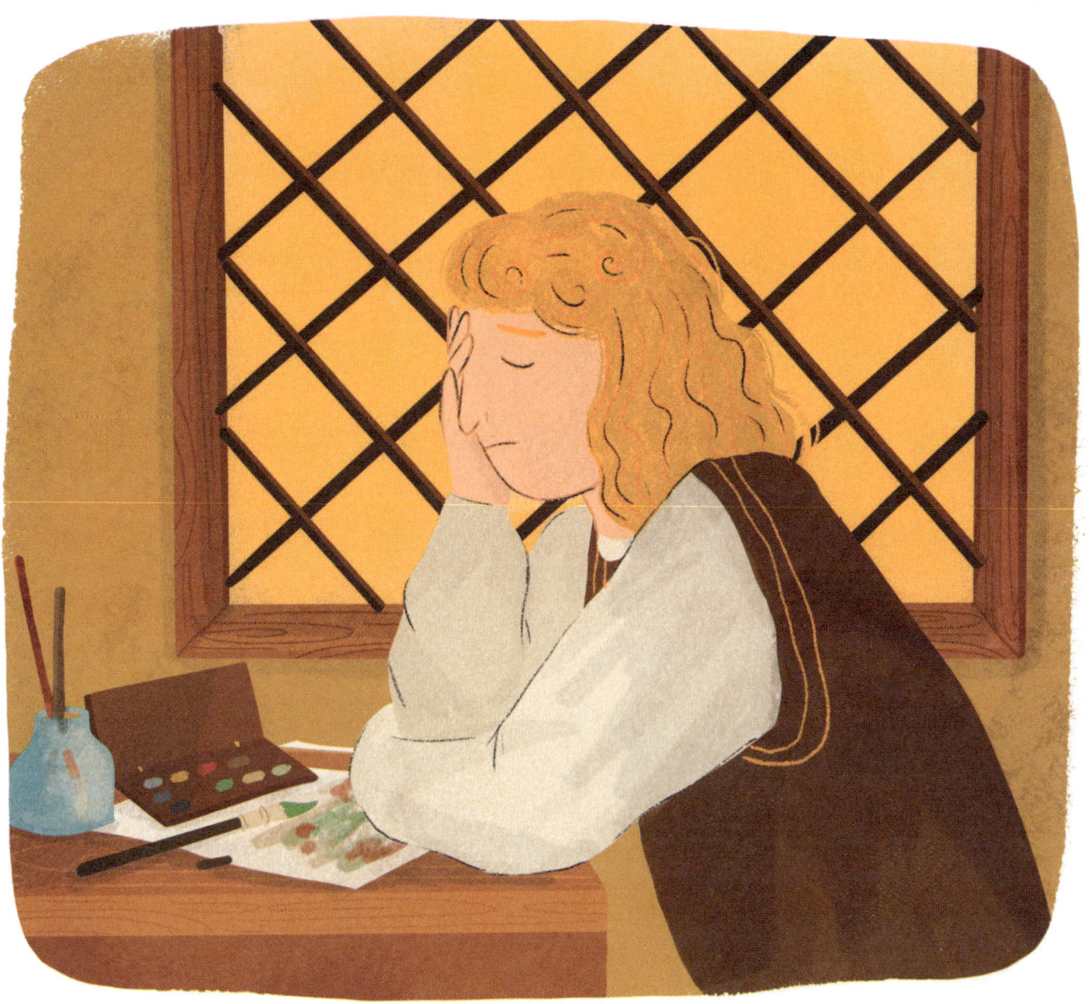

Leonardo wasn't sure what he wanted to do next. But he had lots of ideas.

Leonardo decided to open his own workshop in 1477. He also took on a few apprentices to help.

He hoped to find enough artistic work to keep the workshop running. This is often called "commissioned" work. A commission is an agreement to create art in return for something else, usually money.

Unfortunately, Leonardo did not get many commissions for his workshop. While many knew him to be brilliant, he was also known as somewhat unreliable.

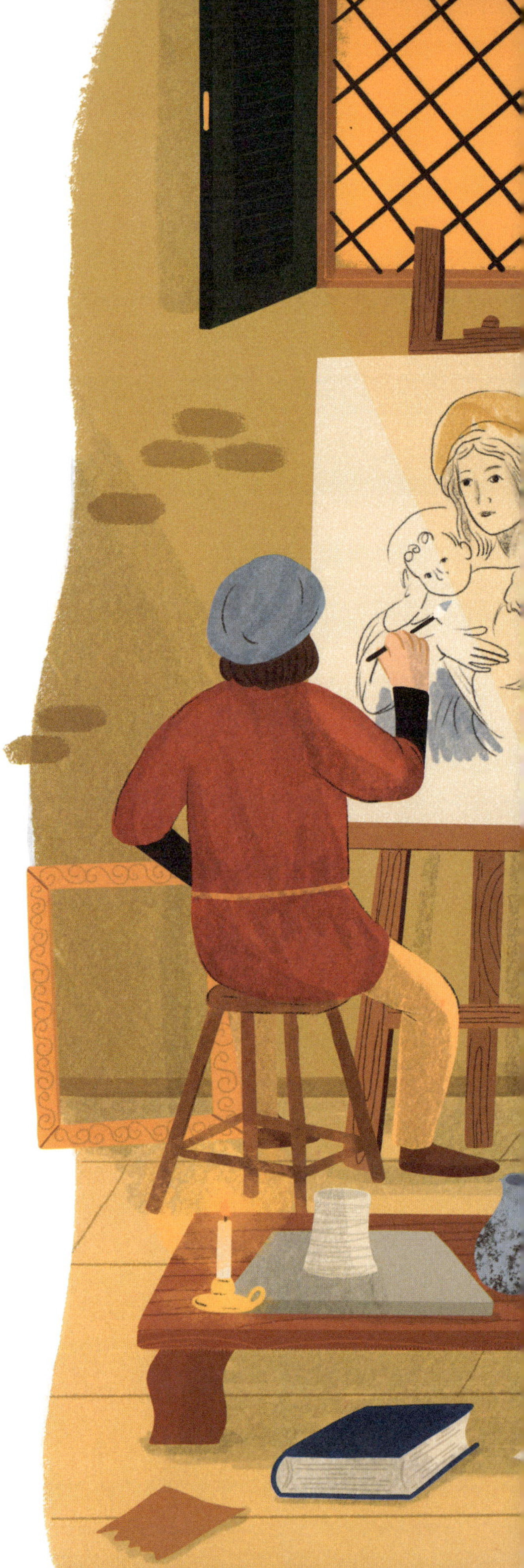

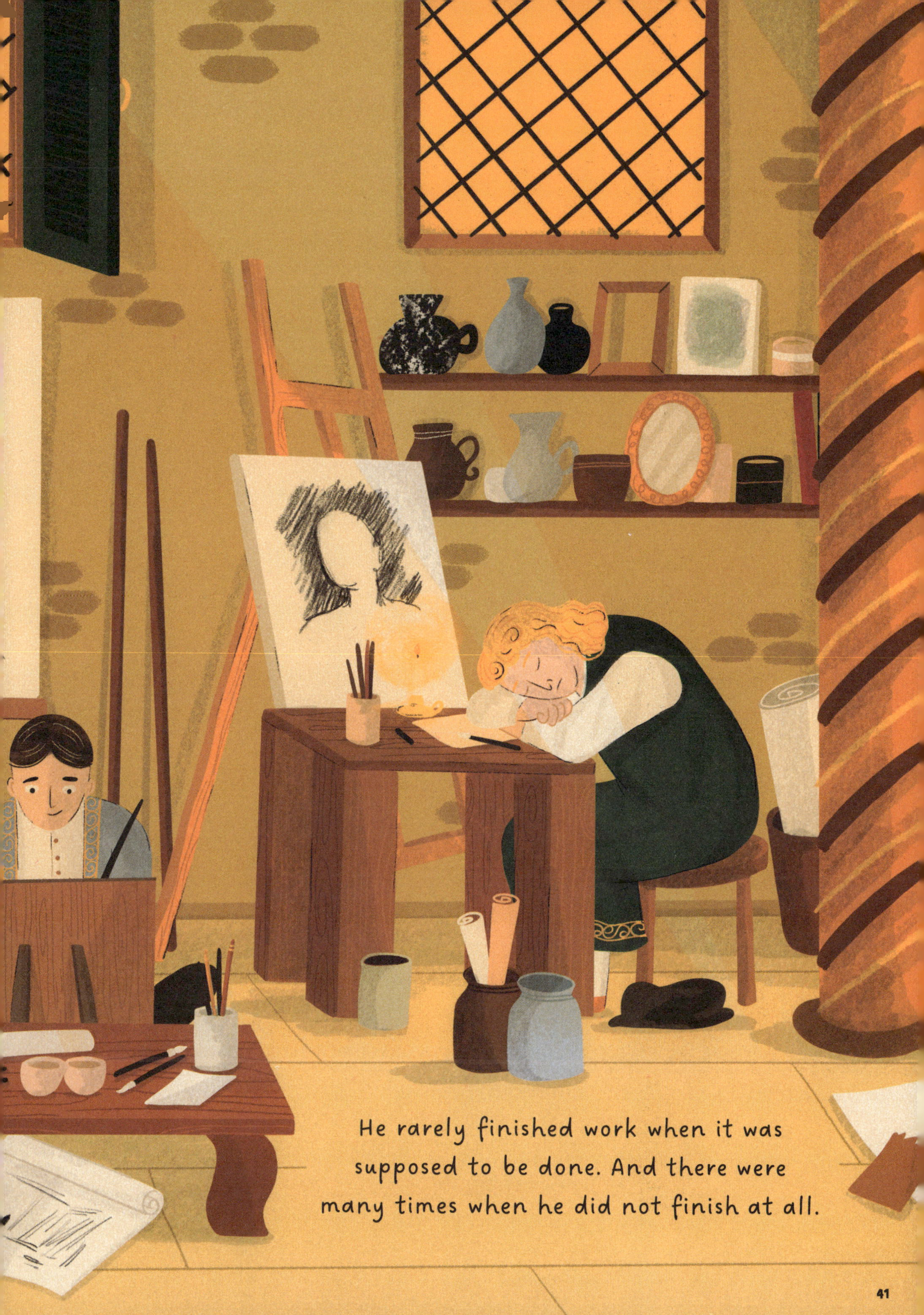

He rarely finished work when it was supposed to be done. And there were many times when he did not finish at all.

Leonardo's father, Piero, worried about his son.

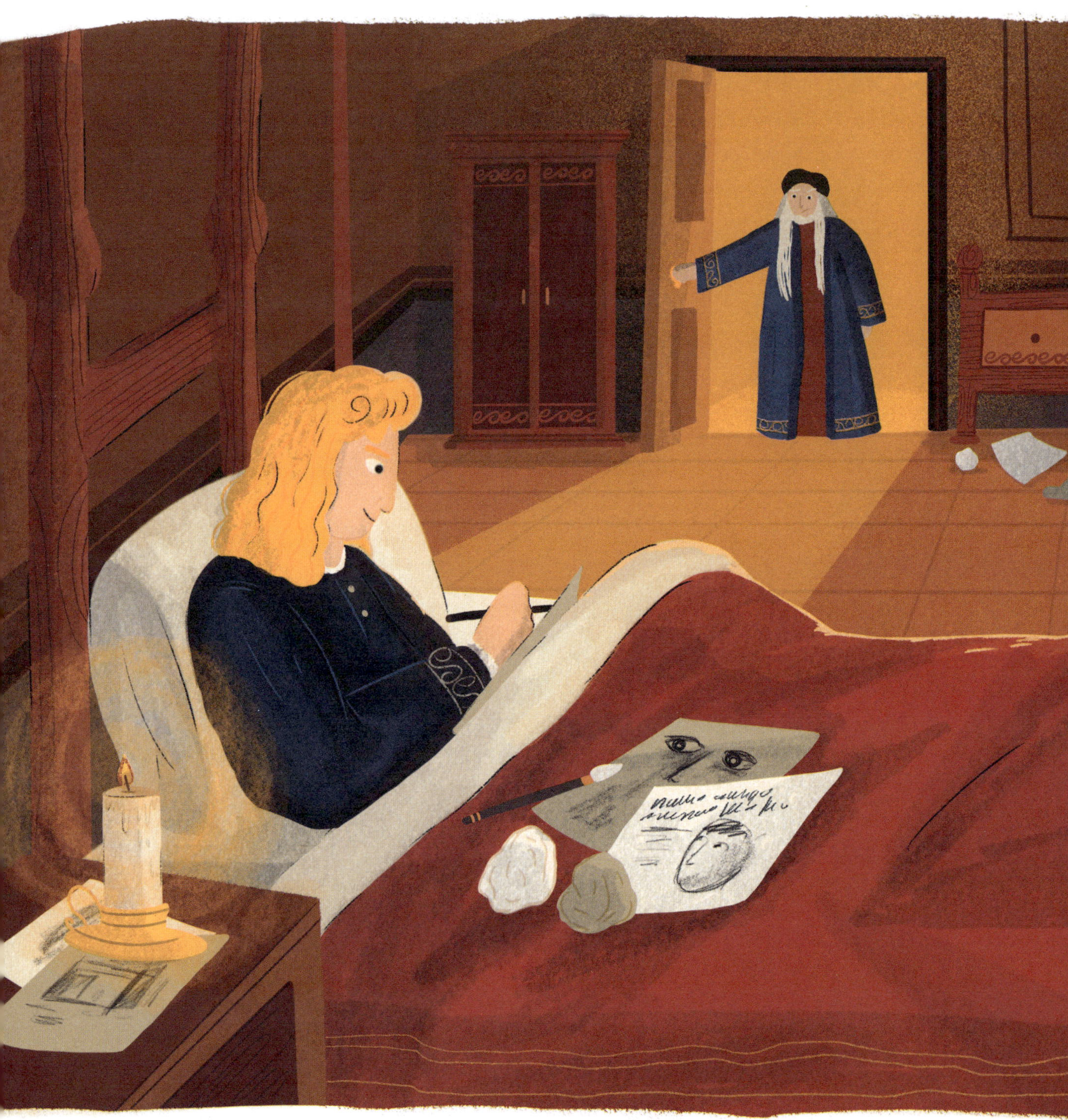

Piero arranged for Leonardo to do a painting for a church in 1478. When Leonardo did not finish the work, Piero was deeply disappointed.

Perhaps the greatest disappointment came from a piece called *The Adoration of the Magi*. This was commissioned to Leonardo in 1481.

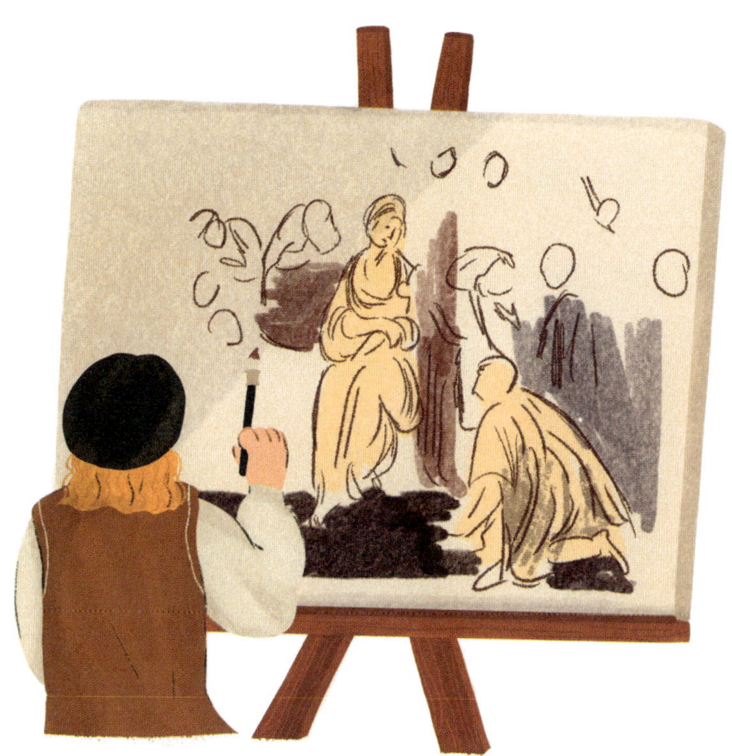

It was a very large religious image showing a number of people as well as a few animals. Leonardo was allowed more than two years to finish it—and he still didn't!

He spent much of that time making sketches for it, some of which were brilliant. But he never finished the work.

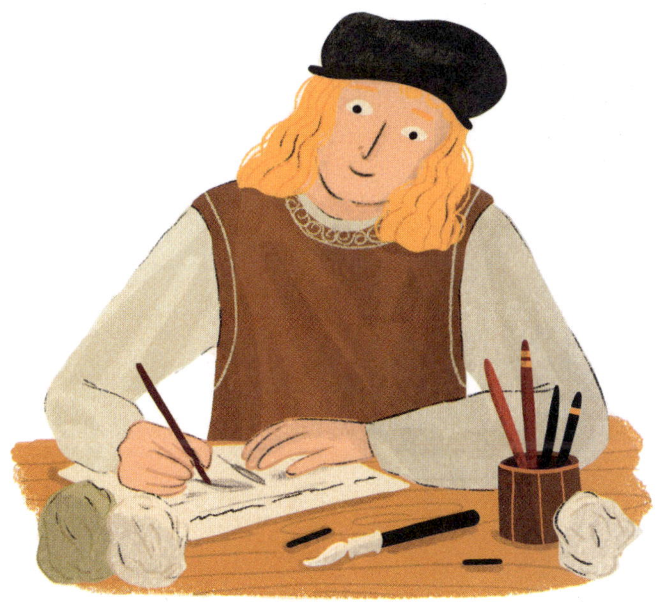

In 1482, Leonardo decided to move away from Florence. He wanted to explore other interests, like science and engineering.

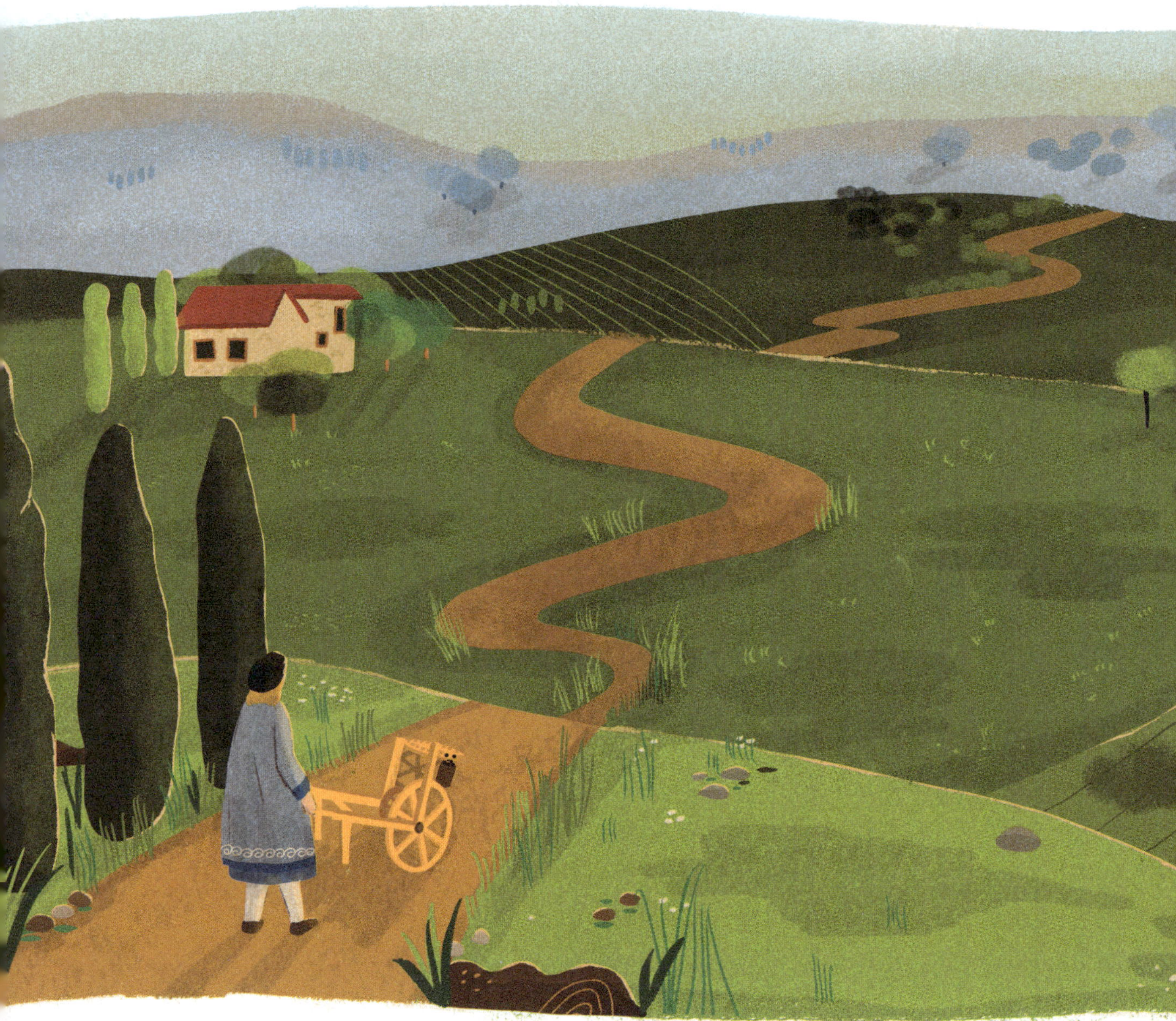

Leonardo went to the town of Milan, which is about 180 miles away. Leonardo knew this because he probably measured the distance with the odometer he built! It had a large wheel at the front and looked like a cart.

Each time the wheel turned, the machine measured the distance that it rolled. A machine like this had been designed about 1500 years earlier. But Leonardo wanted to make his better.

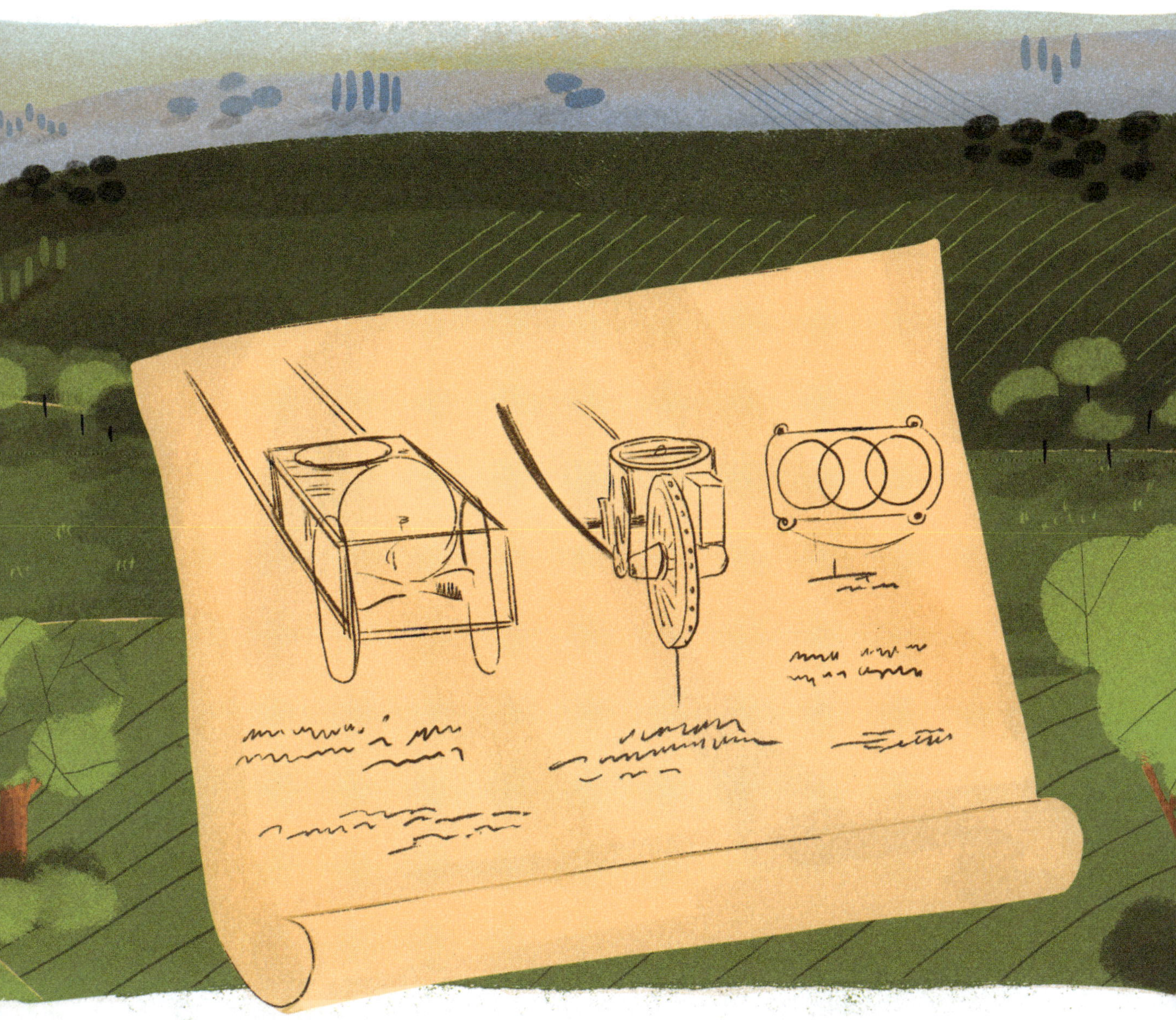

The odometer was just one of many inventions Leonardo would produce during his lifetime.

Measuring DISTANCES

Modern odometers still have the same purpose as Leonardo's—to measure distances. Their design has improved greatly since then. But the basic idea has not changed.

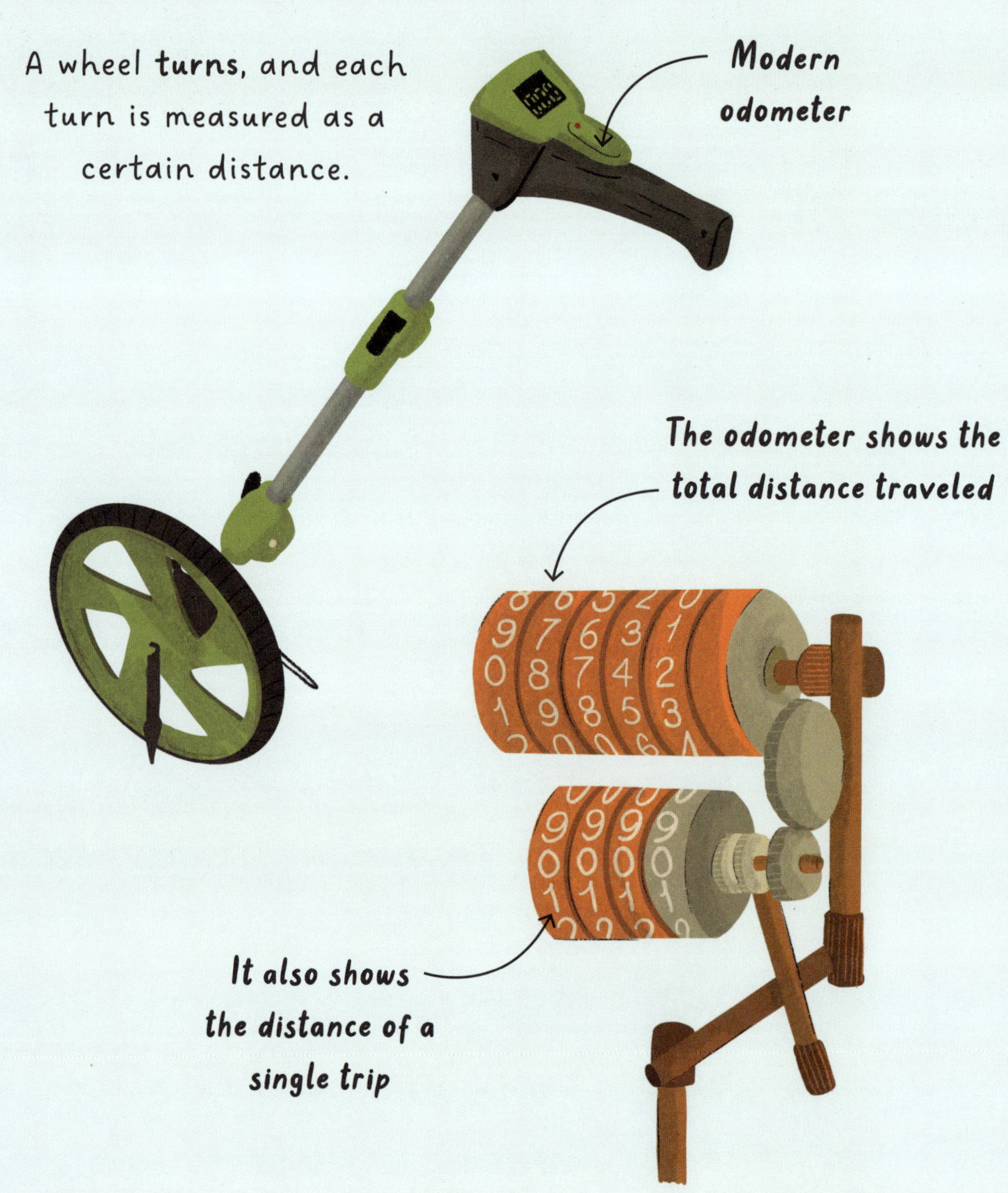

An odometer can be helpful in many ways. It can tell a driver how far a car has **traveled** from one point to another. It can also keep track of how many miles a car has gone since it was first built.

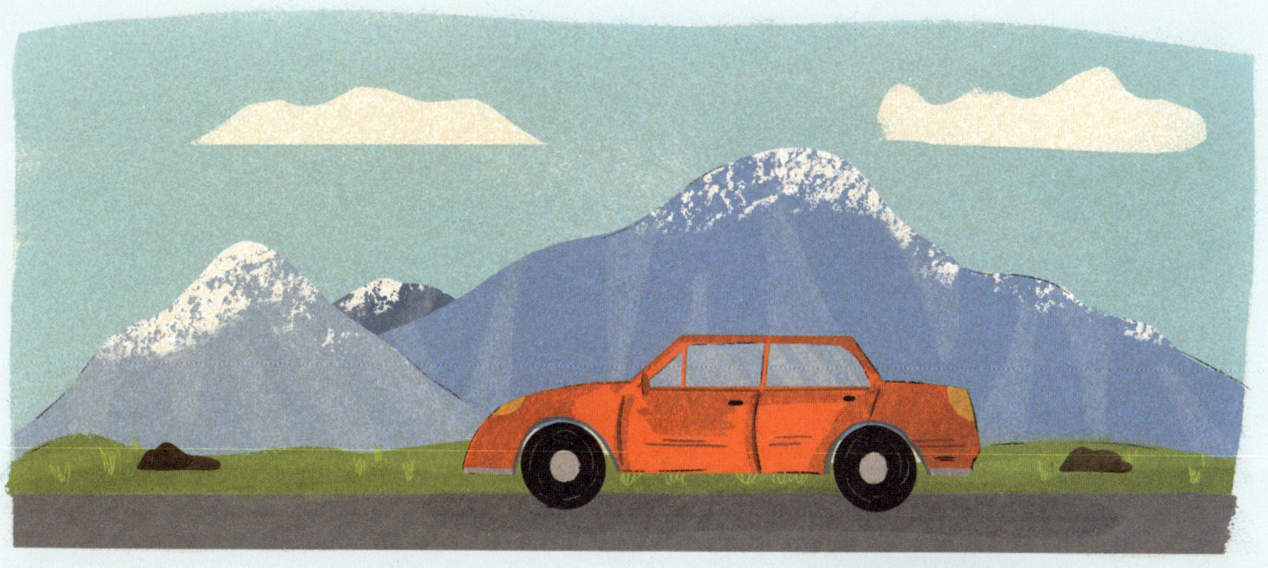

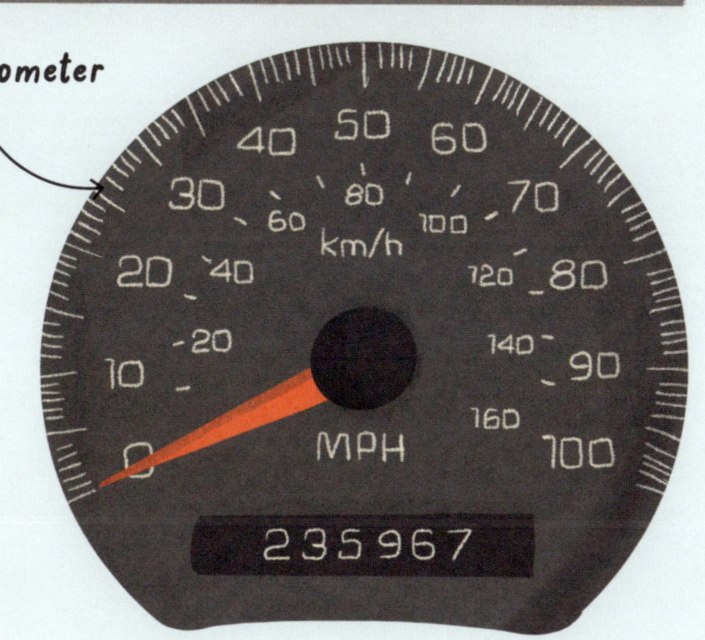

The word "odometer" is based on a Greek word—***hodómetron***. This means "to measure a way."

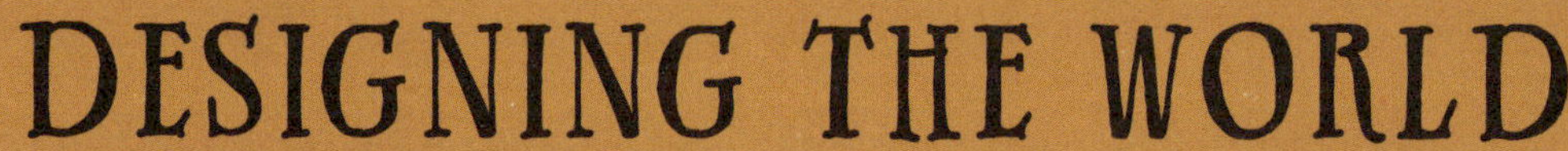

DESIGNING THE WORLD

From Architect to Map Maker

Leonardo had long been fascinated by architecture. He read through the writings of some of the best architects of the time.

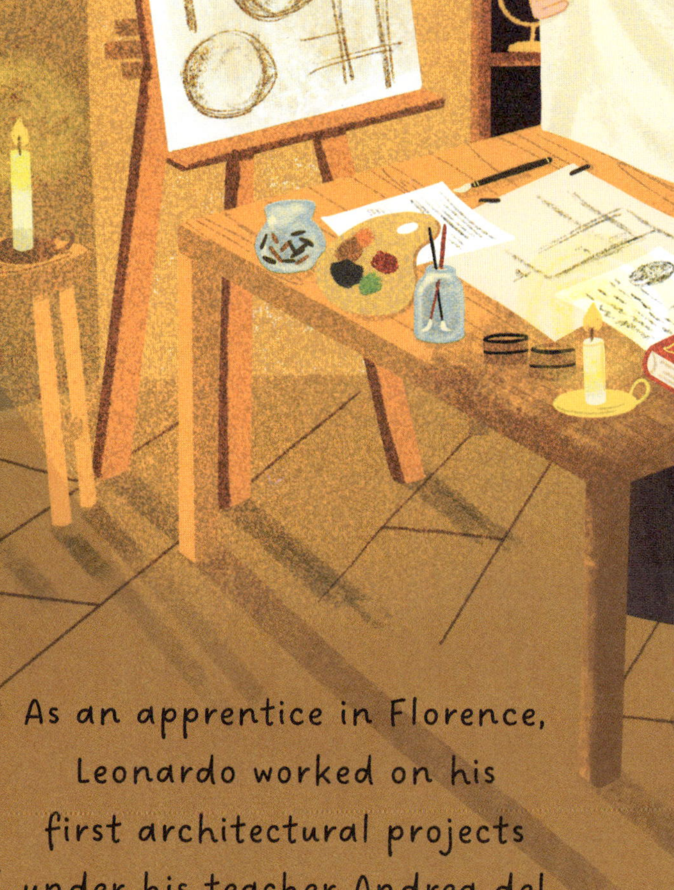

As an apprentice in Florence, Leonardo worked on his first architectural projects under his teacher Andrea del Verrocchio's guidance.

Verrocchio created a giant golden ball made of stone that weighed more than two tons. They had to work out how to put it on top of a church called the Cathedral of Santa Maria del Fiore.

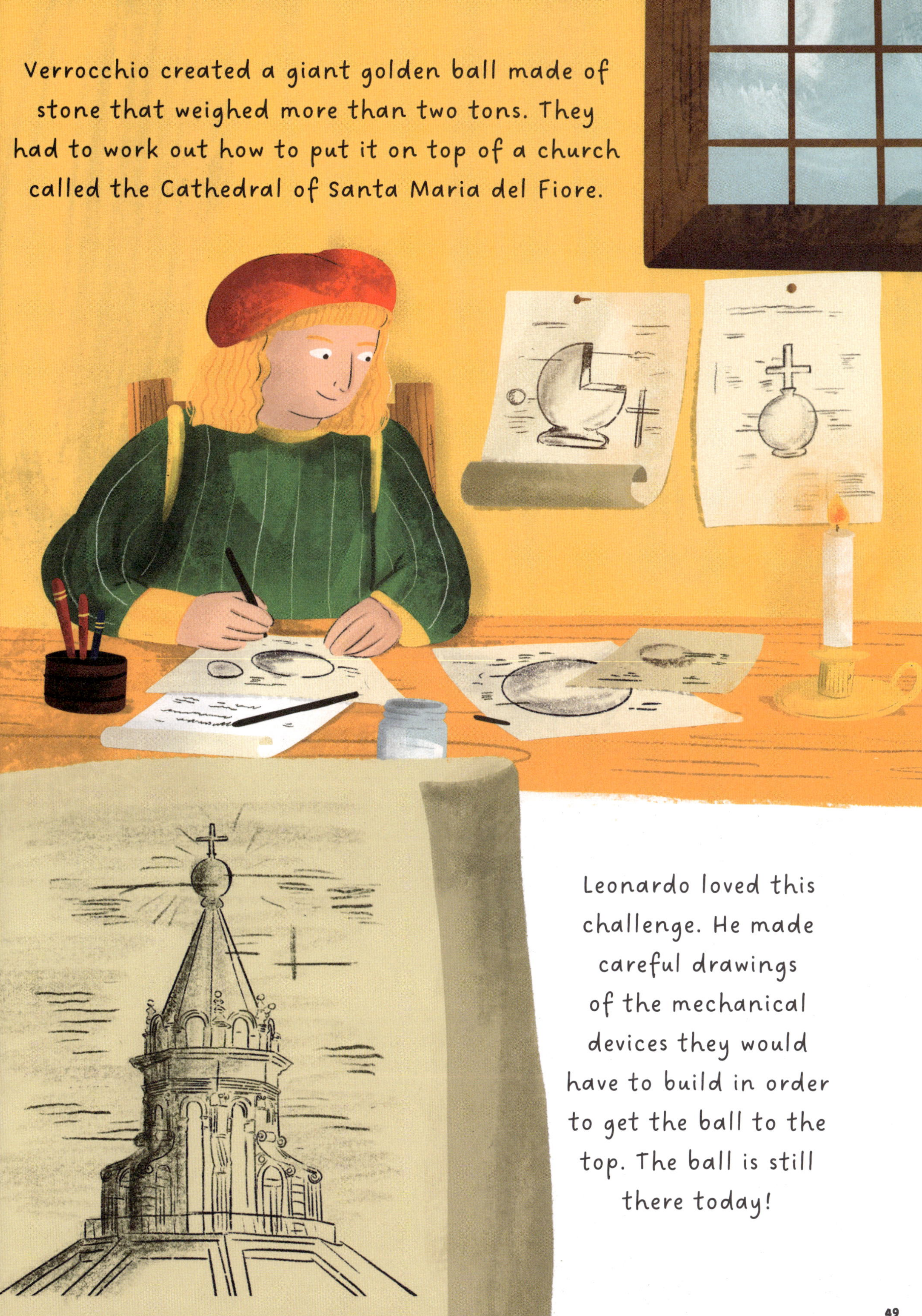

Leonardo loved this challenge. He made careful drawings of the mechanical devices they would have to build in order to get the ball to the top. The ball is still there today!

Leonardo took his architectural experience and interest with him to Milan, where he arrived in 1482 at the age of thirty.

He hoped to work for the Duke of Milan, a man named Ludovico Sforza.

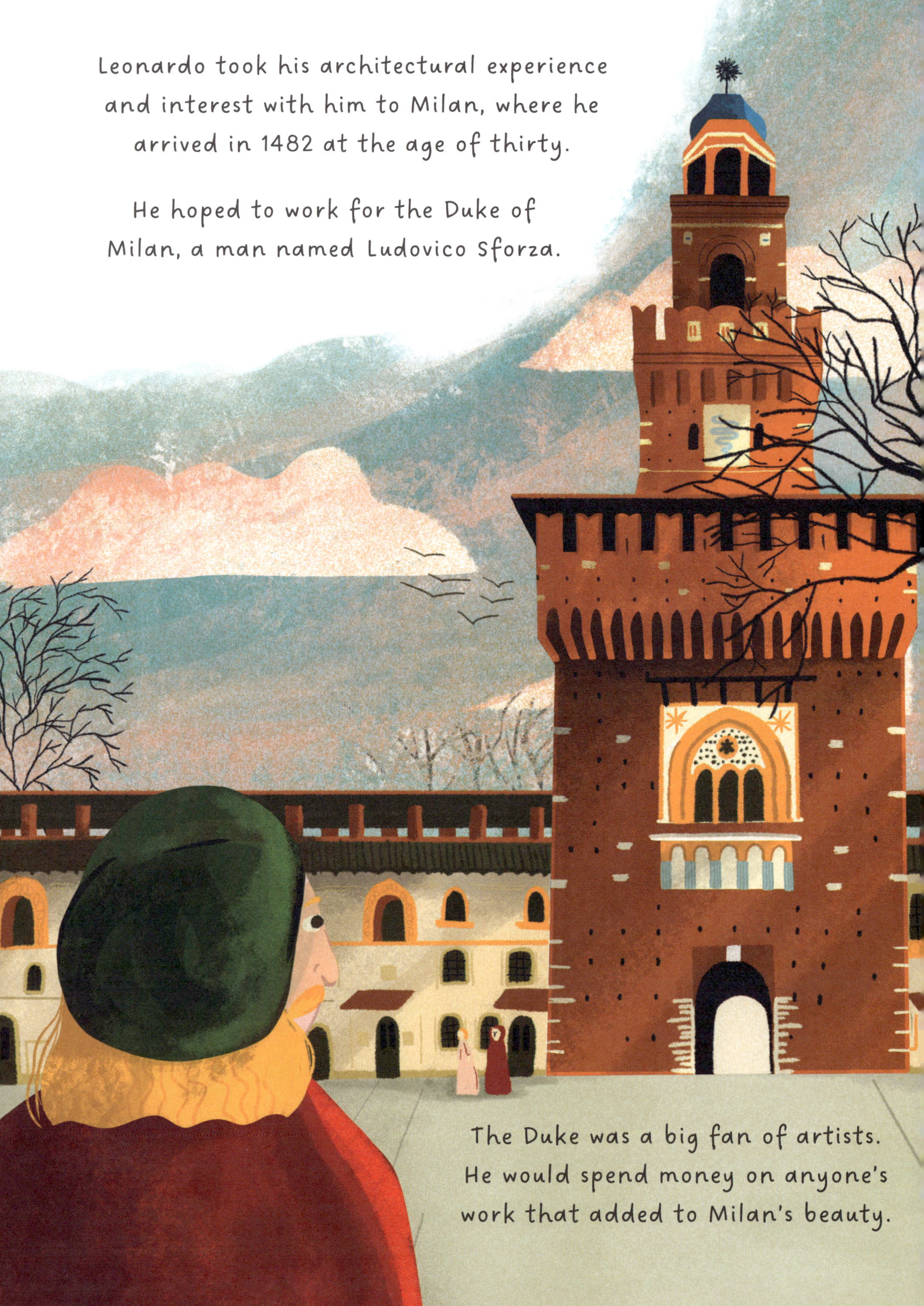

The Duke was a big fan of artists. He would spend money on anyone's work that added to Milan's beauty.

Leonardo wanted to do all sorts of things for the Duke—including architecture.

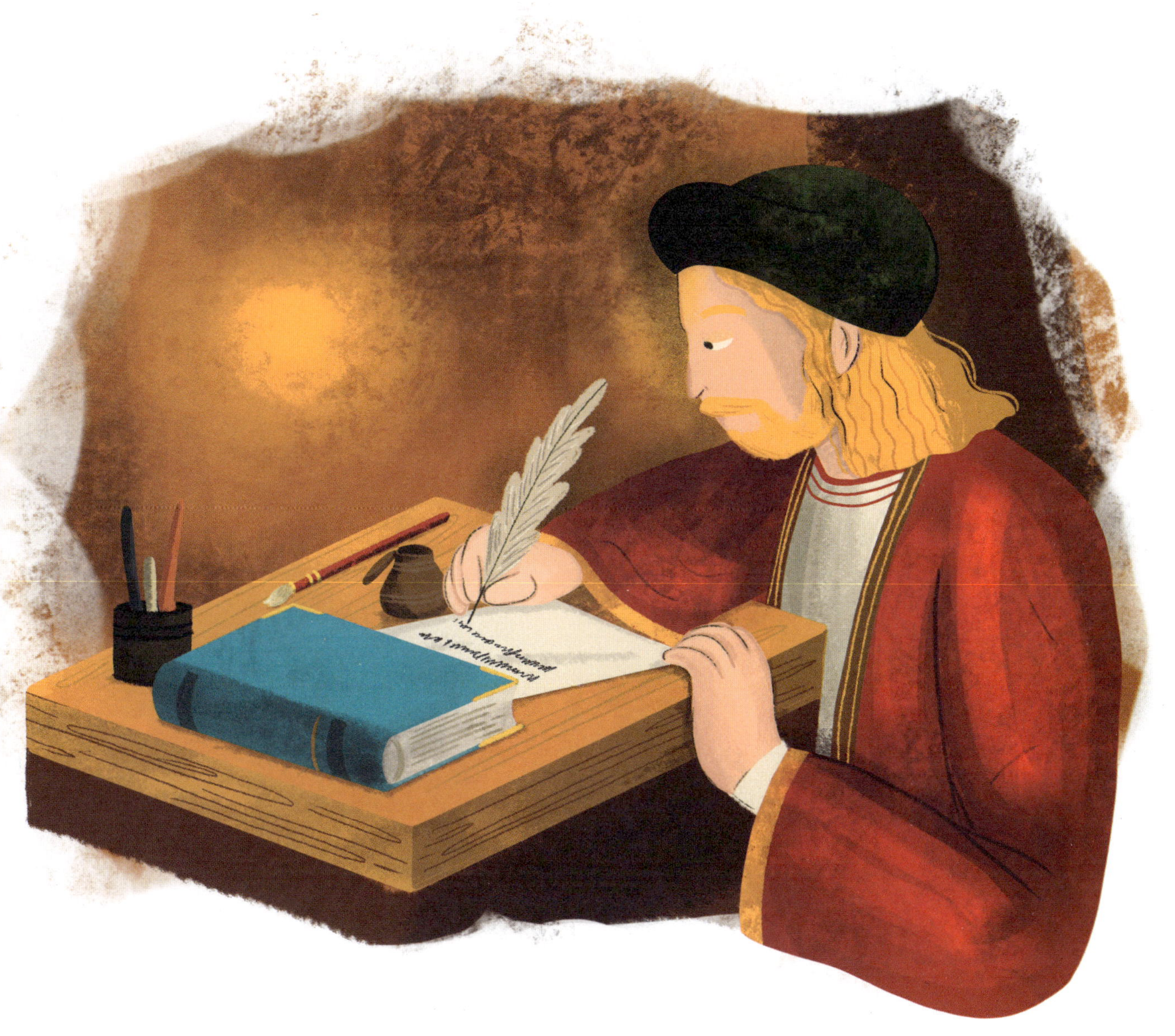

In his first letter to the Duke, Leonardo claimed,

"I can give perfect satisfaction and be the equal of any other in architecture and the composition of buildings..."

By the time he was in his mid-thirties, Leonardo was ready to put his architectural skills to good use. In 1487, he designed an entire imaginary city.

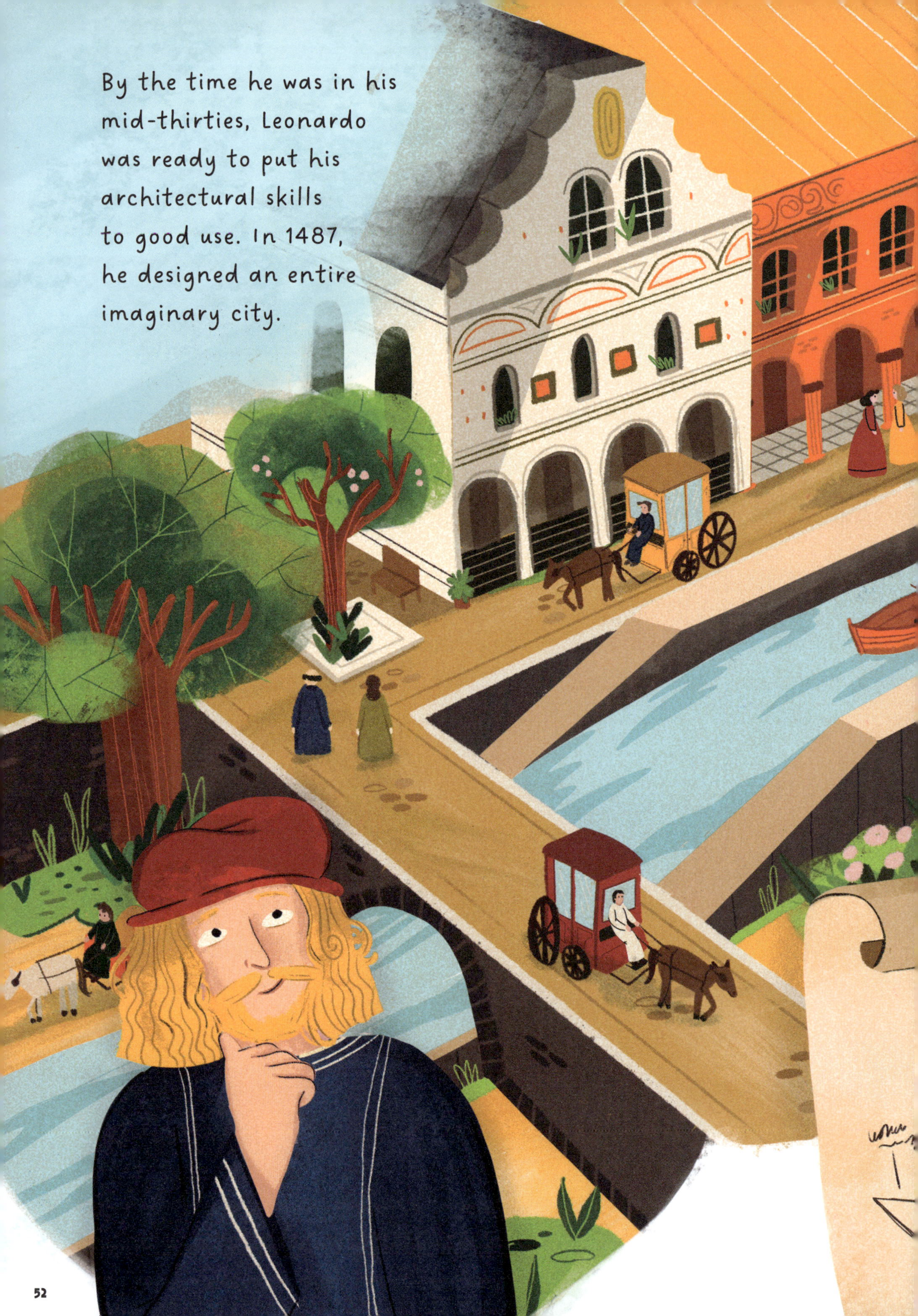

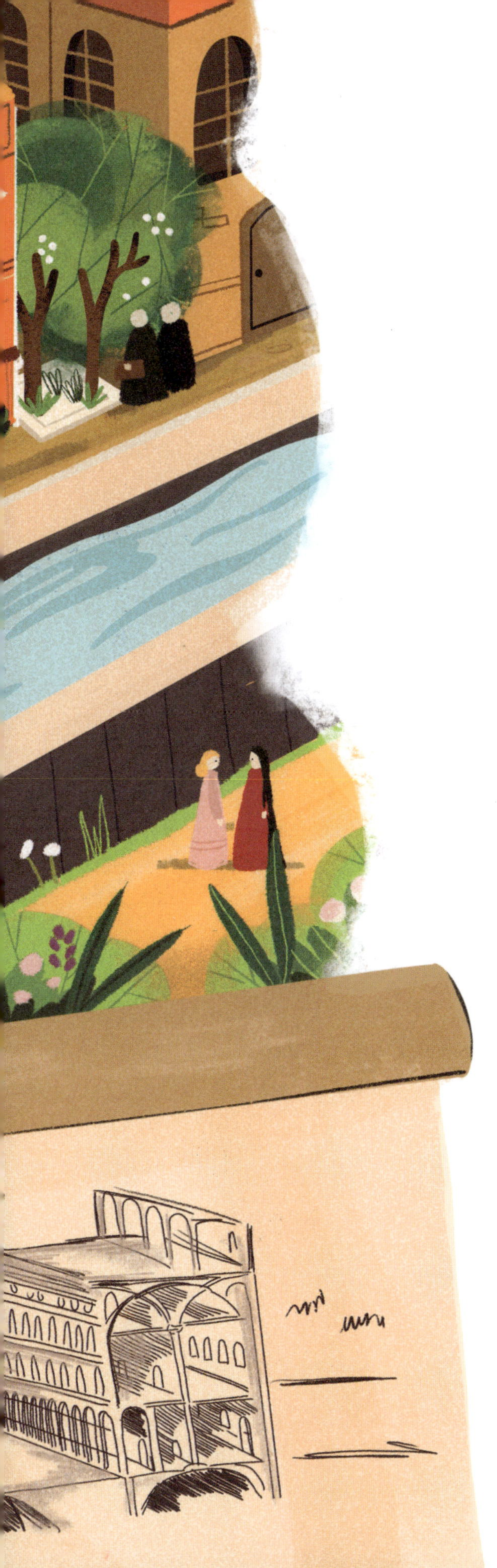

Leonardo spent time walking around Milan and making notes.

One problem he noticed was that it was too crowded. There was filth everywhere, which made people sick.

He thought his new city should have different levels. The lower levels would be for workers and other tradespeople to carry out their daily business. The upper levels would be cleaner and more beautiful, with colorful gardens and wide streets.

Leonardo also wanted his city to have waterways called canals. People could travel around by boat.

While Leonardo's ideas were interesting, they were also too hard to build back then. So his ideal city had to stay in his notebooks.

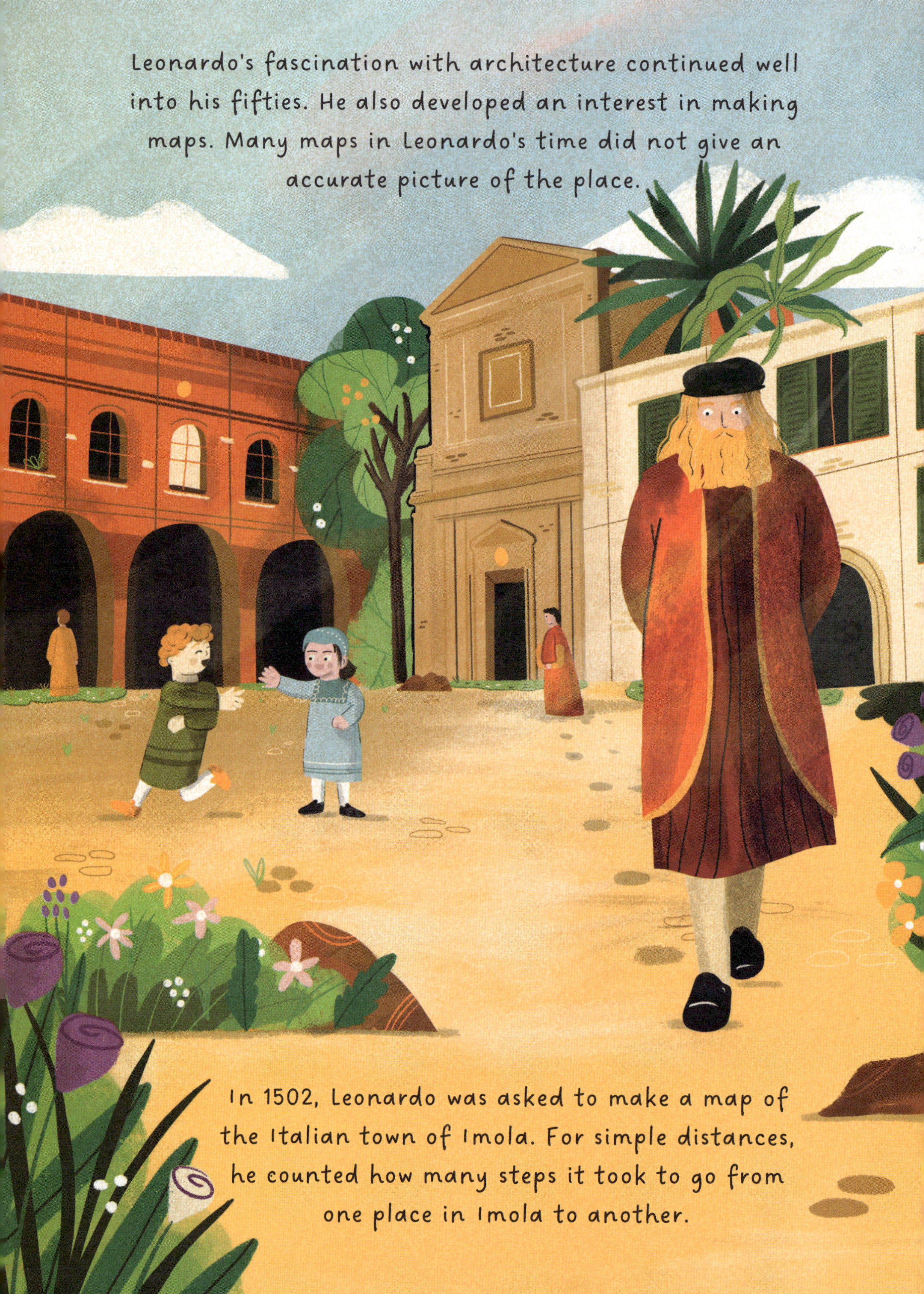

Leonardo's fascination with architecture continued well into his fifties. He also developed an interest in making maps. Many maps in Leonardo's time did not give an accurate picture of the place.

In 1502, Leonardo was asked to make a map of the Italian town of Imola. For simple distances, he counted how many steps it took to go from one place in Imola to another.

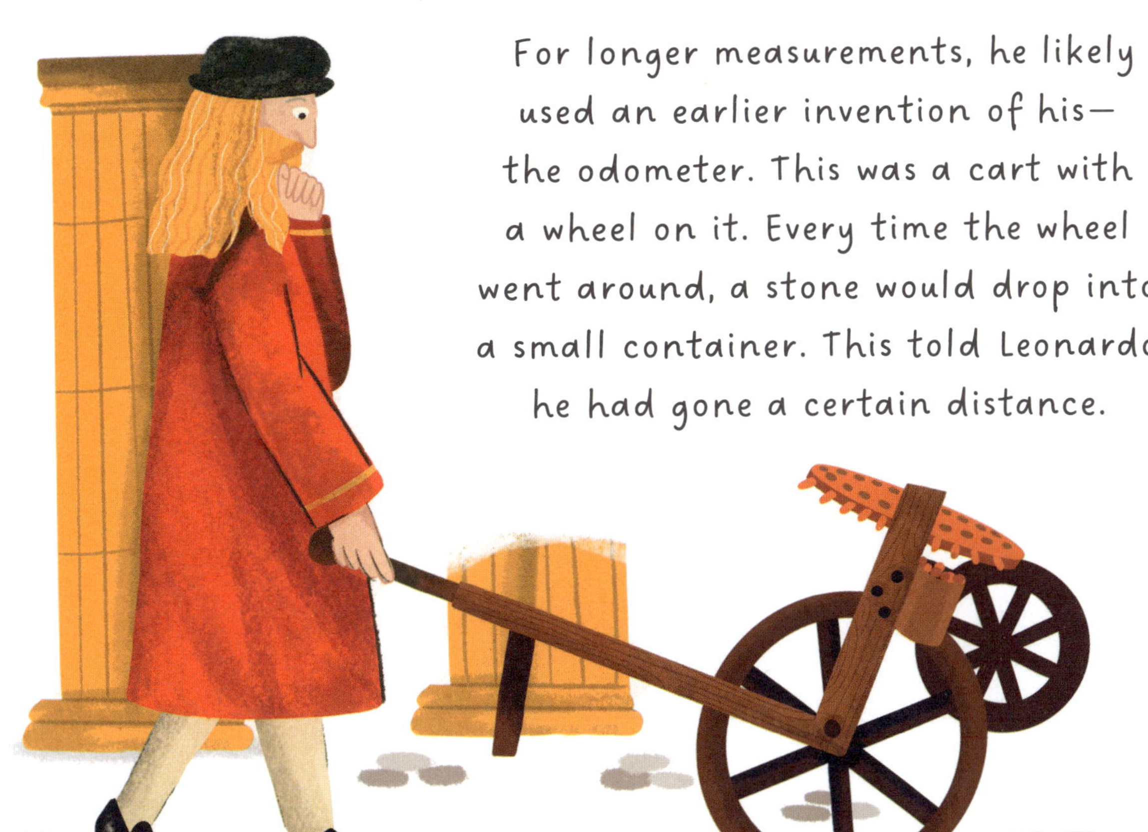

For longer measurements, he likely used an earlier invention of his—the odometer. This was a cart with a wheel on it. Every time the wheel went around, a stone would drop into a small container. This told Leonardo he had gone a certain distance.

Leonardo carefully colored the Imola map. Water was blue and the houses were red. It was one of the most artistic maps of its time.

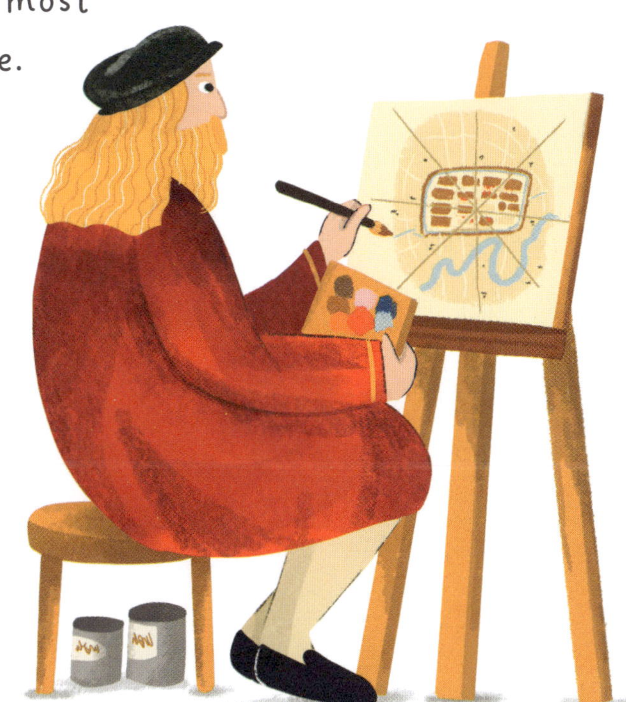

By combining his problem-solving and artistic skills, Leonardo changed the way people thought about designing and mapping cities.

Mapping the WORLD

Leonardo's desire to understand the world helped others better understand it, too. His map of Imola is a good example of this.

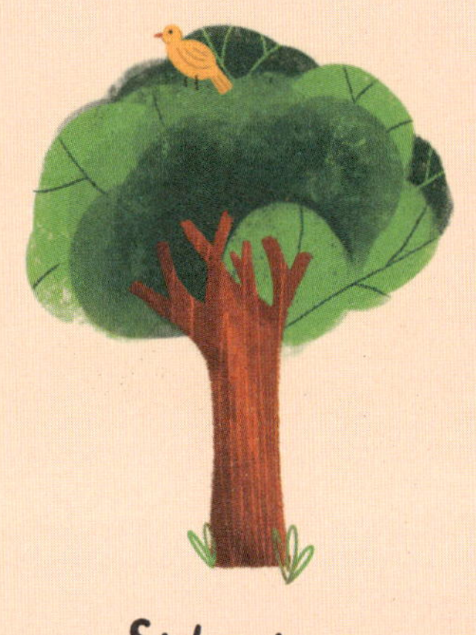

Side view

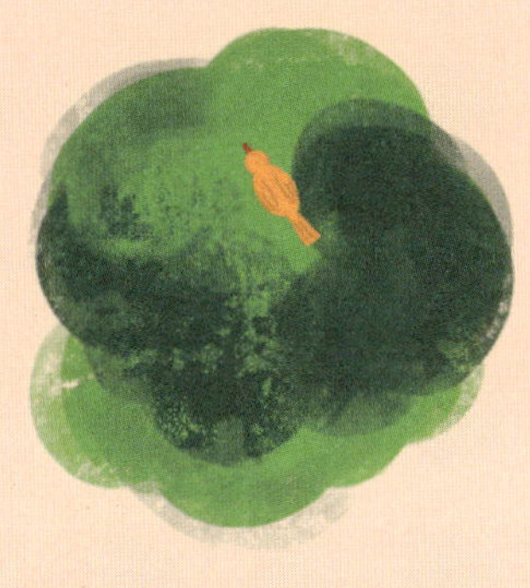

Bird's-eye view

The map was among the first to show an accurate "**bird's-eye view**" of a particular place. It wasn't long before other mapmakers were doing the same thing.

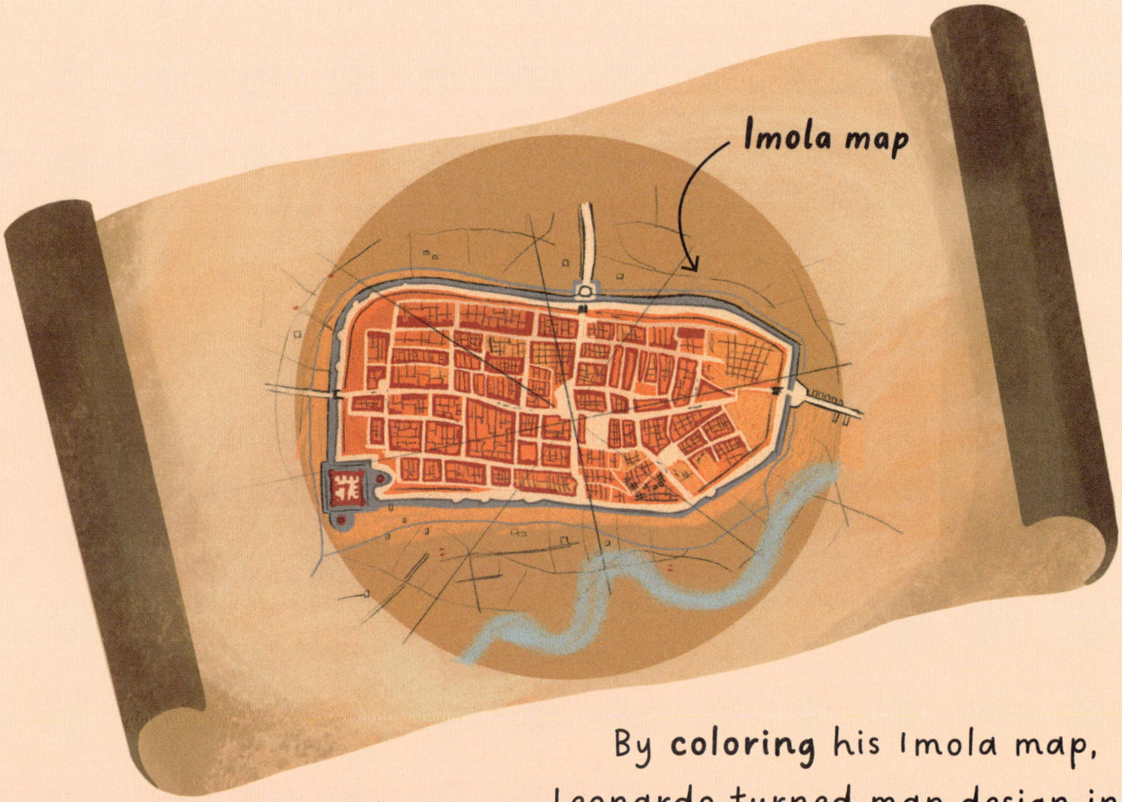

Imola map

By **coloring** his Imola map, Leonardo turned map design into a new kind of art form.

Blue indicates water such as rivers and lakes

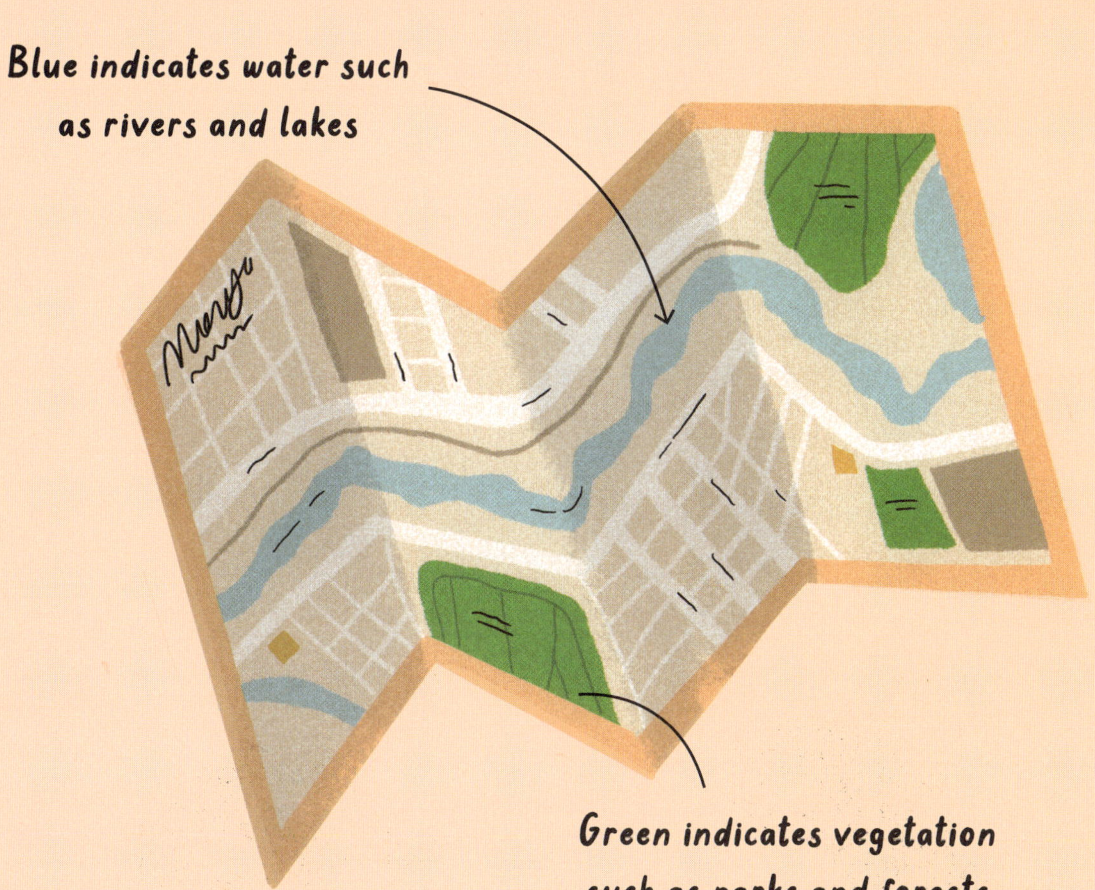

Green indicates vegetation such as parks and forests

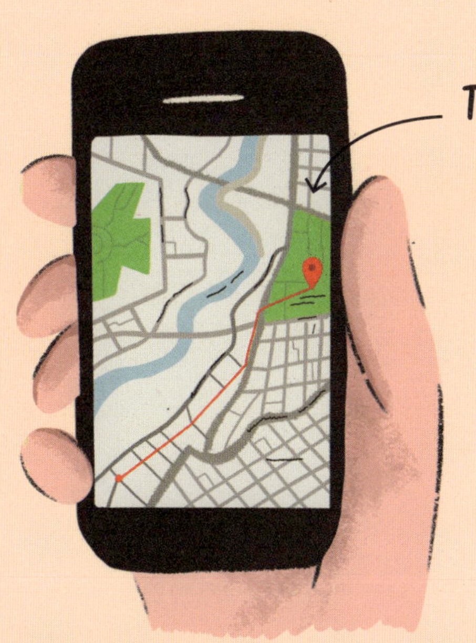

The colors are clear, even on smartphone screens

Different **colors** show different things, but they also make a map something that's lovely to look at.

Leonardo's brilliant ideas led to **improvements in mapmaking**. Today, almost all maps are drawn this way.

MIGHTY MACHINES

Leonardo Prepares for Battle

Leonardo was fascinated by military engineering—the design of equipment used during times of war, such as vehicles and weapons. He had lots of ideas for new machines.

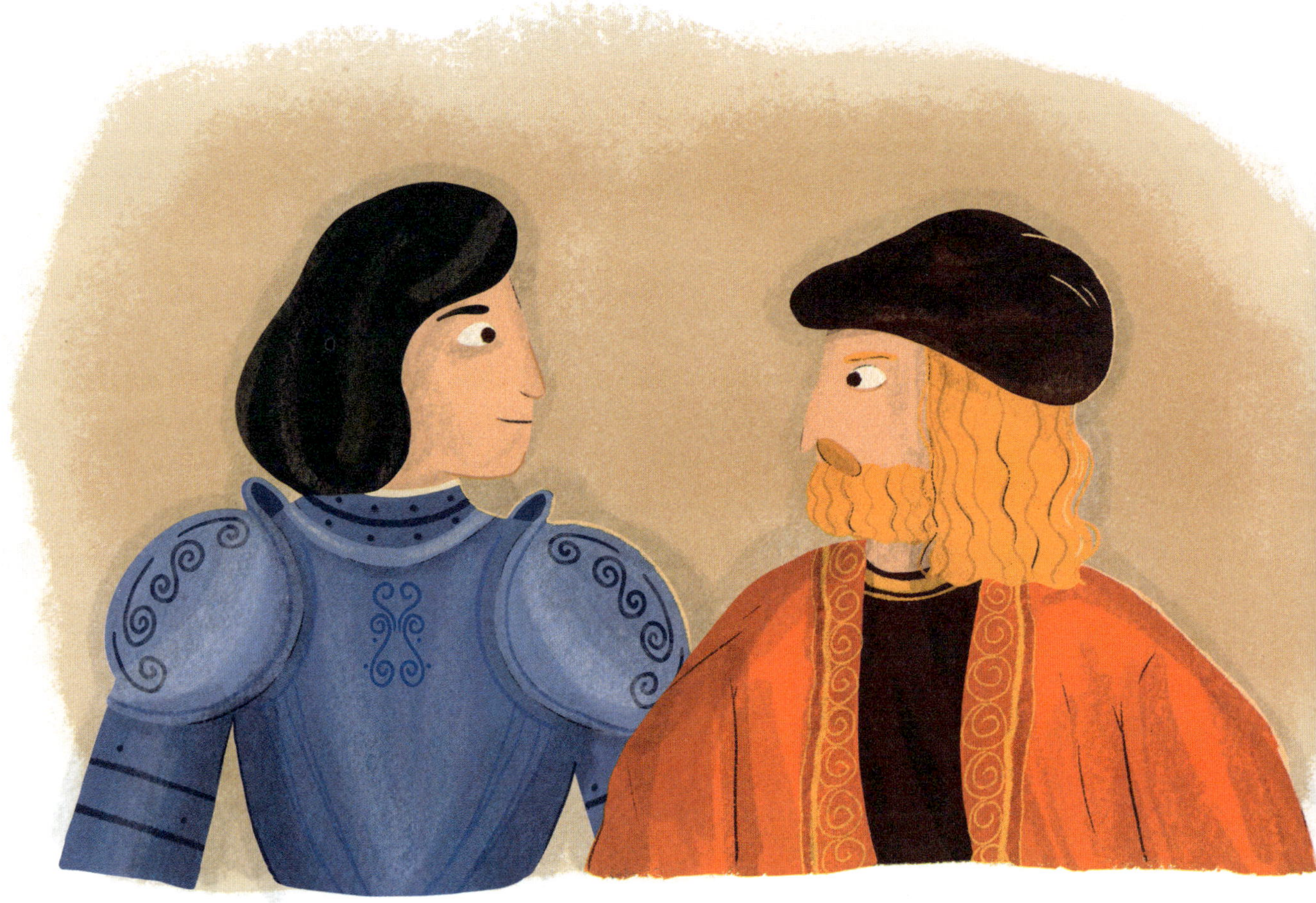

Leonardo was trying his best to get on the good side of the Duke of Milan, Ludovico Sforza. The Duke and the rest of his family had become powerful in Milan, mostly through force.

Many people had died in the Italian War (1494–1495), during which Ludovico took power as the Duke of Milan.

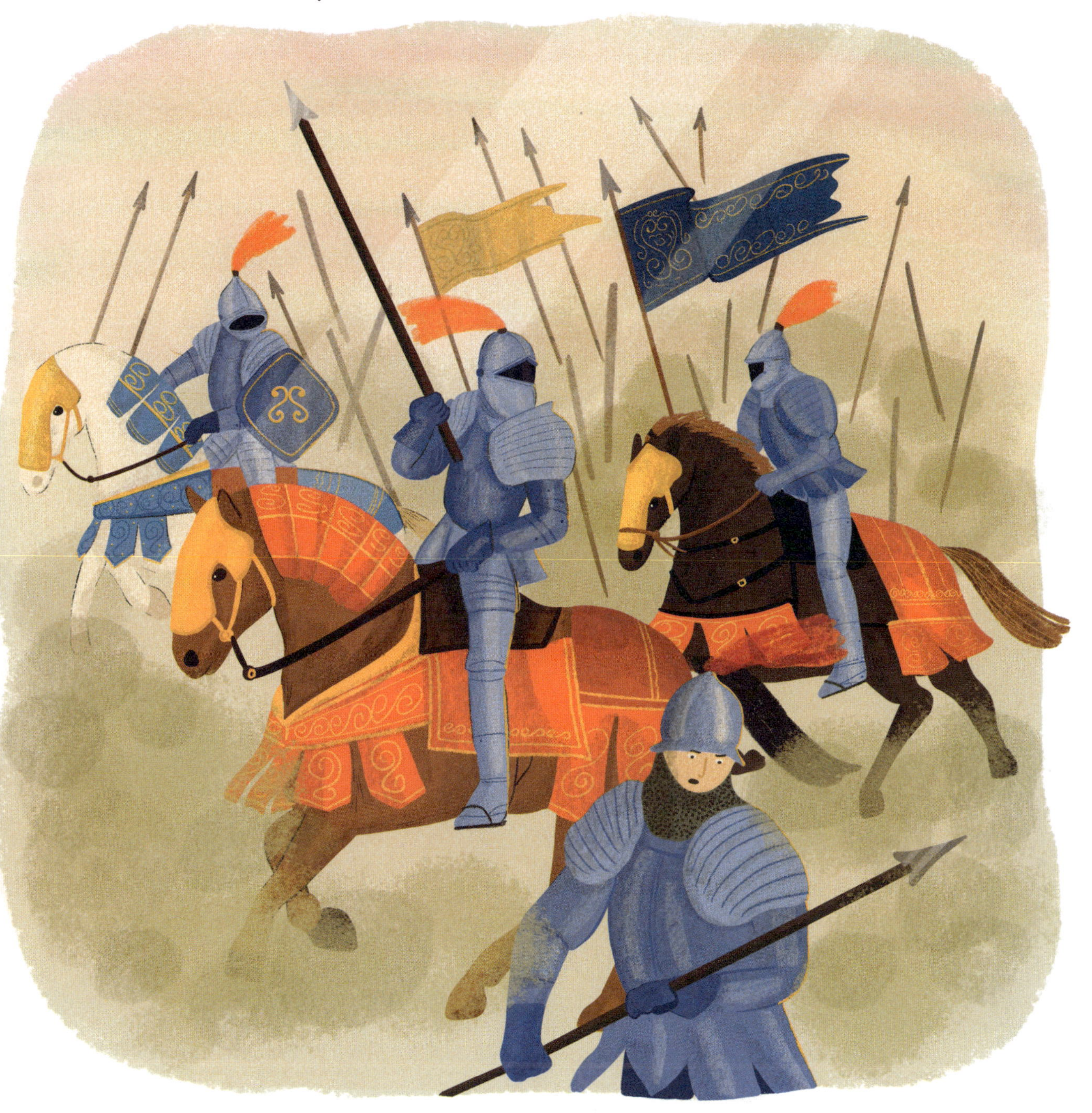

It also meant Ludovico spent a lot of time worrying about who might try to take power from him in the same way!

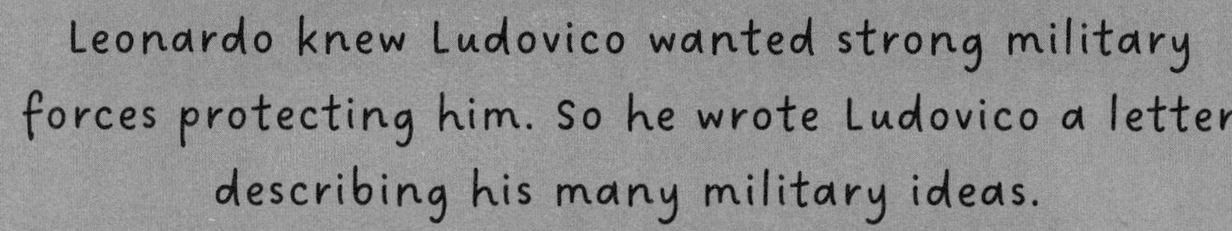

Leonardo knew Ludovico wanted strong military forces protecting him. So he wrote Ludovico a letter describing his many military ideas.

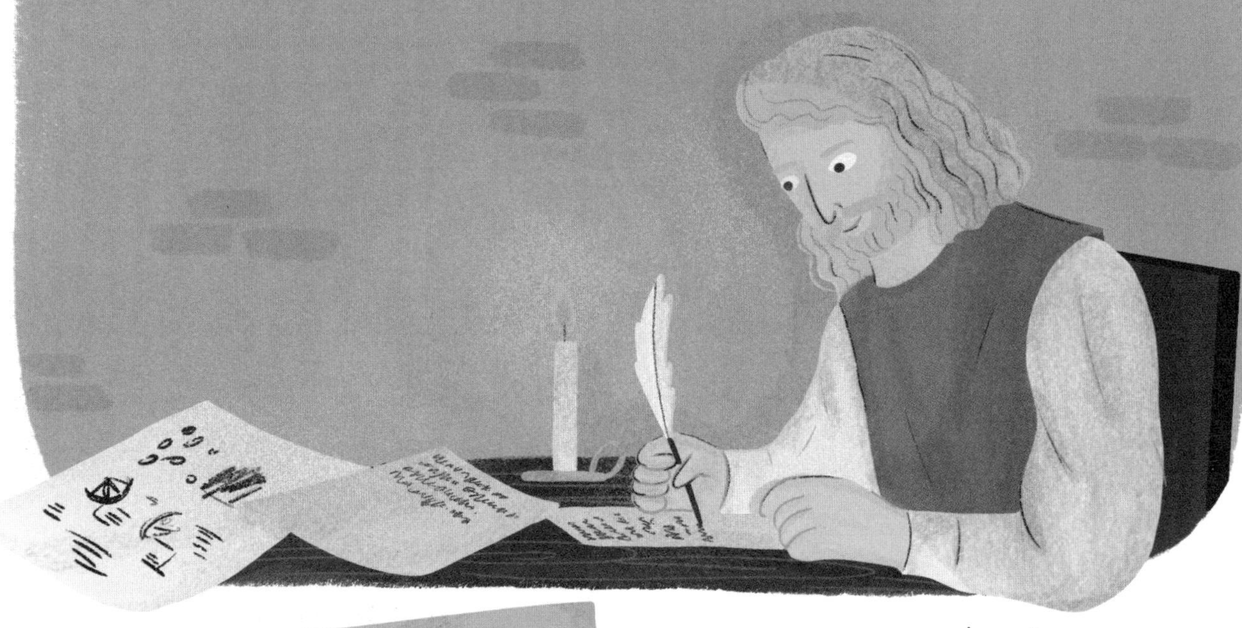

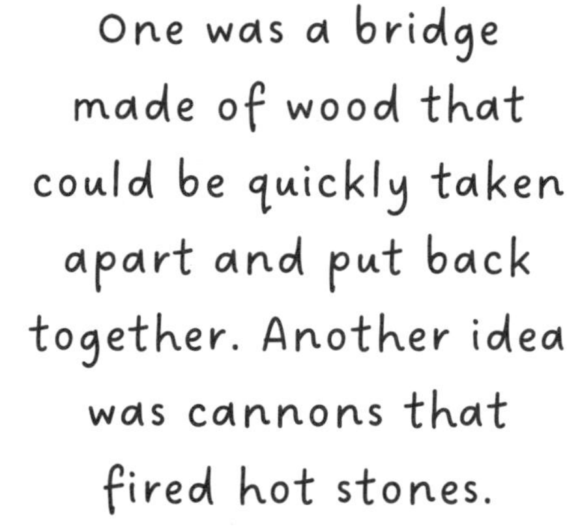

One was a bridge made of wood that could be quickly taken apart and put back together. Another idea was cannons that fired hot stones.

Leonardo had an idea for a diving suit. A solider could wear the suit underwater and breathe through a hose attached to a container filled with air. Then the soldier could attack enemy ships from beneath.

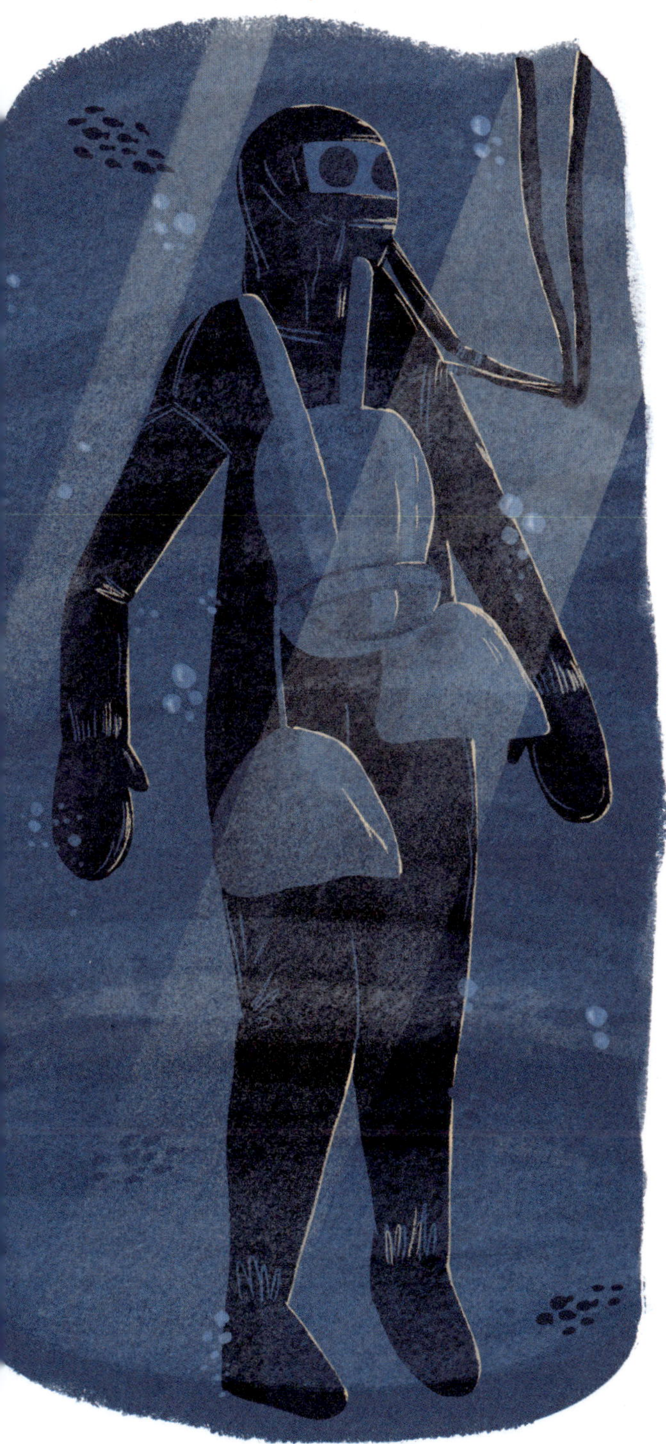

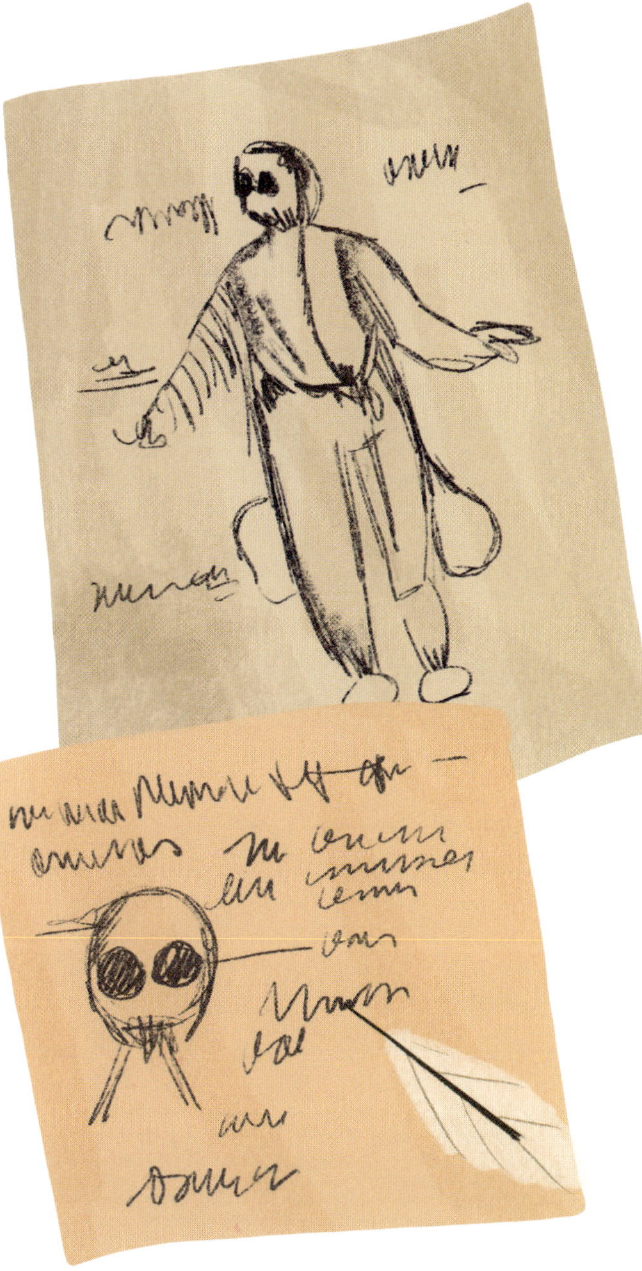

Leonardo also wrote out a detailed description of how Ludovico's men could quickly dig tunnels. This way they could get into an enemy fort without being noticed.

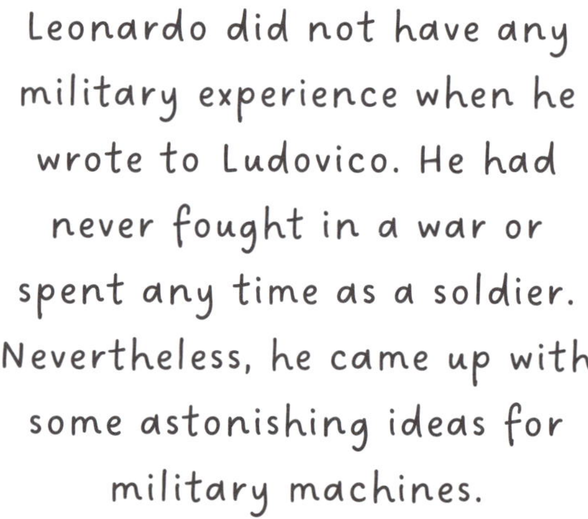

Leonardo did not have any military experience when he wrote to Ludovico. He had never fought in a war or spent any time as a soldier. Nevertheless, he came up with some astonishing ideas for military machines.

One was a device that knocked down ladders with enemy soldiers on it. Another had spinning blades that hit soldiers if they climbed too high on the ladders.

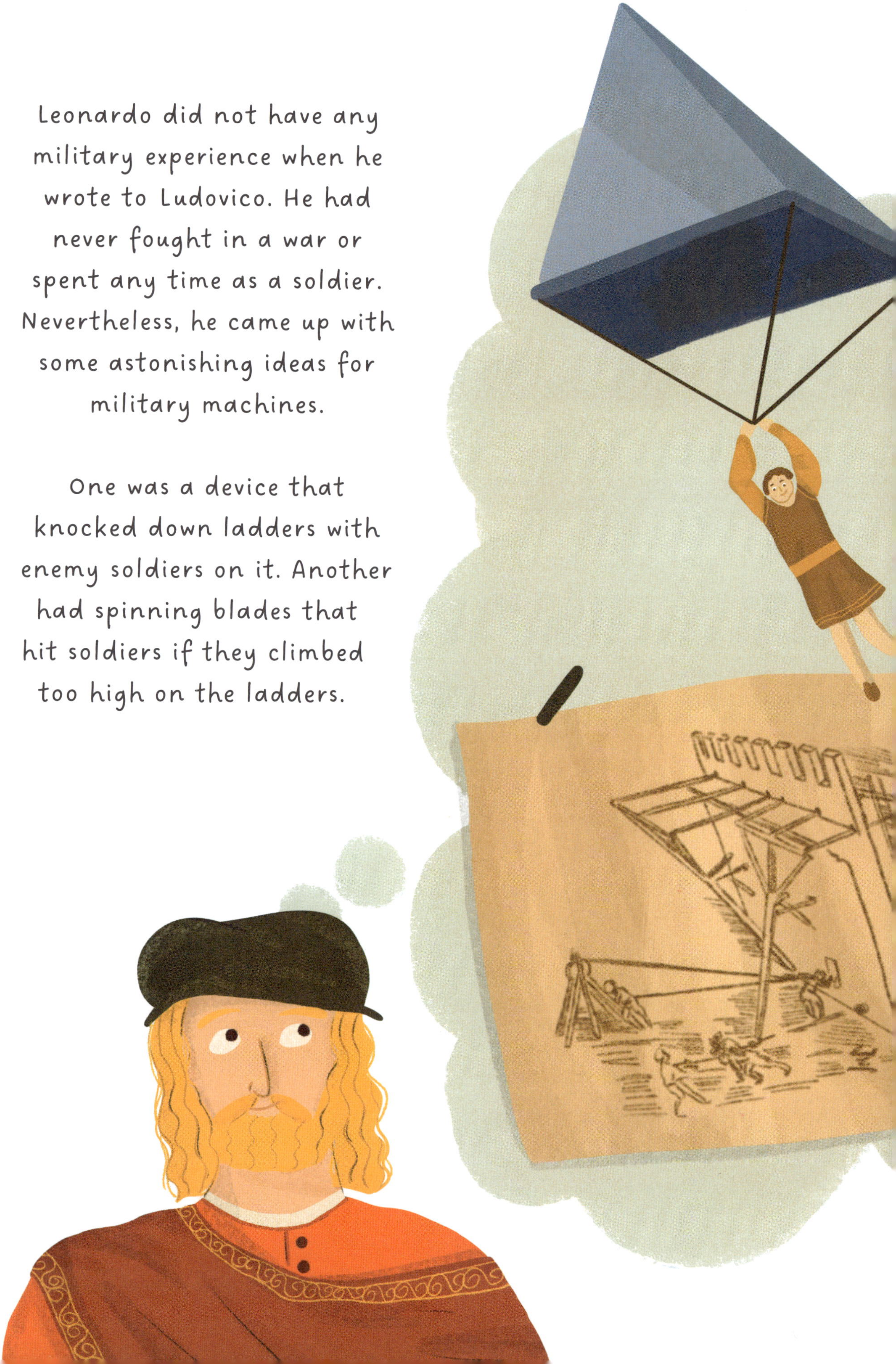

Leonardo also wanted to build a flying machine. Such a machine would be helpful to soldiers during battle. A blade shaped like a screw was attached over the place where the pilot sat. When it spun, the machine was supposed to lift into the air.

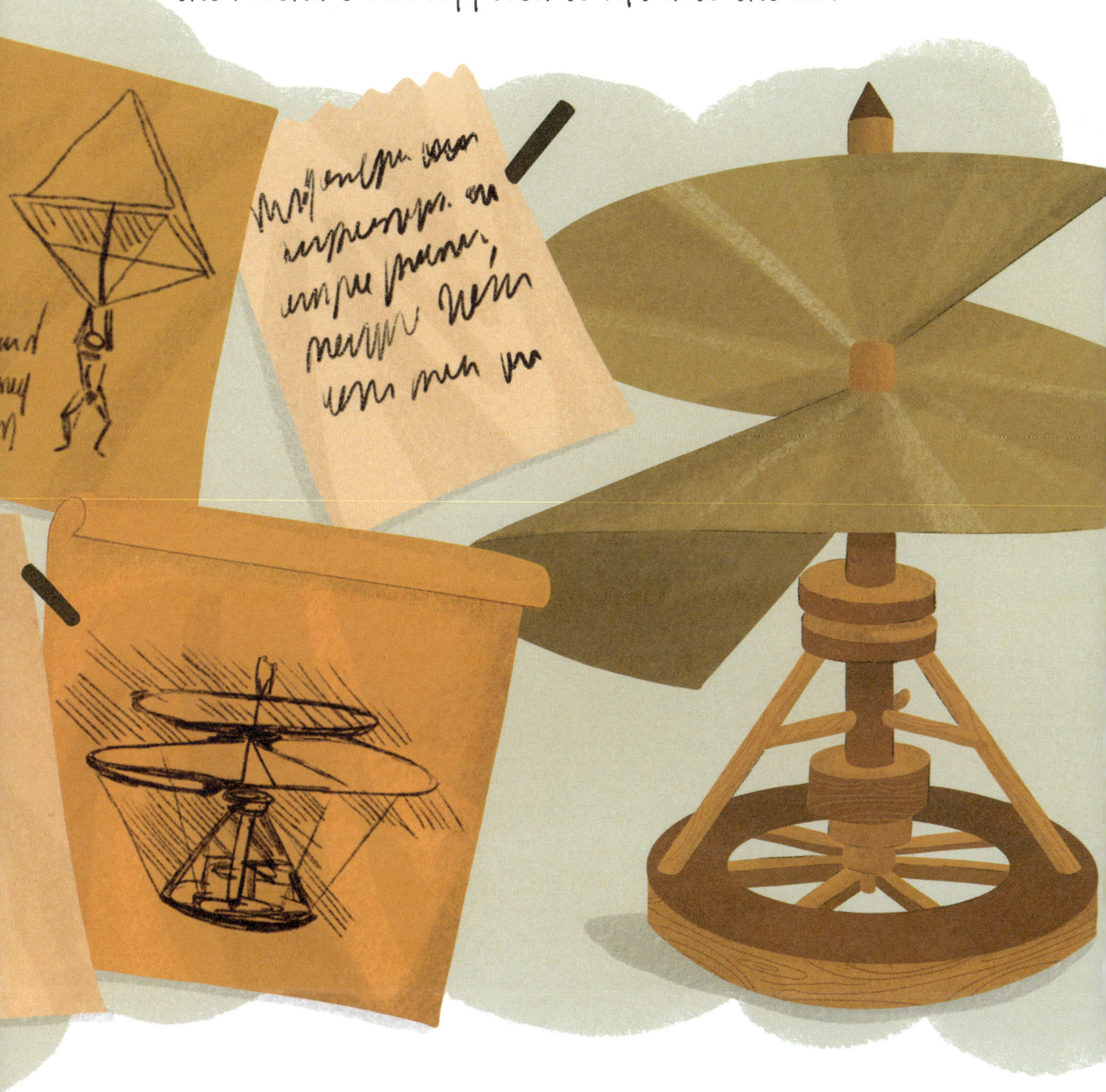

Leonardo's design was similar to today's helicopters. And if the pilot had to jump out, Leonardo also designed an early version of the parachute!

One of Leonardo's most famous military designs was for a vehicle that protected soldiers riding inside. It was shaped like a wide cone and made from strong metal plates. Anything fired at it, such as arrows, would simply bounce off.

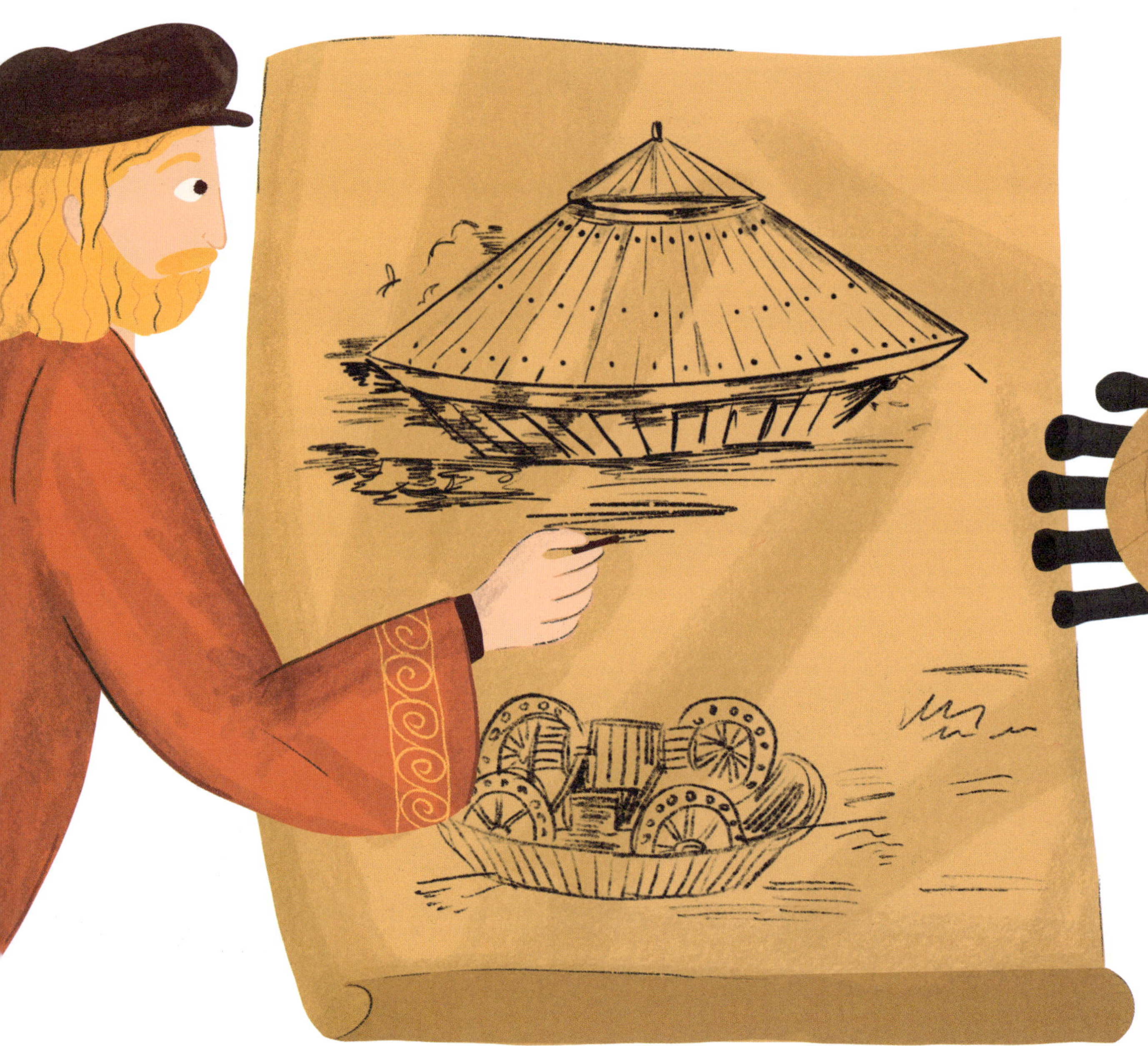

It also had wheels. The soldiers turned a set of hand-cranks inside, which then made the wheels turn.

There were also cannons built into it. Soldiers could use these to fire back at their enemies.

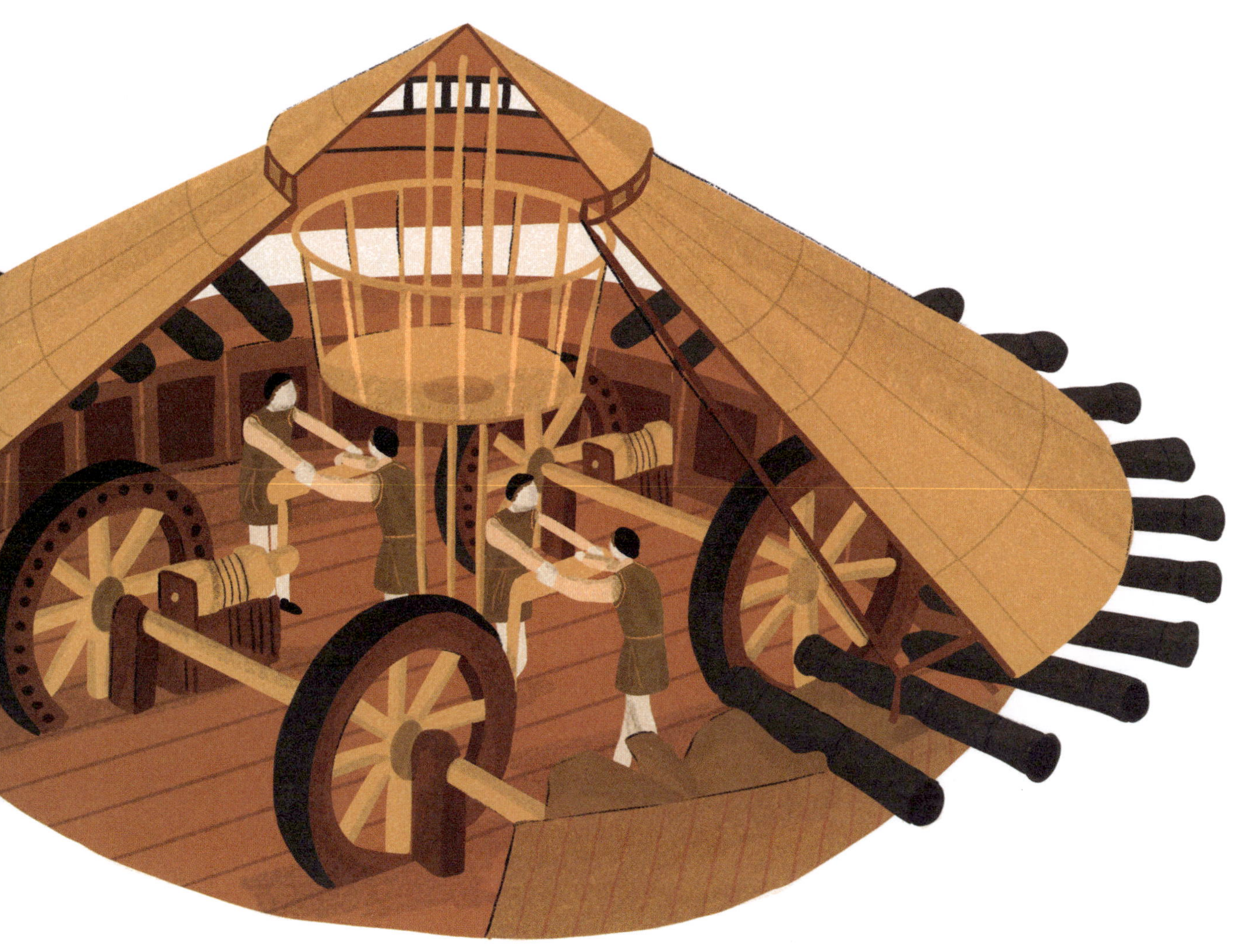

Leonardo's design may have inspired the first military tanks that were built hundreds of years later.

In the AIR

Leonardo was fascinated by the flight of birds and studied them for years. This came in handy when he began thinking about ways that people might fly.

One of Leonardo's earliest ideas about human flight was based on bird anatomy. He sketched out a set of **wings** that could be attached directly to a person's body.

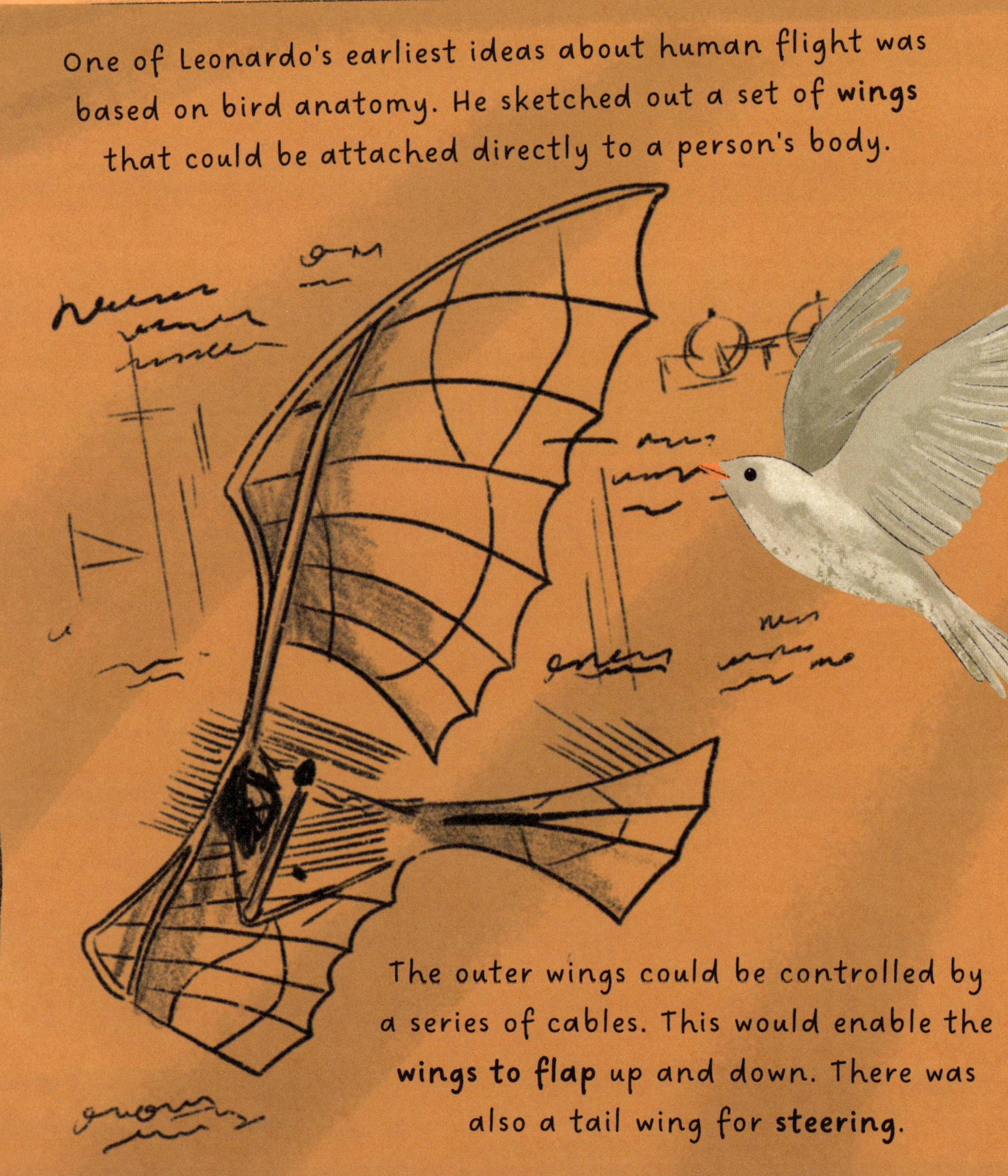

The outer wings could be controlled by a series of cables. This would enable the **wings to flap** up and down. There was also a tail wing for **steering**.

The wings of a modern **hang glider** do not flap. The flyer simply soars through the air.

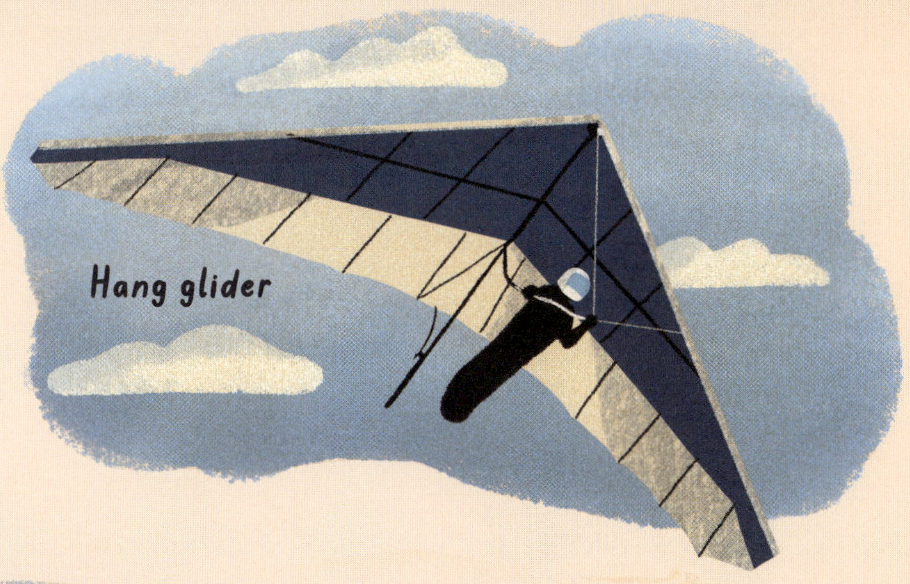

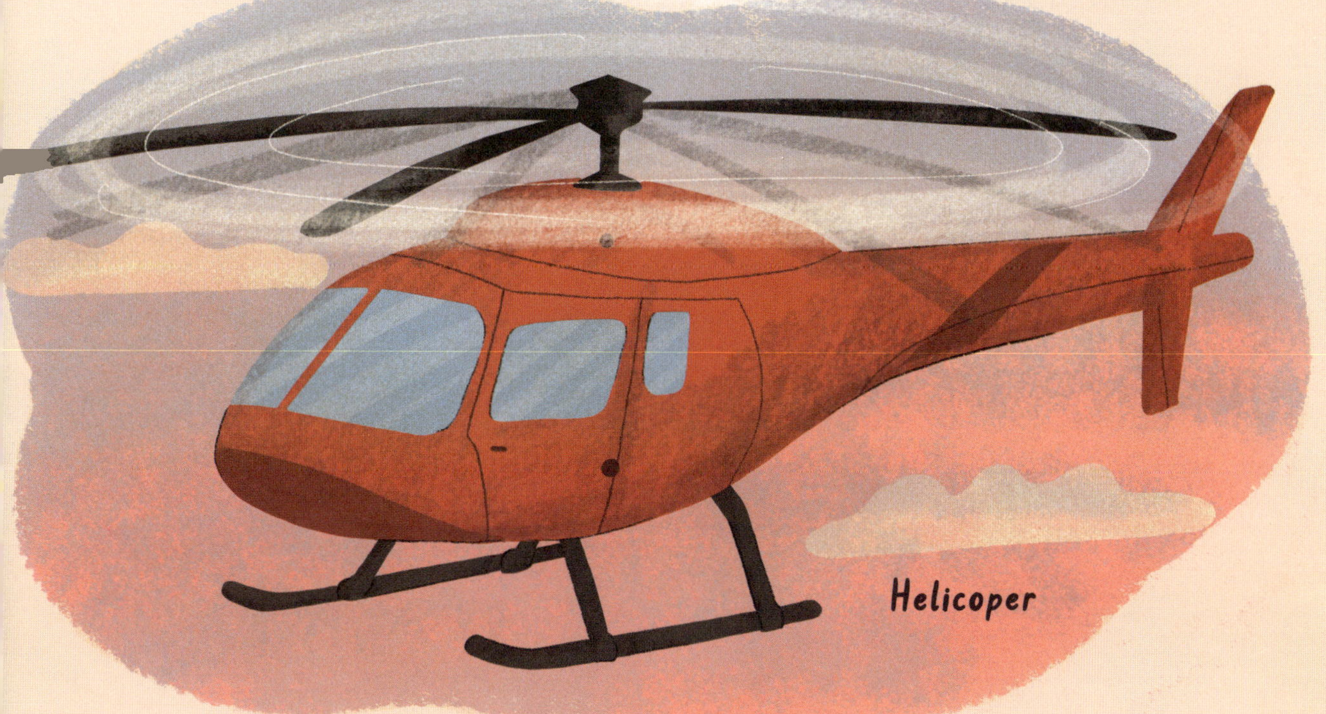

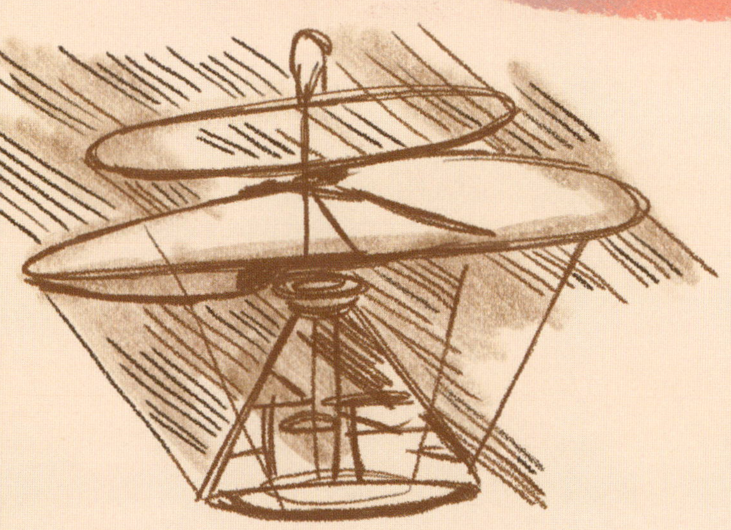

Leonardo had another idea called the "aerial screw." A working model was never built, but it inspired the idea for the modern **helicopter** hundreds of years later.

TAKING TO THE STAGE

Leonardo Becomes a Showman

Leonardo did not experience much artistic culture in his hometown of Vinci. There were no theaters or museums. Nevertheless, Leonardo would go on to invent devices that make putting on shows easier and more efficient to this day.

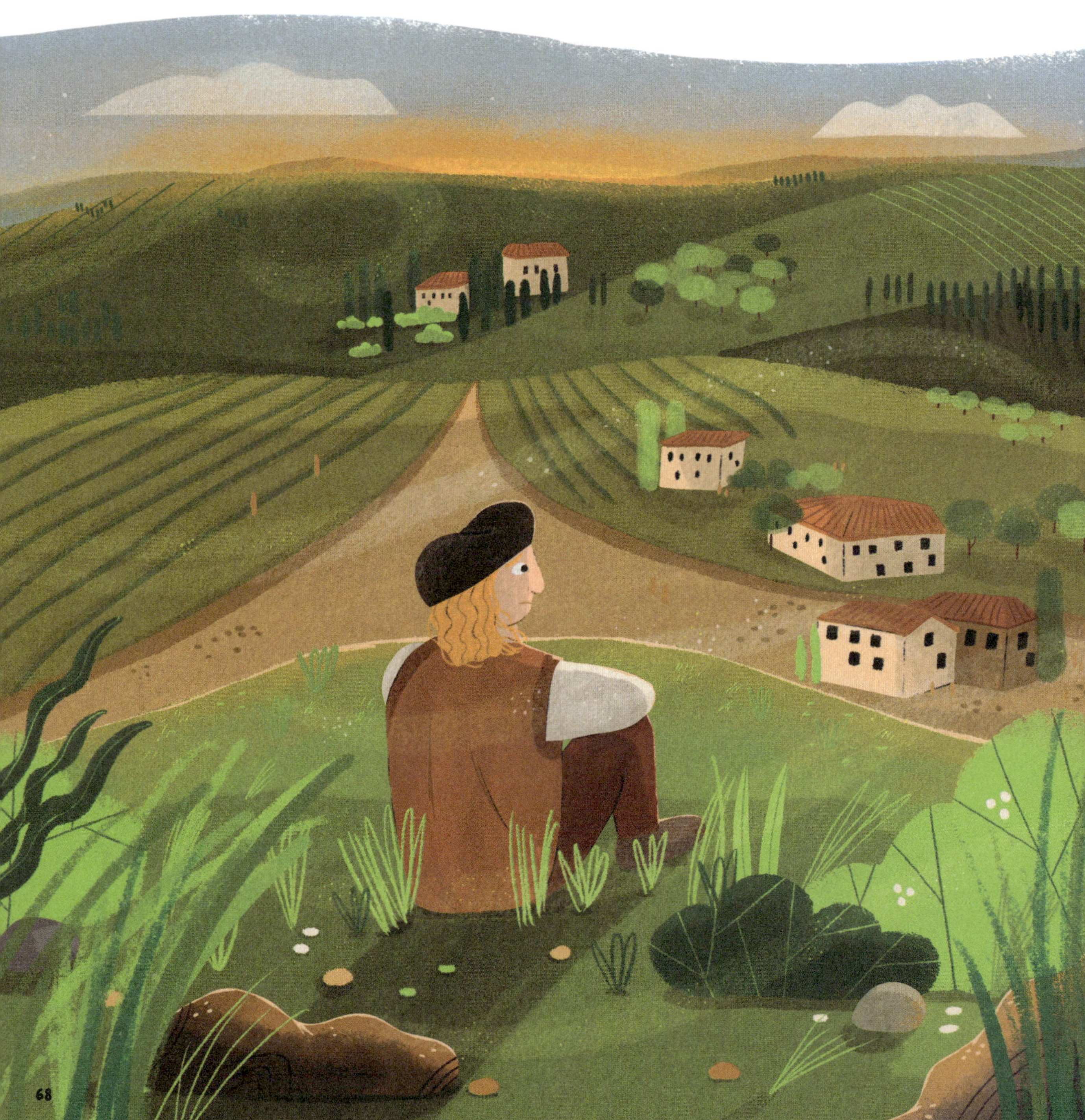

Leonardo had a restless creativity, and was always interested in the creations of others.

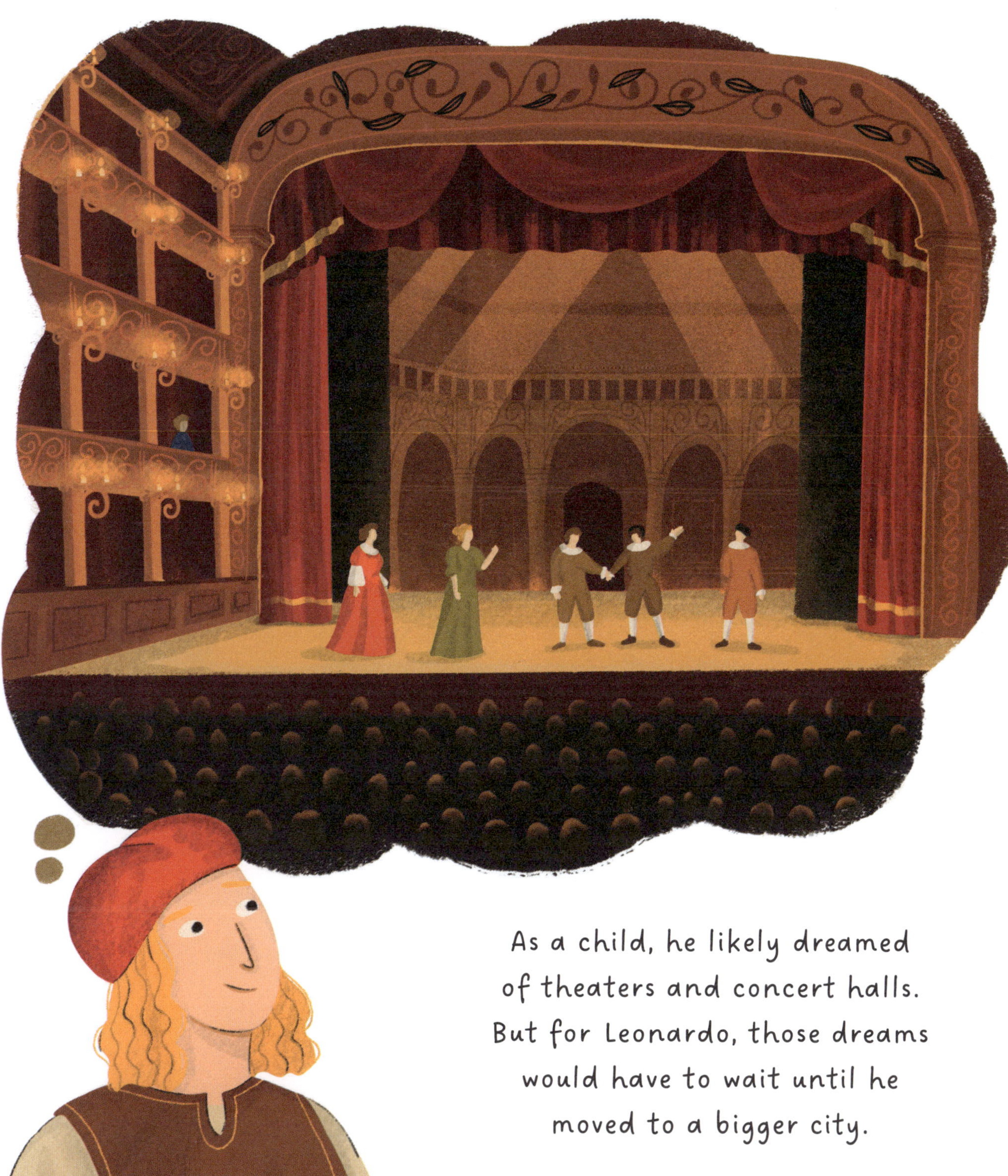

As a child, he likely dreamed of theaters and concert halls. But for Leonardo, those dreams would have to wait until he moved to a bigger city.

When Leonardo moved to Florence as a teenager, he was given the chance to work in a busy artists' workshop.

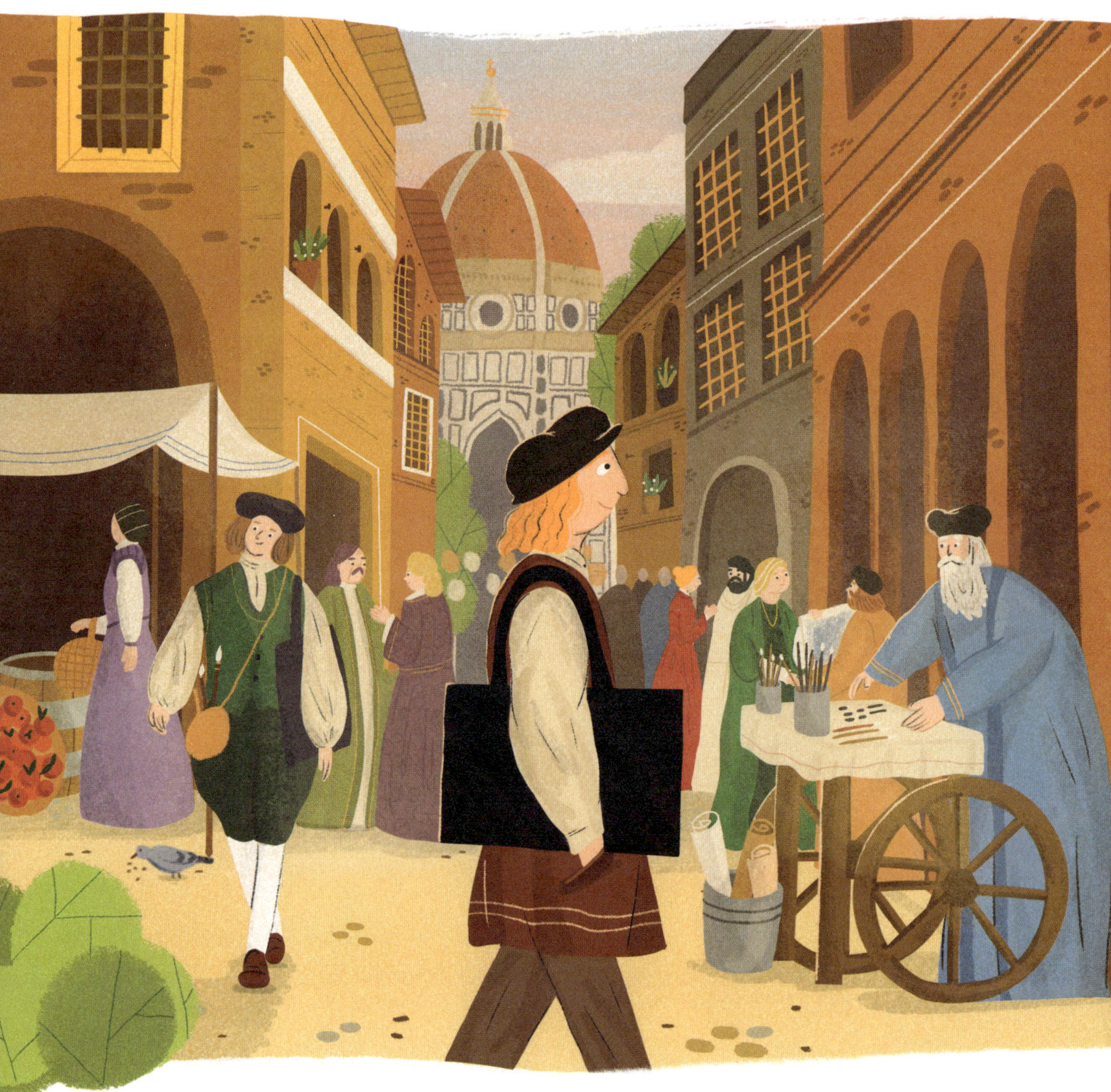

Florence also had a bustling community of actors and musicians. Young Leonardo was able to see many plays and concerts. It had a powerful effect on his own creative ambitions.

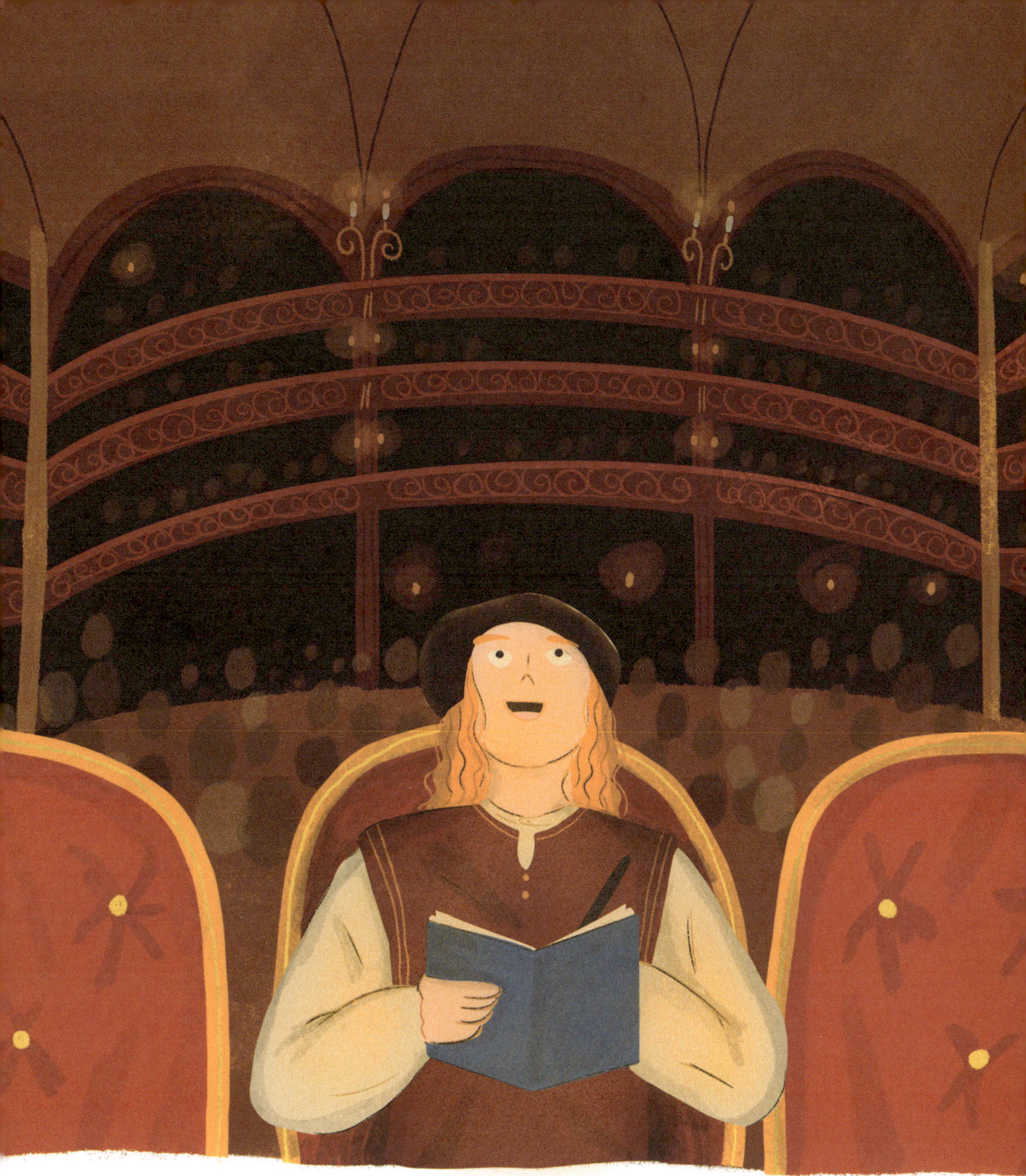

Young Leonardo was delighted to be in such an exciting and energetic place. Florence sparked his imagination and creativity, and he carried his notebook everywhere. Leonardo began making notes and sketches, and thought about producing his own plays.

The Duke of Milan, Ludovico Sforza, was a supporter of the arts. He loved to put on plays for his people. This meant he was often looking for fresh talent to help with new productions.

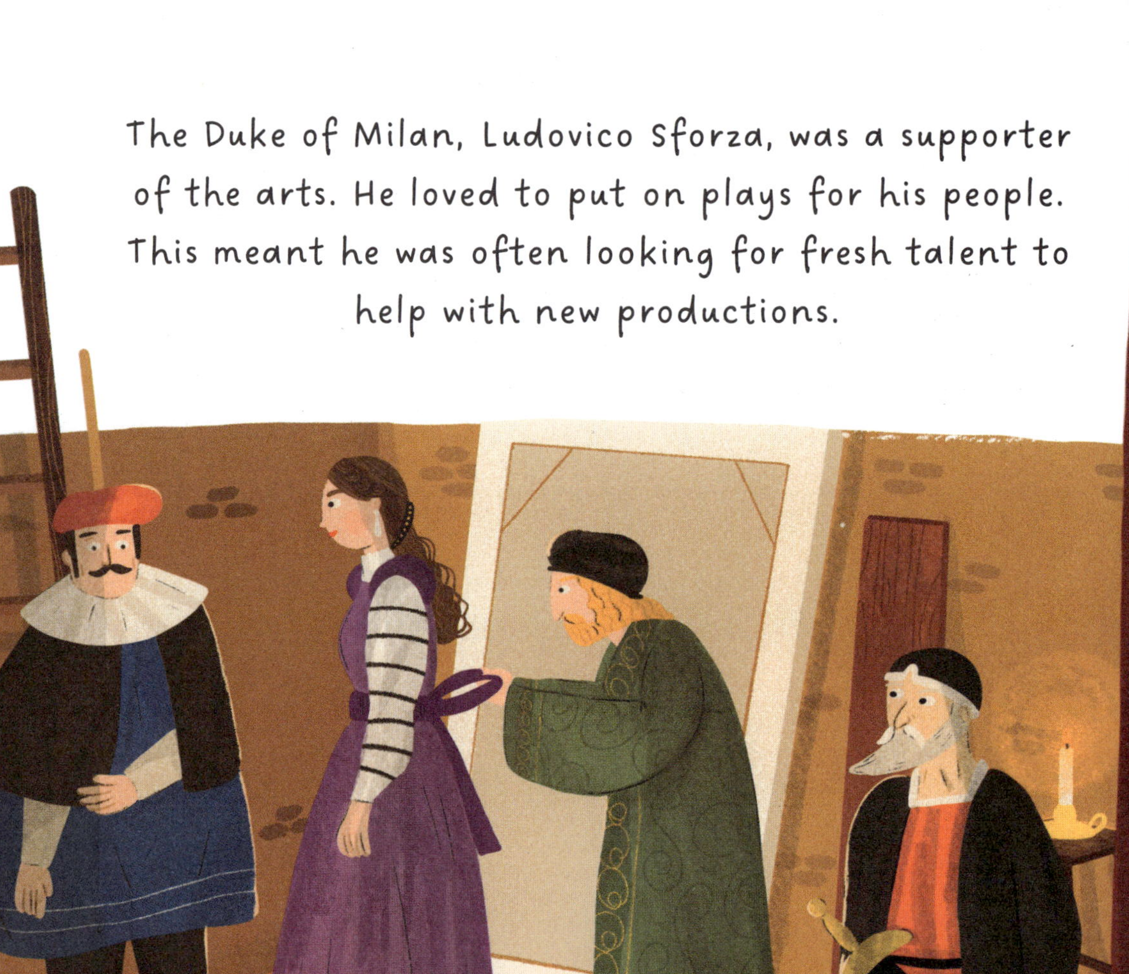

It wasn't long before Ludovico realized Leonardo would be perfect for the theater. Leonardo loved every part of putting on a play.

He enjoyed designing the costumes and building the sets. He liked working with the actors and the musicians. He even wanted to help figure out the best way to arrange the dancing.

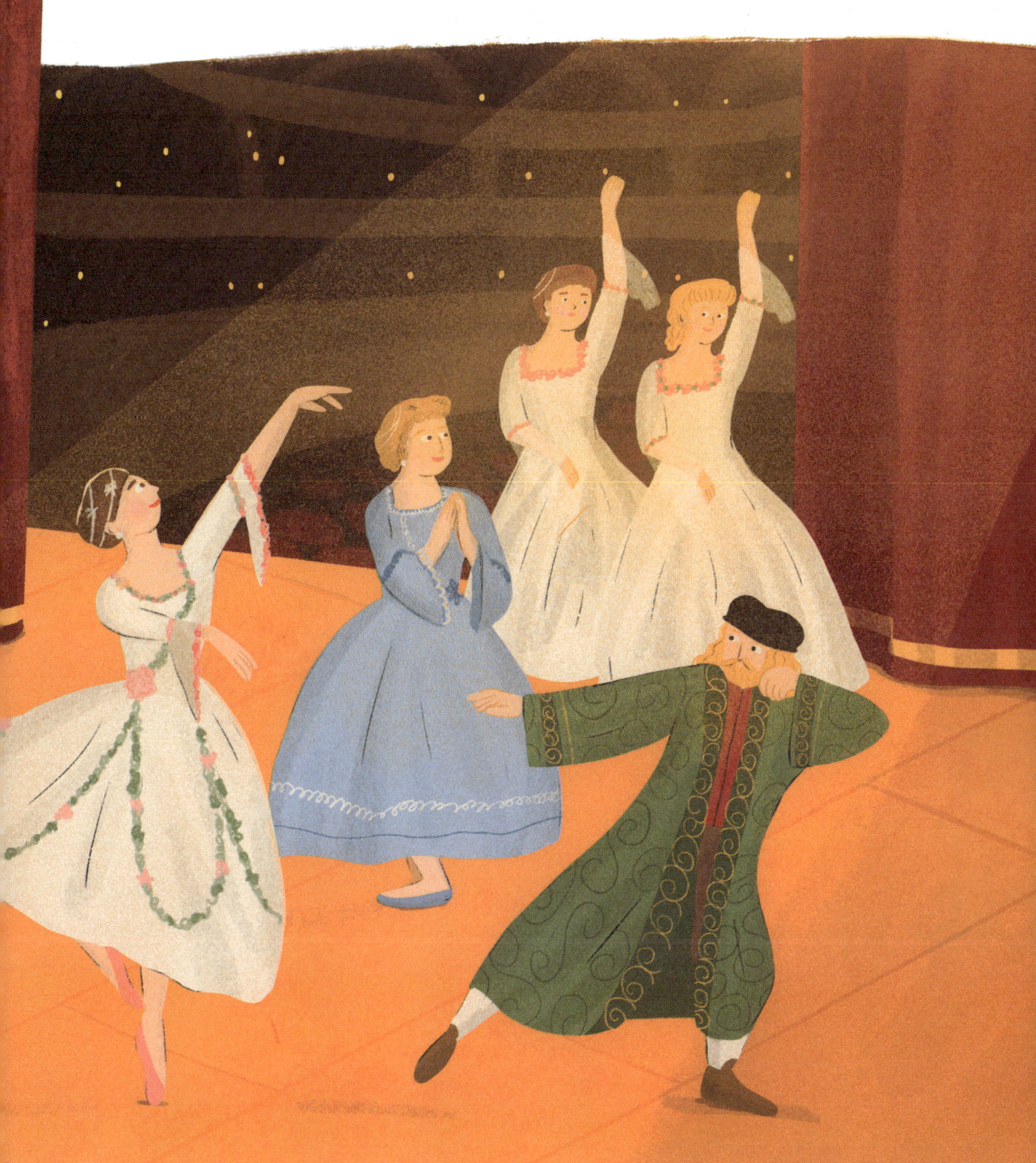

Leonardo began working on different productions for Ludovico. He was thrilled to put so many of his talents to use at the same time.

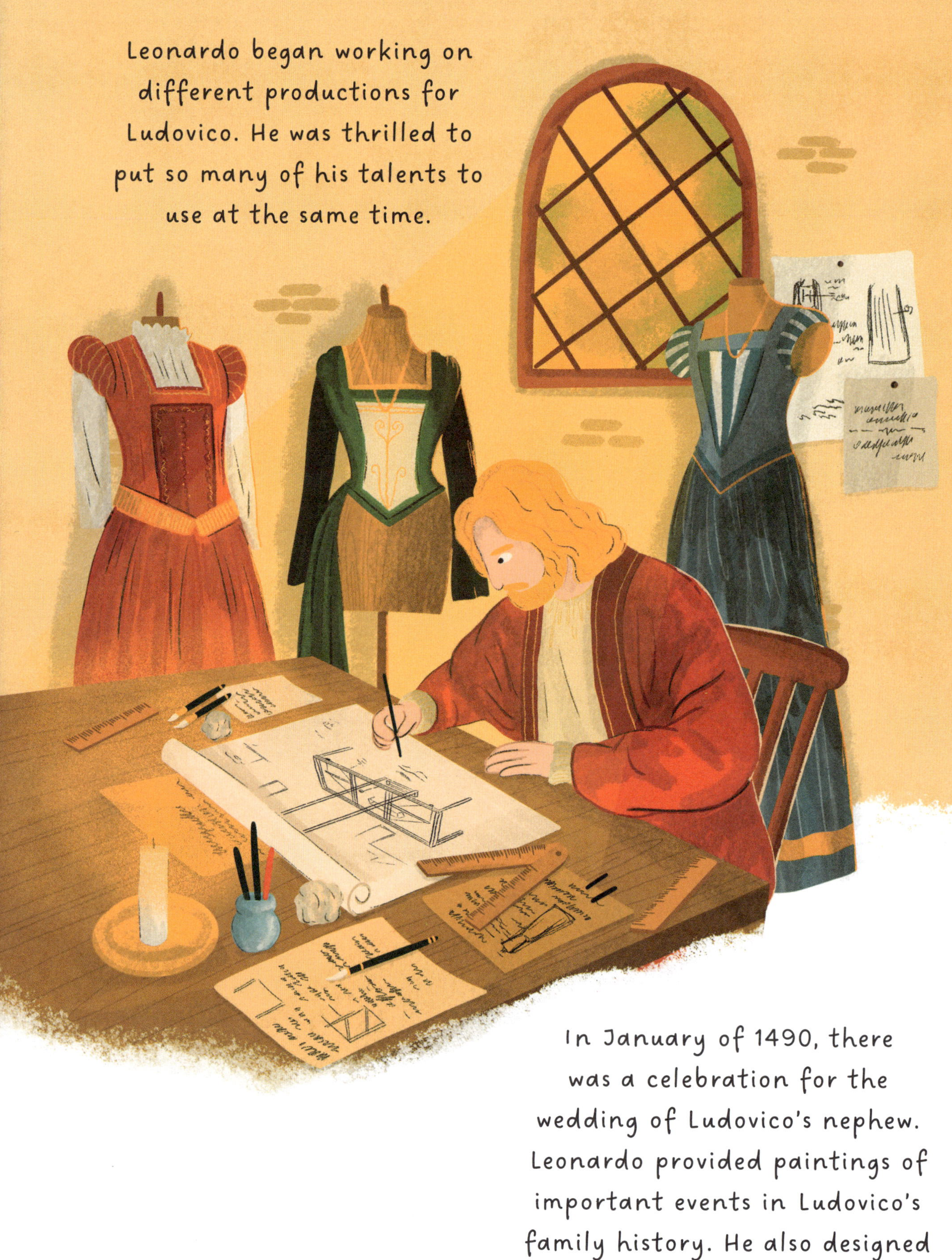

In January of 1490, there was a celebration for the wedding of Ludovico's nephew. Leonardo provided paintings of important events in Ludovico's family history. He also designed some of the actors' costumes.

In early 1496, Leonardo had the idea for a stage that turned so it would be easier to go from one set to the next. He also designed a system of cables and pulleys to create the illusion of actors flying through the air!

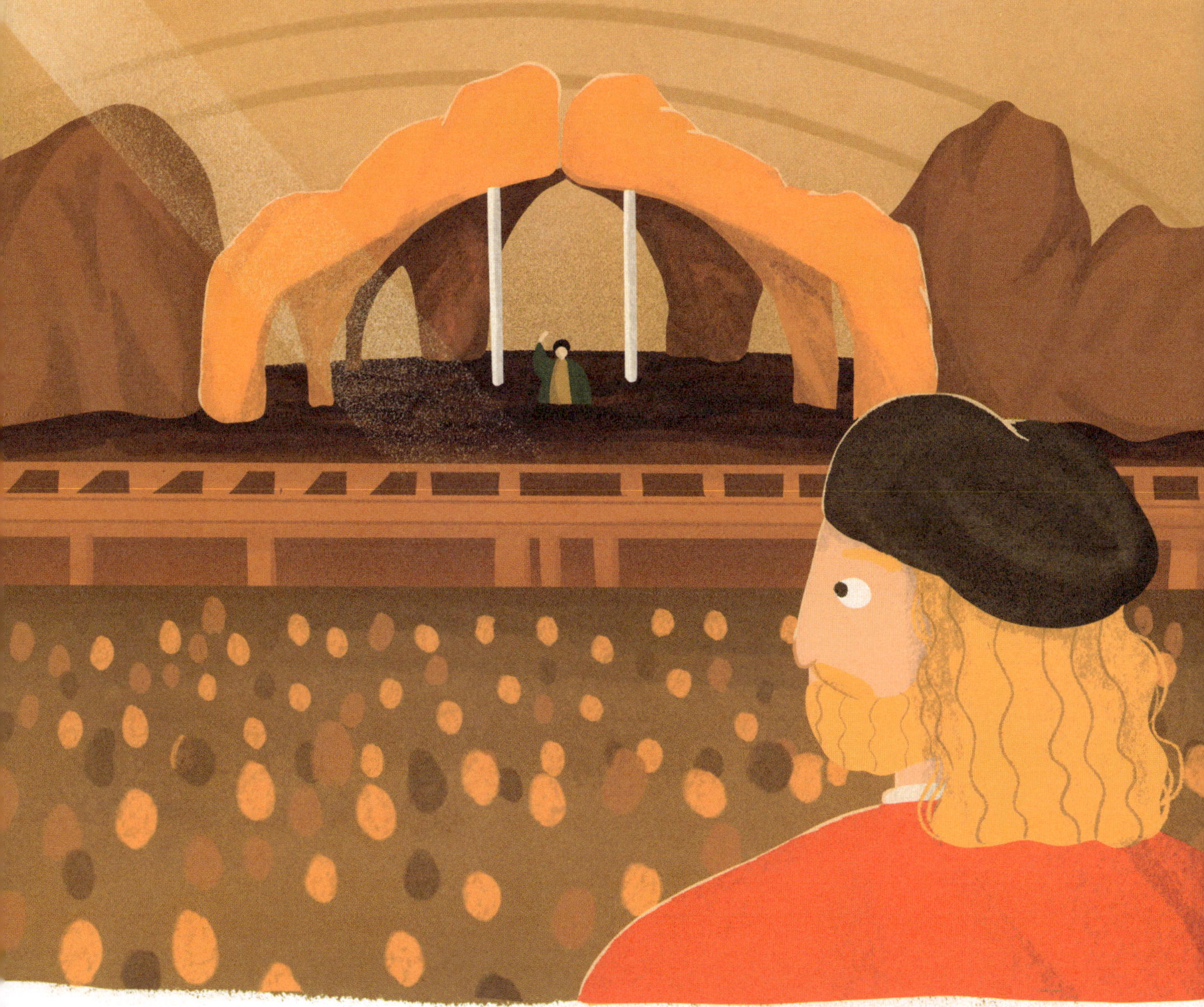

Today, revolving stages are common in theater production, and are proof of Leonardo's combination of astounding mechanical knowledge and creativity.

Scenic DESIGN

The production of a play is difficult work. It requires people who know how to act, direct, write, design costumes, build sets, control sound, and much more.

A modern play, for example, is often based on a story that may need **special effects**.

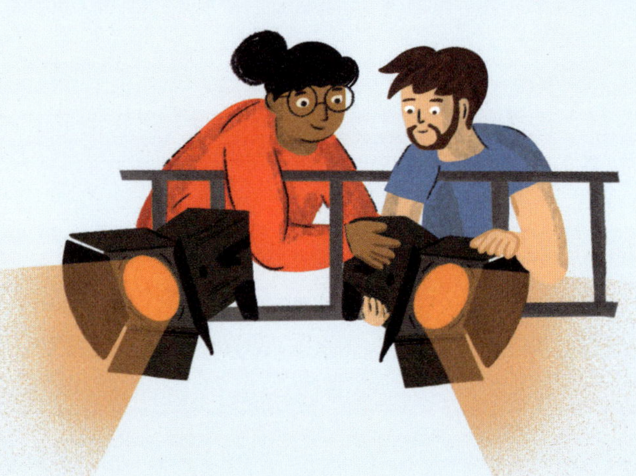

Lighting

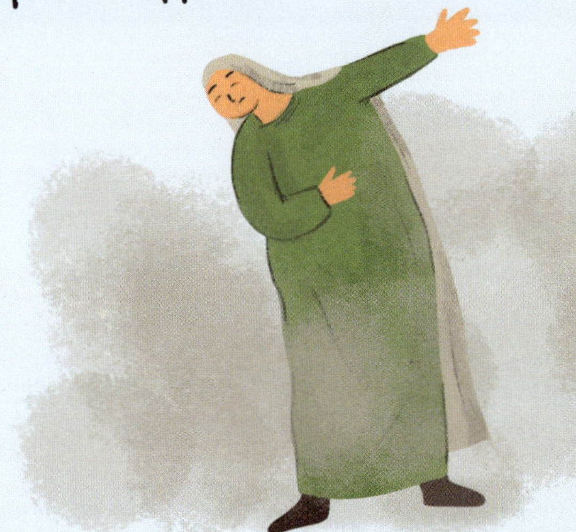

Fog

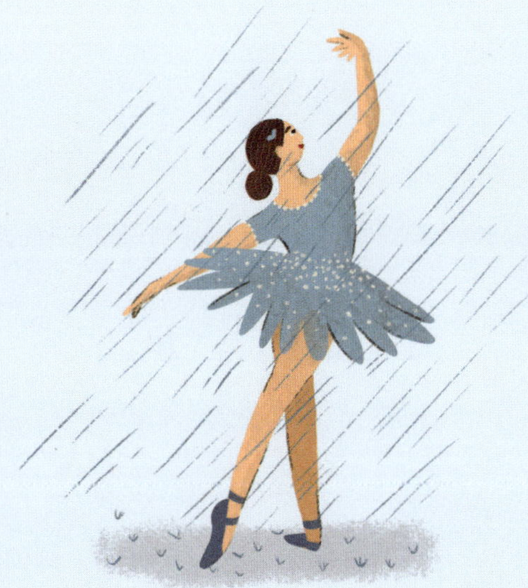

Rain

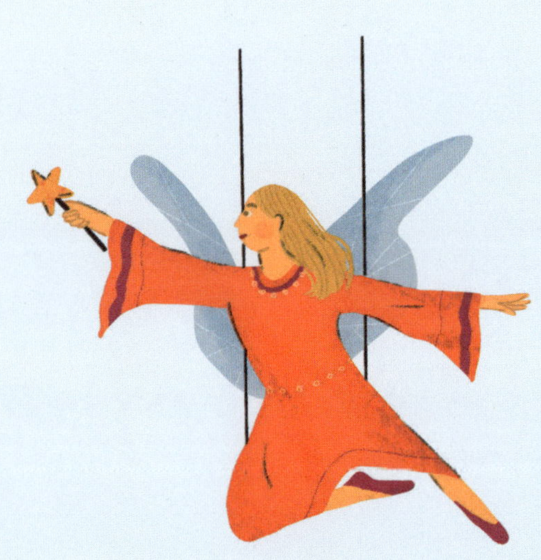

Flying

It may also need more than one **setting**. This means changes to the stage have to be made very quickly. Sometimes in a matter of minutes!

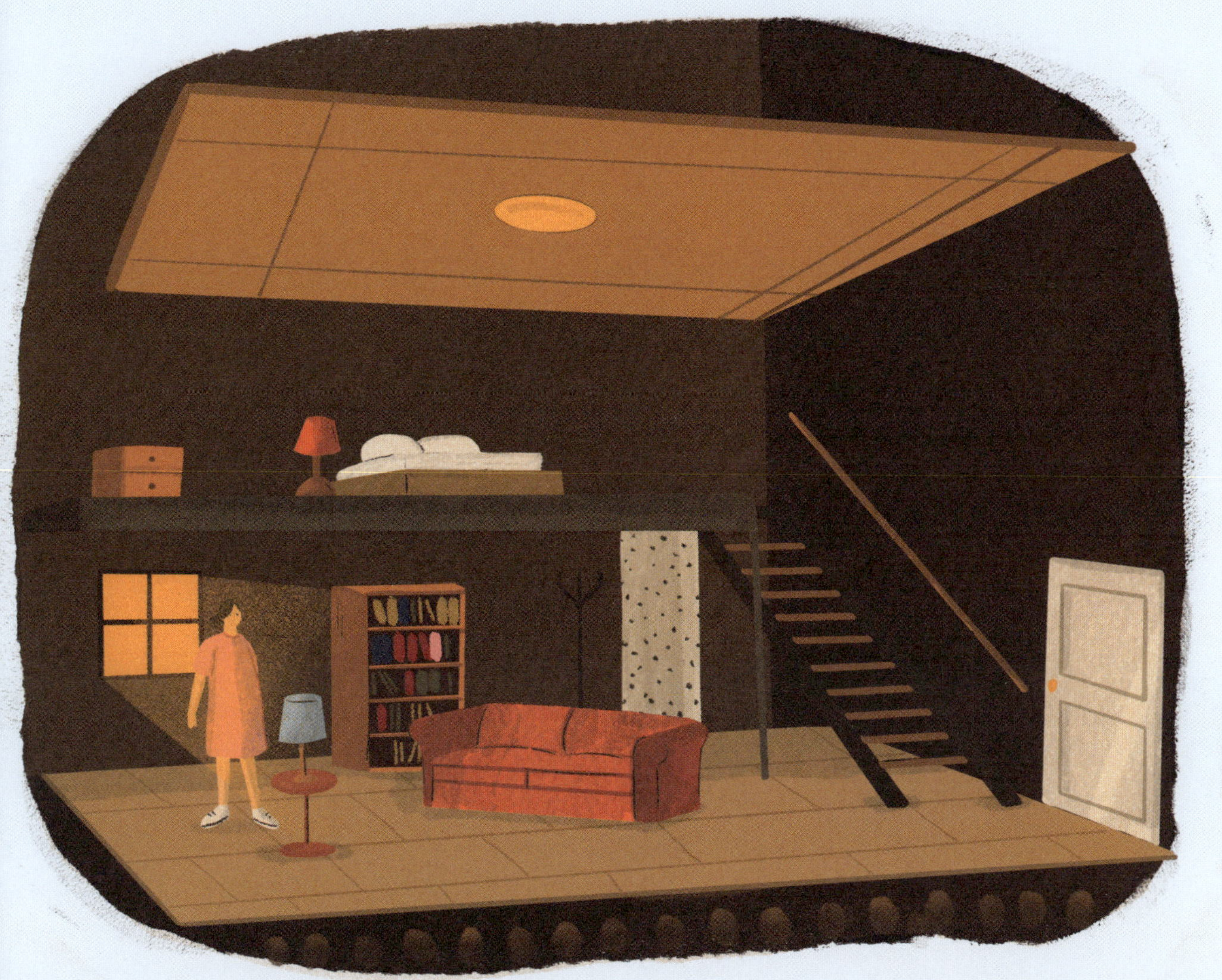

Leonardo's idea for a **revolving stage** that provided different sets would have saved a great deal of time between scenes. Today's stages are even more advanced. They can open and close, turn over, and change shape.

MUSICAL GIFTS

A Performance to Remember

Leonardo had a great love of music all his life. There is no record of him having any formal music lessons. Yet he had a tremendous amount of natural musical talent.

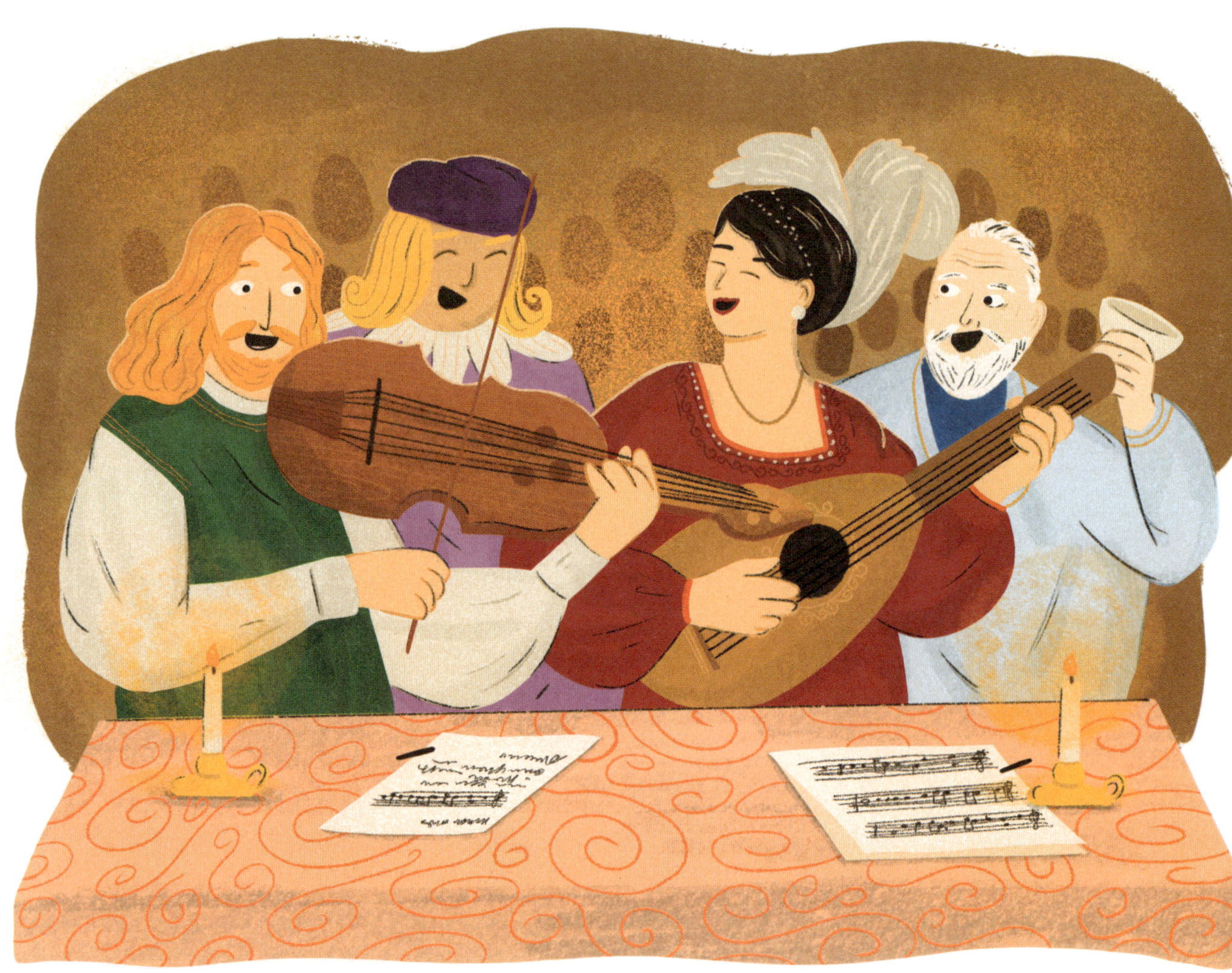

Leonardo taught himself to play an instrument called the lira. A typical lira of the time looked very similar to today's violins. It had a pear-shaped body, a long neck, and a set of strings.

The strings could be played one of two ways. The musician could pluck them with their fingers, producing notes that were short and quick. Or they could slide a bow across them, creating notes that were longer and fuller.

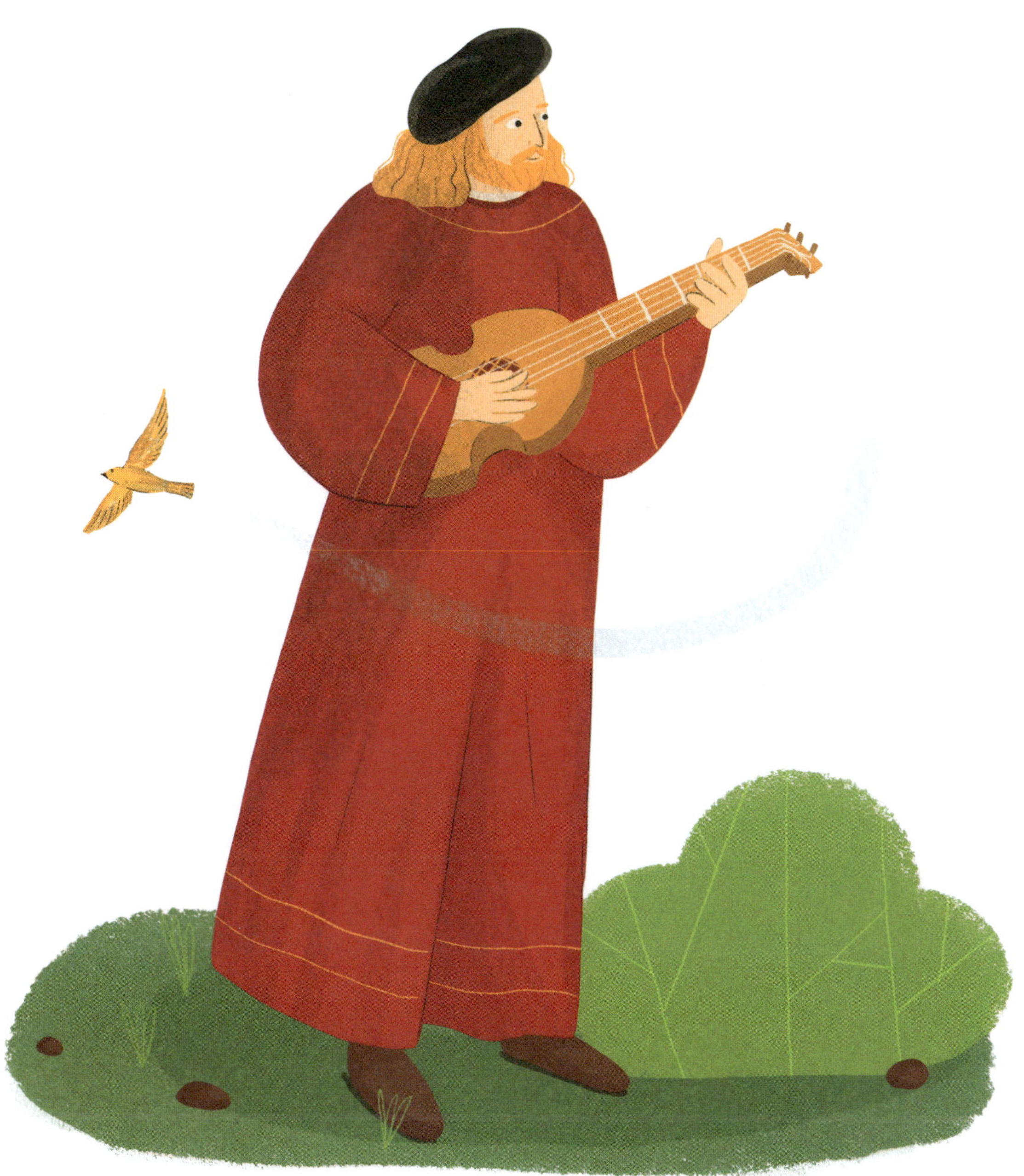

Leonardo often practiced the lira in his spare time, and he became very good.

Leonardo was also excellent at singing. People who knew him wrote about what a beautiful voice he had. It was clear and strong, with a high range.

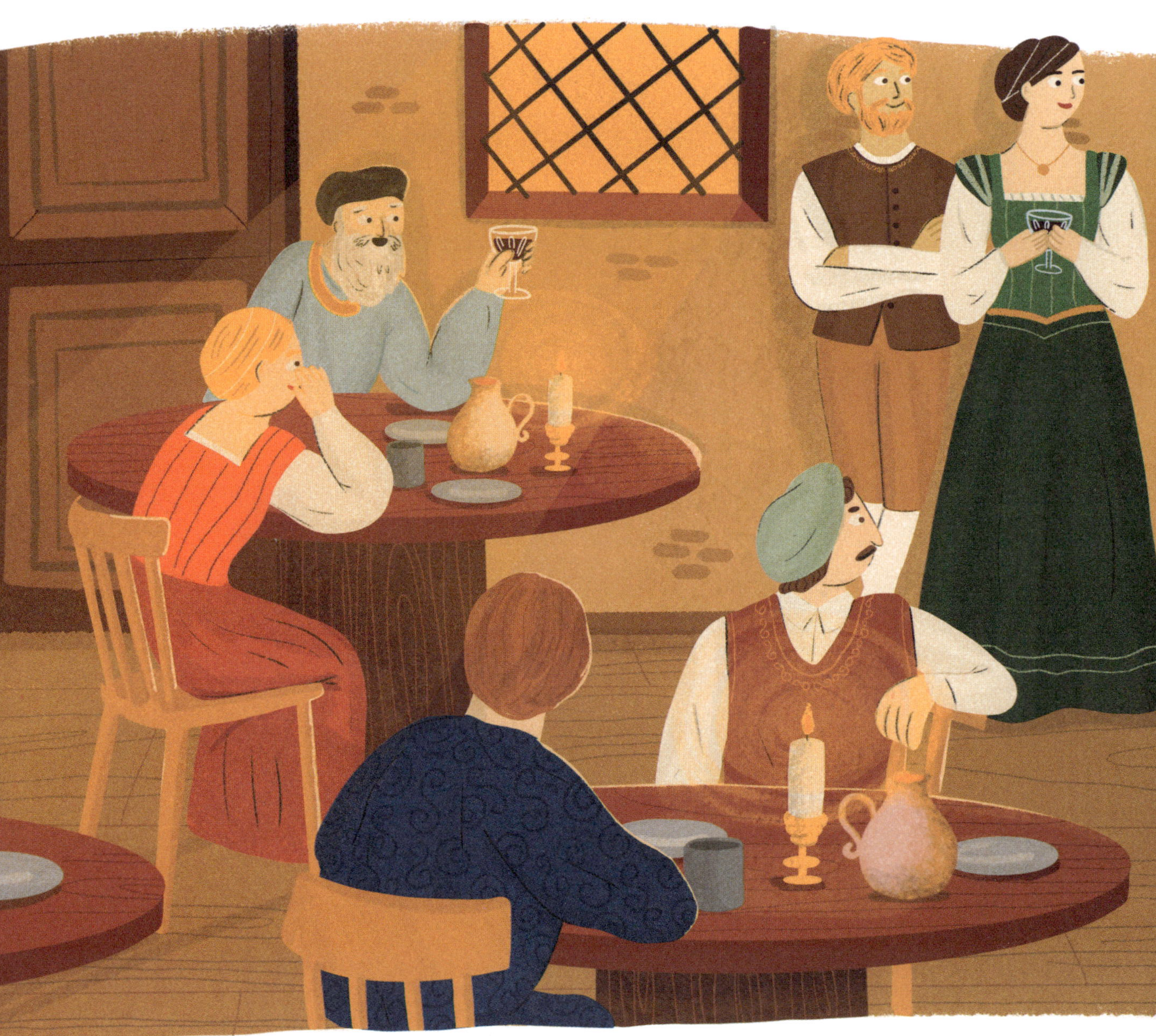

Leonardo had the gift of improvisation, too. This meant he could make something up without any practice or preparation.

Leonardo could play an instrument without any sheet music in front of him. He would craft songs on the spot.

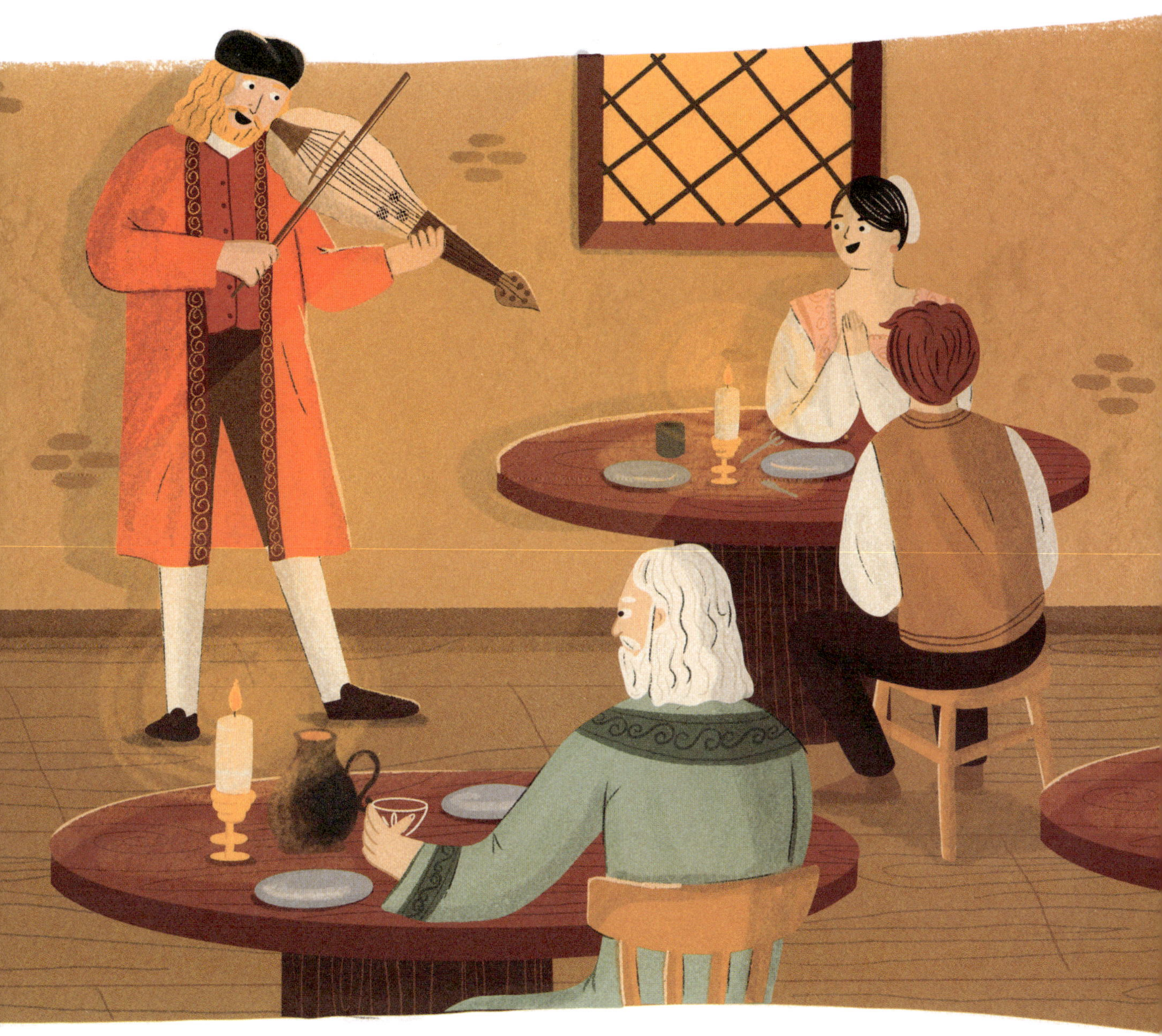

Then he would sing lyrics as he played. Sometimes these were words from popular poems. Other times he would tell funny stories. When he was a teenager, Leonardo won a contest for his ability to play the lira and sing along to it.

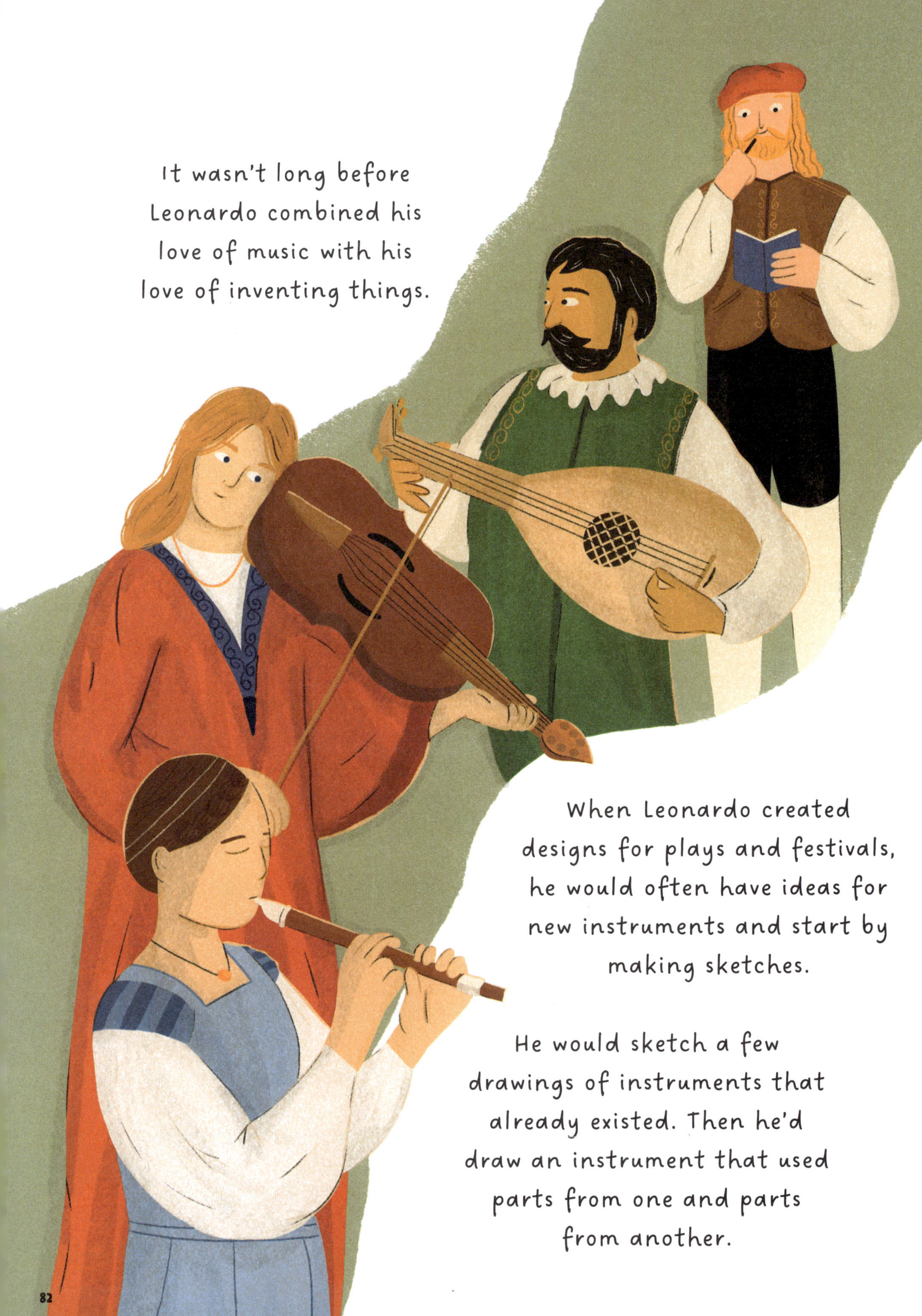

It wasn't long before Leonardo combined his love of music with his love of inventing things.

When Leonardo created designs for plays and festivals, he would often have ideas for new instruments and start by making sketches.

He would sketch a few drawings of instruments that already existed. Then he'd draw an instrument that used parts from one and parts from another.

Leonardo liked to decorate his drawings with things he found in nature. For example, he might use feathers from a colorful bird to decorate an instrument.

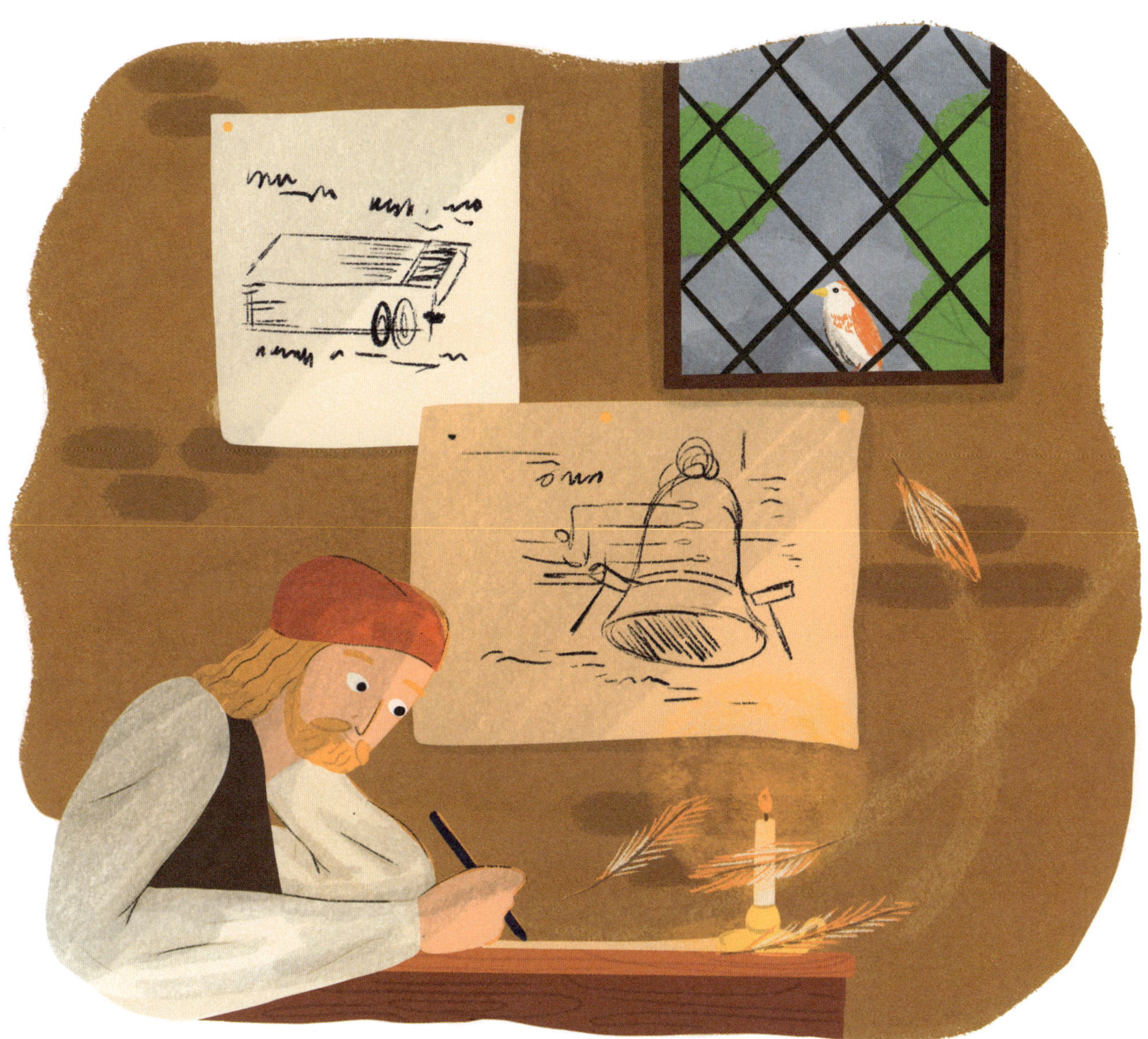

Leonardo also spent hours thinking up new ways of playing an instrument to get different sounds out of it. He would add strings to a lira, change the holes on flutes, loosen or tighten the head of a drum—anything to produce a sound that hadn't been heard before.

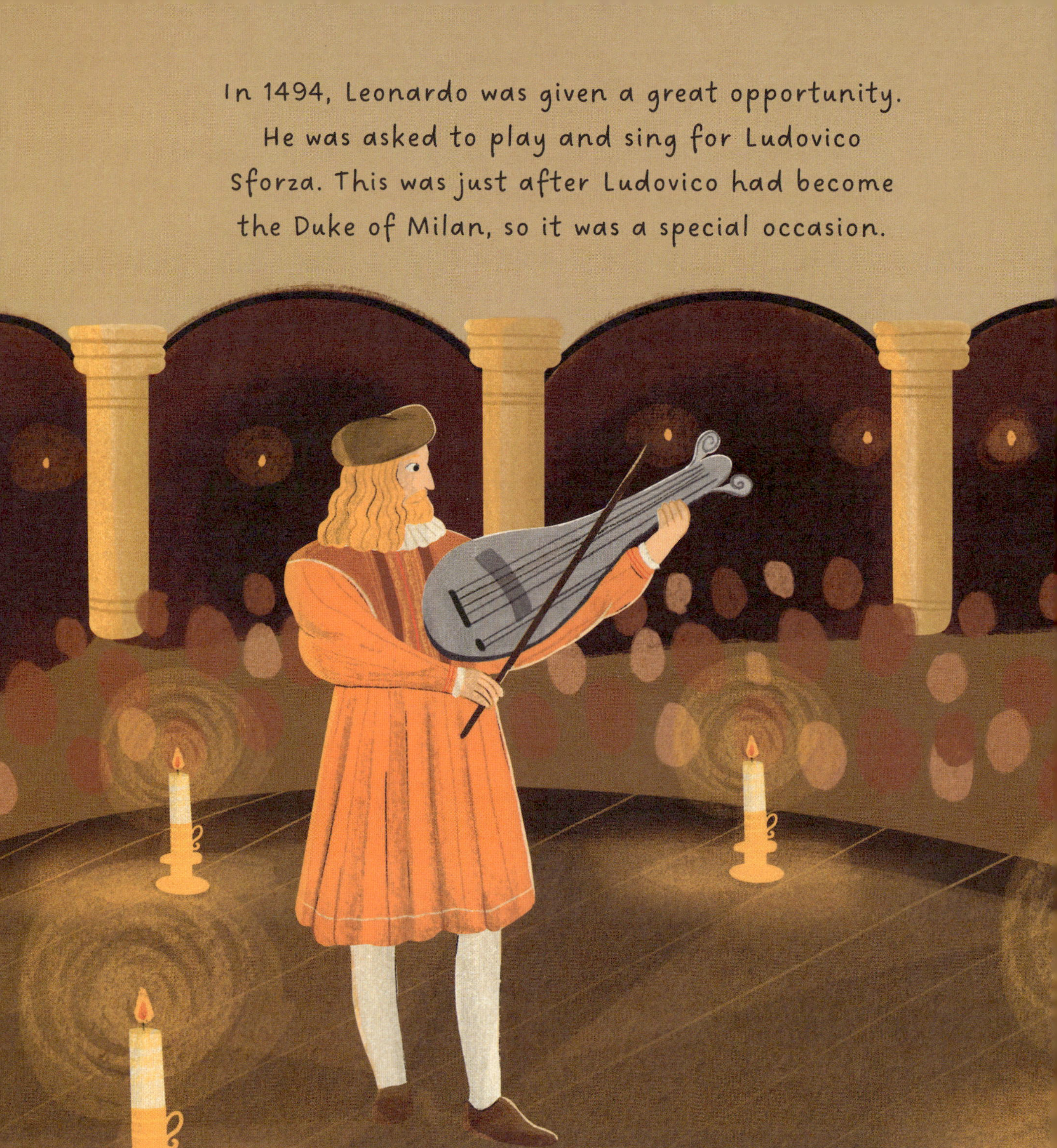

In 1494, Leonardo was given a great opportunity. He was asked to play and sing for Ludovico Sforza. This was just after Ludovico had become the Duke of Milan, so it was a special occasion.

Leonardo knew that Ludovico loved the sound of the lira. But Leonardo wanted his performance to sound even better.

So he brought along an instrument that he had designed and built himself. It had two sets of strings. One set was to be plucked with the fingers. The other strings were played with a bow.

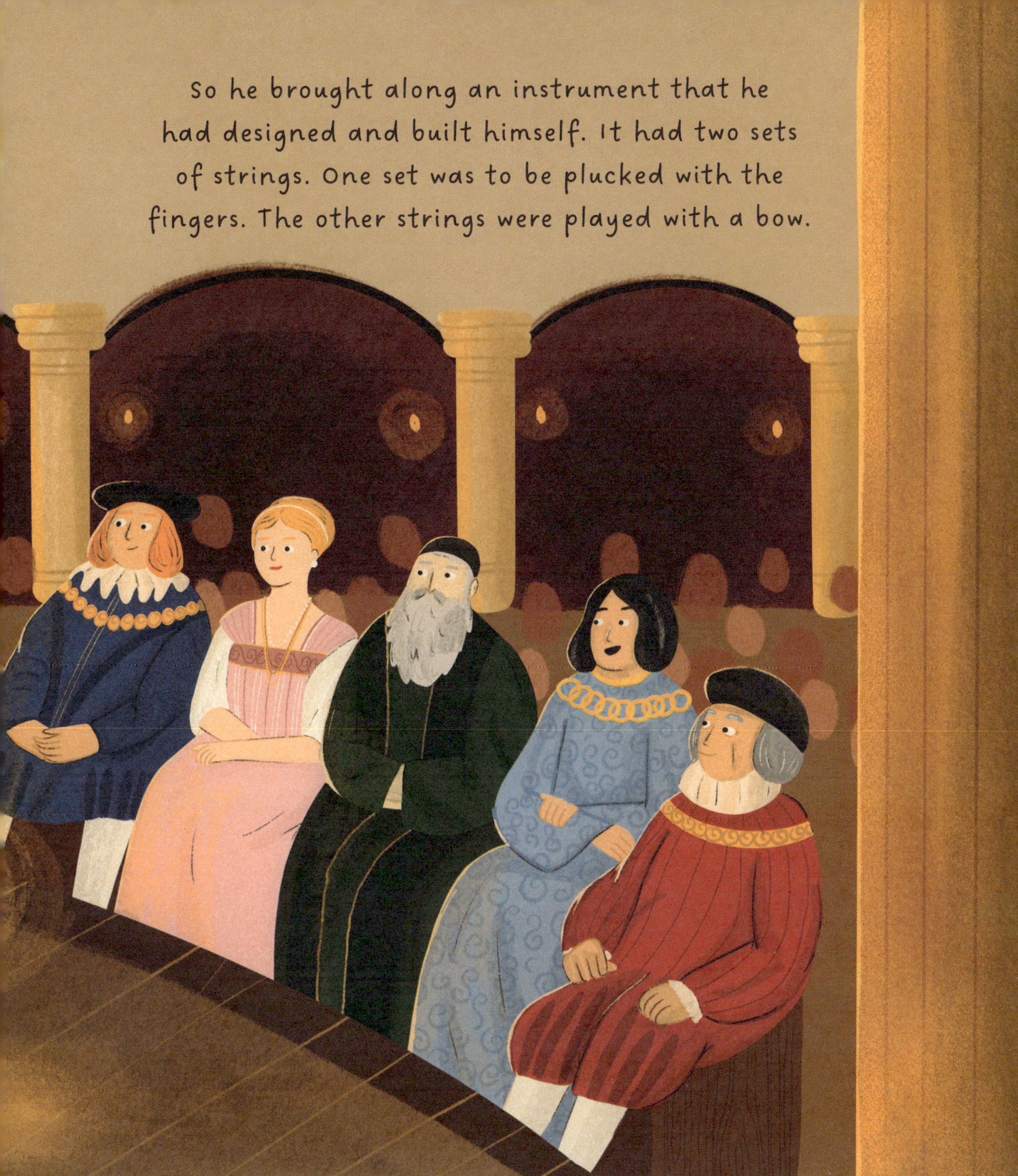

Leonardo's performance was magnificent.

Stringed INSTRUMENTS

A stringed instrument has a set of strings that are pulled tight across one side of the instrument's surface. Each string is tuned to produce a different note.

The strings **vibrate** when they are played. The sound comes from these vibrations.

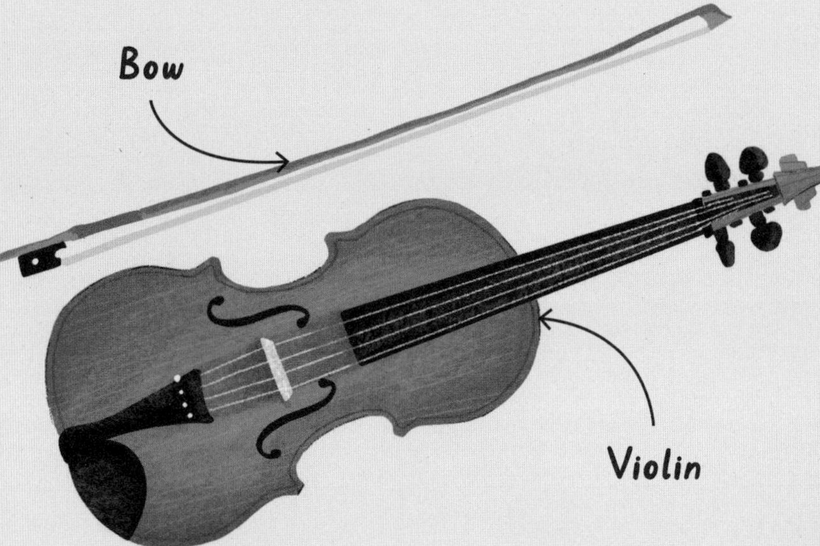

A sitar is plucked

Many stringed instruments are **hollow**, which allows the vibrations to sound deeper and fuller.

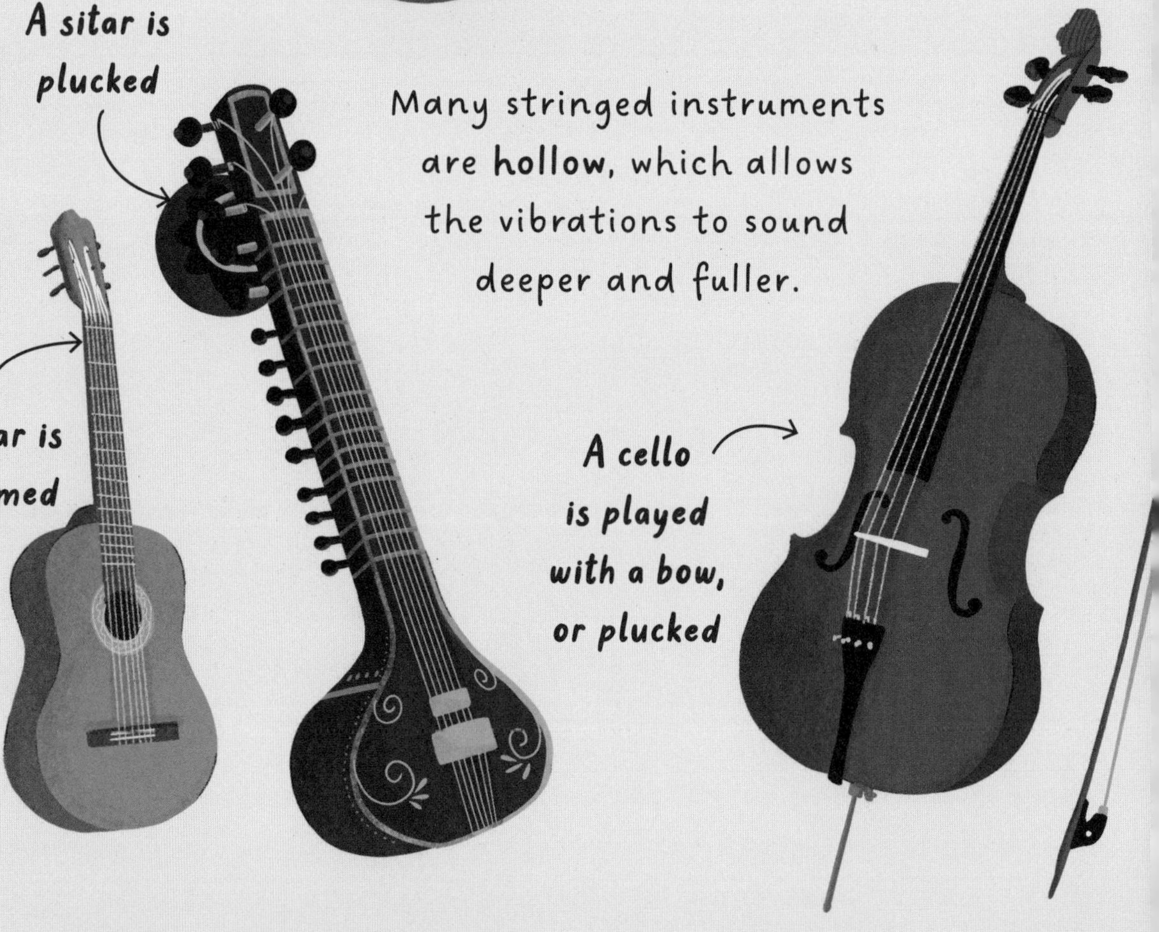

A guitar is strummed

A cello is played with a bow, or plucked

Most modern strings are made of either **steel or nylon**. Steel strings give a more metallic sound, while nylon strings produce a softer, warmer sound.

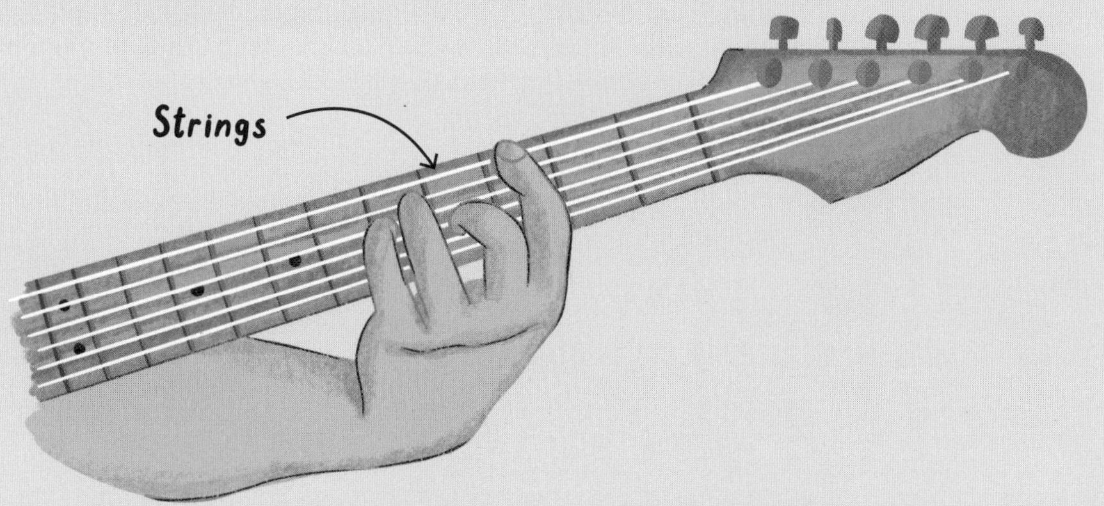

Strings produce **different notes** depending on their length, weight, and tightness.

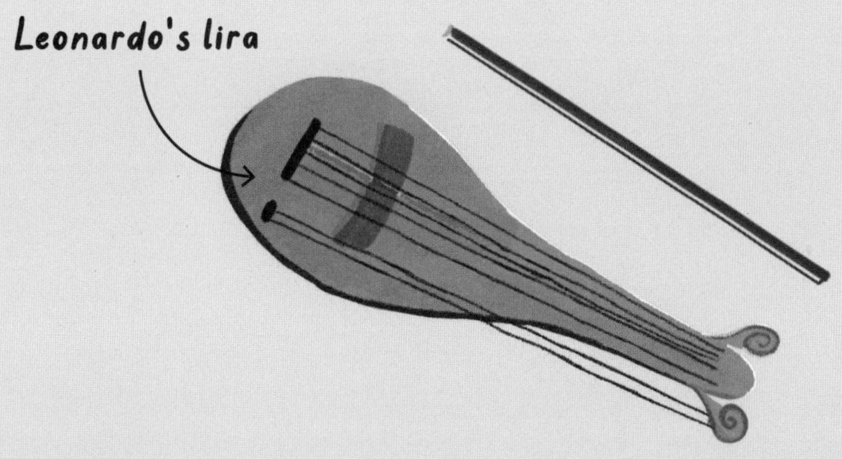

The stringed instrument that Leonardo invented had **two sets of strings** on it. One set was meant to be played with a bow. The other set was for plucking with the fingers.

THE PLASTER PAINTING

Leonardo's Experiment

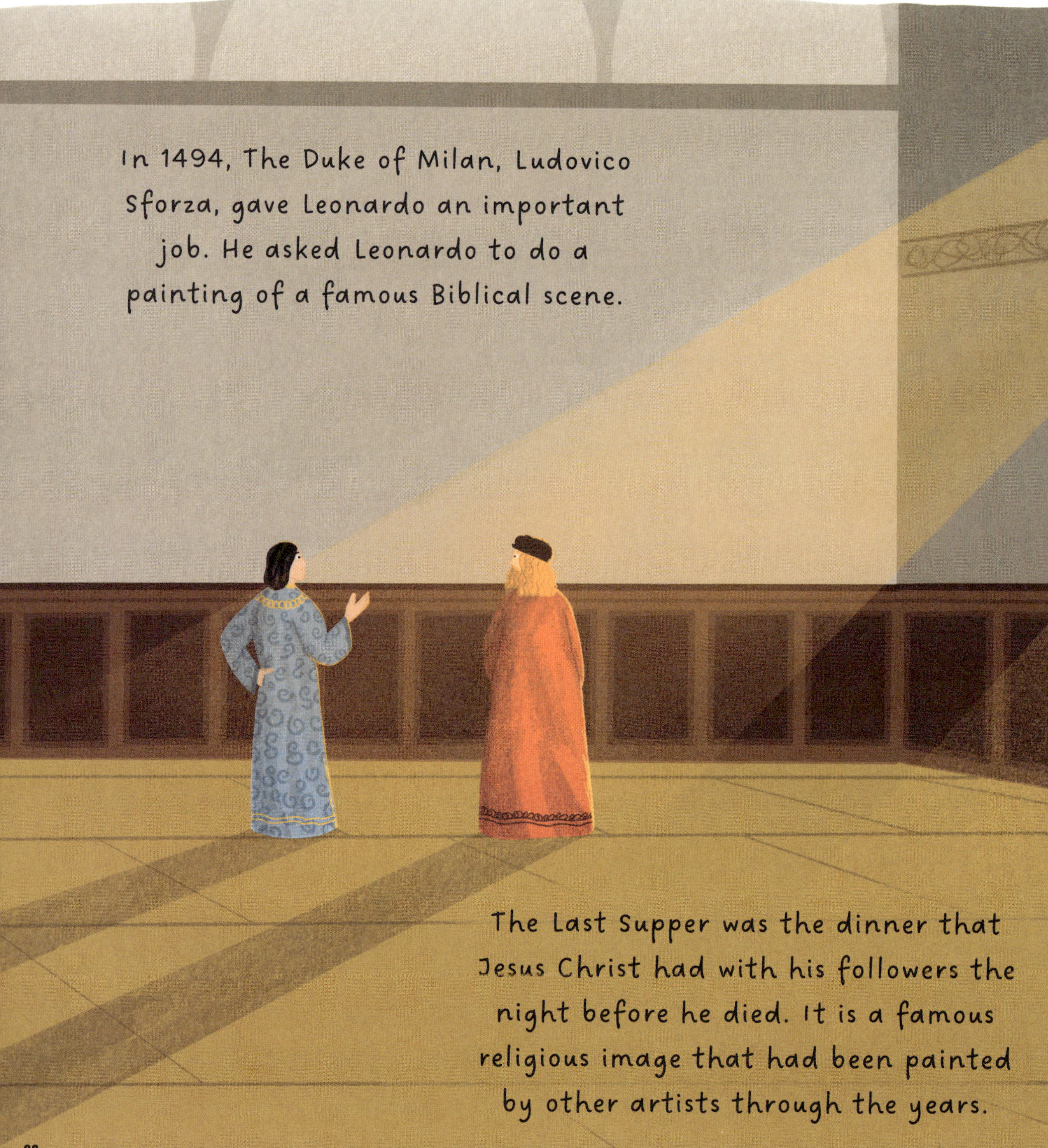

In 1494, The Duke of Milan, Ludovico Sforza, gave Leonardo an important job. He asked Leonardo to do a painting of a famous Biblical scene.

The Last Supper was the dinner that Jesus Christ had with his followers the night before he died. It is a famous religious image that had been painted by other artists through the years.

But Ludovico wanted Leonardo to do a huge version of it. He wanted it painted on the wall of a religious school called the Santa Maria delle Grazie.

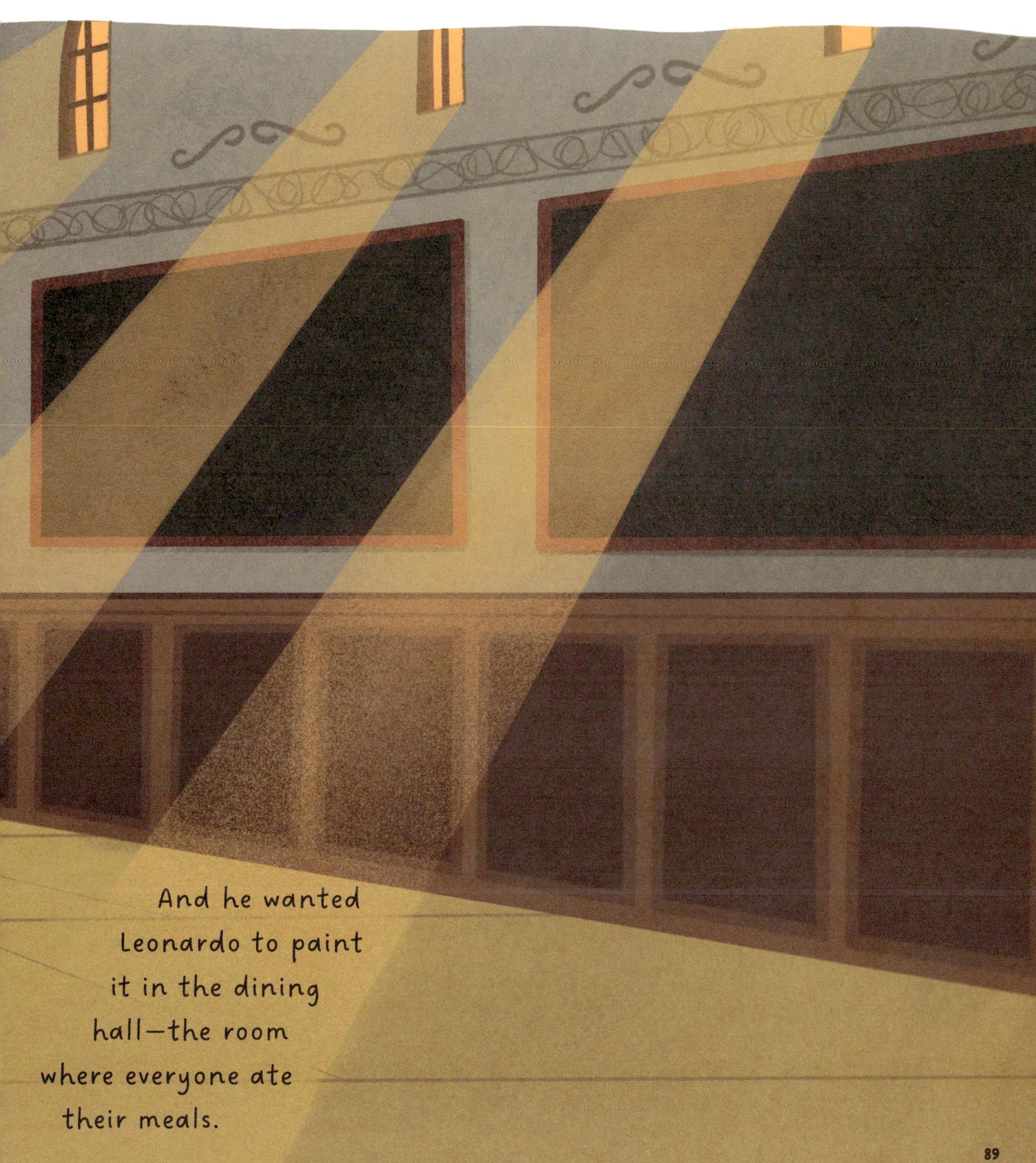

And he wanted Leonardo to paint it in the dining hall—the room where everyone ate their meals.

Leonardo accepted Ludovico's offer. In fact, he was very excited about it.

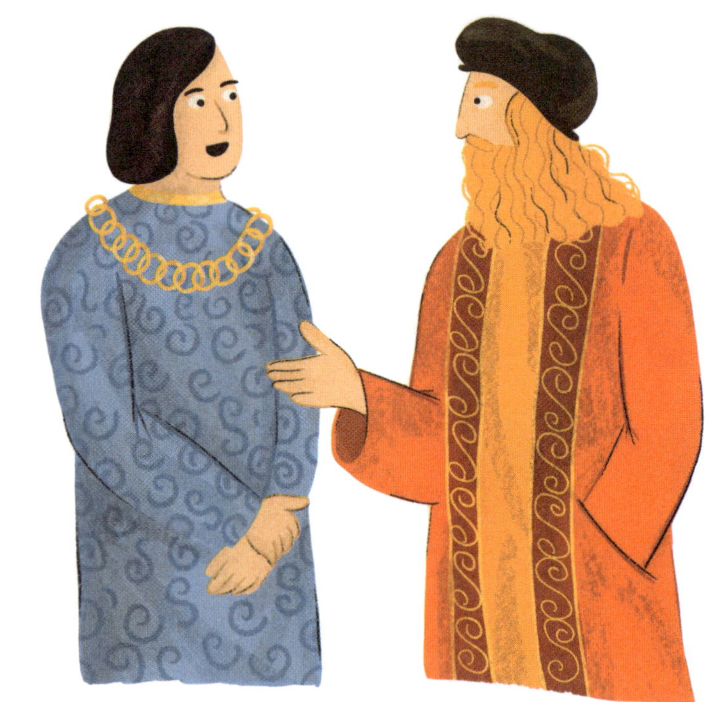

The problem was that Leonardo's work habits often changed from one day to the next.

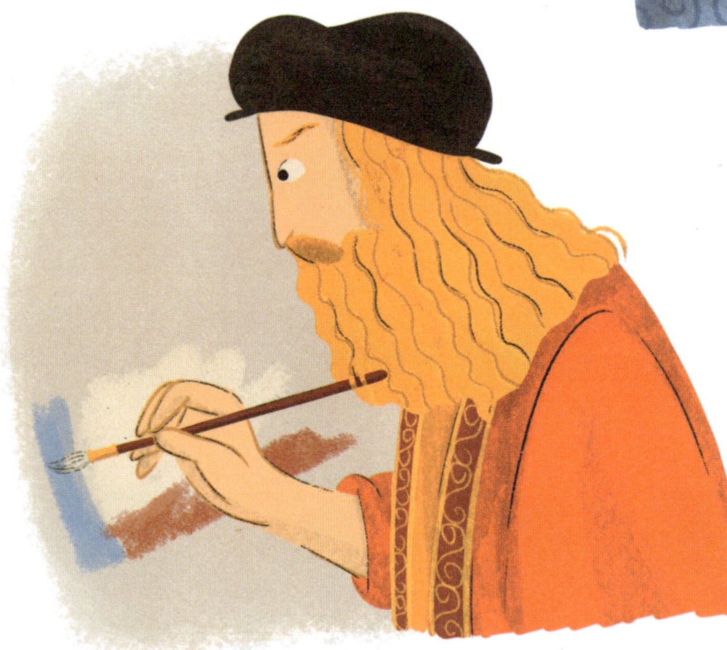

He might come in very early on a Tuesday and paint for hours.

On Wednesday, he might not show up at all.

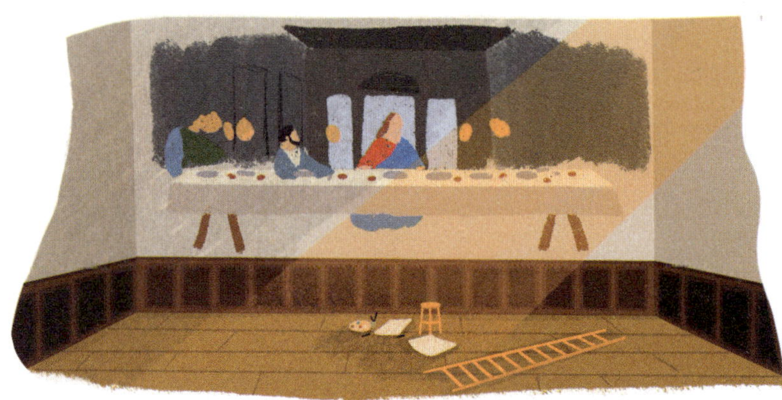

Then he'd be back on Thursday, but he'd stare at the unfinished painting for hours without touching it!

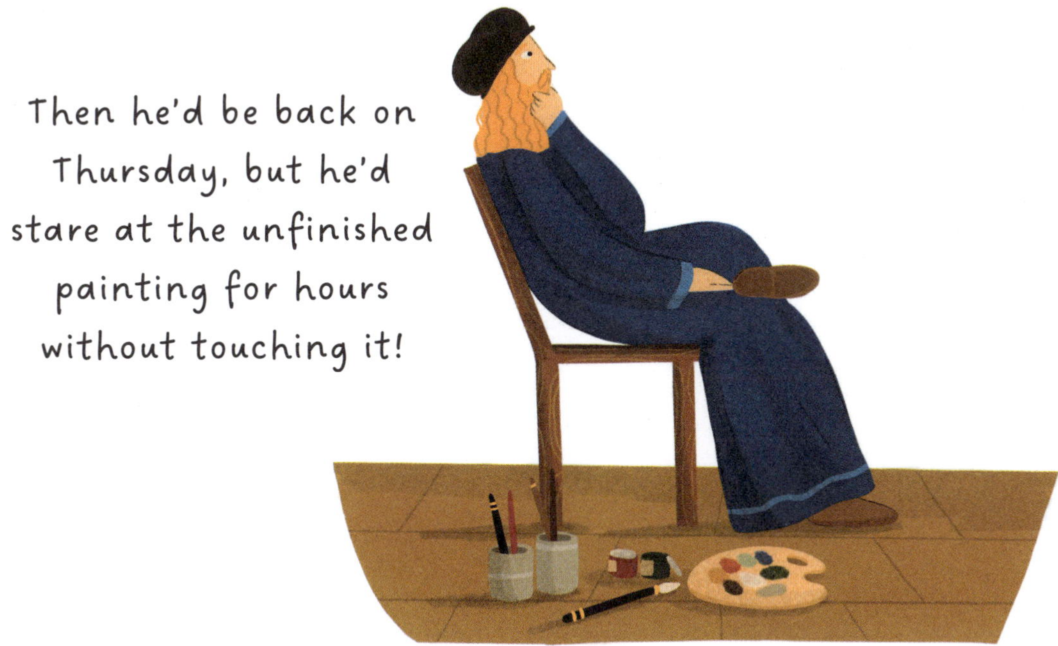

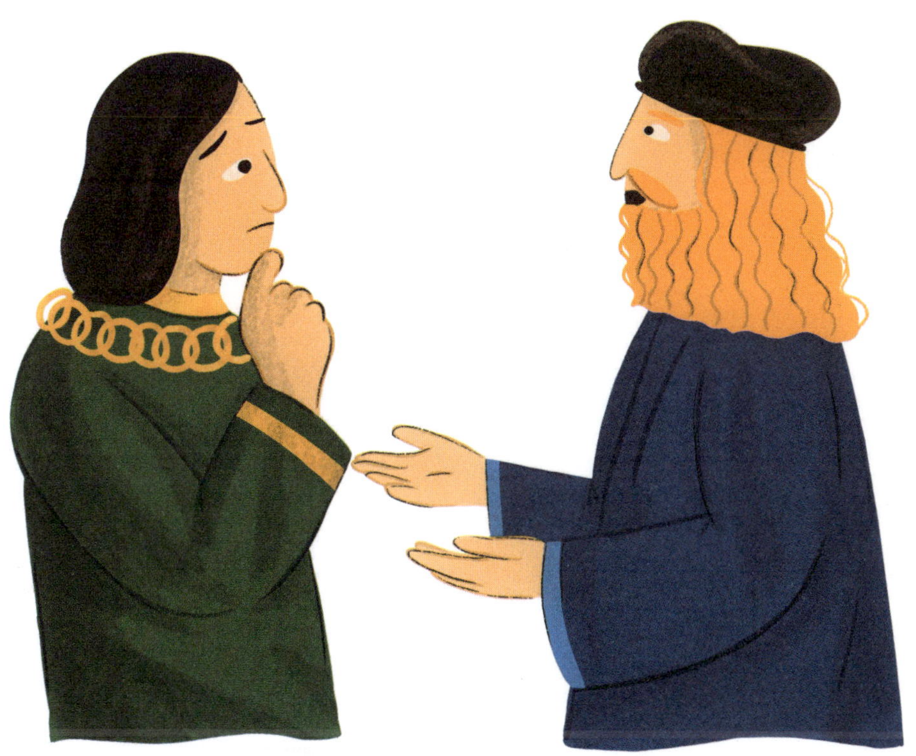

Ludovico worried about Leonardo's work habits. But Leonardo told him that was how artists worked. He reassured Ludovico that the painting would look wonderful in the end.

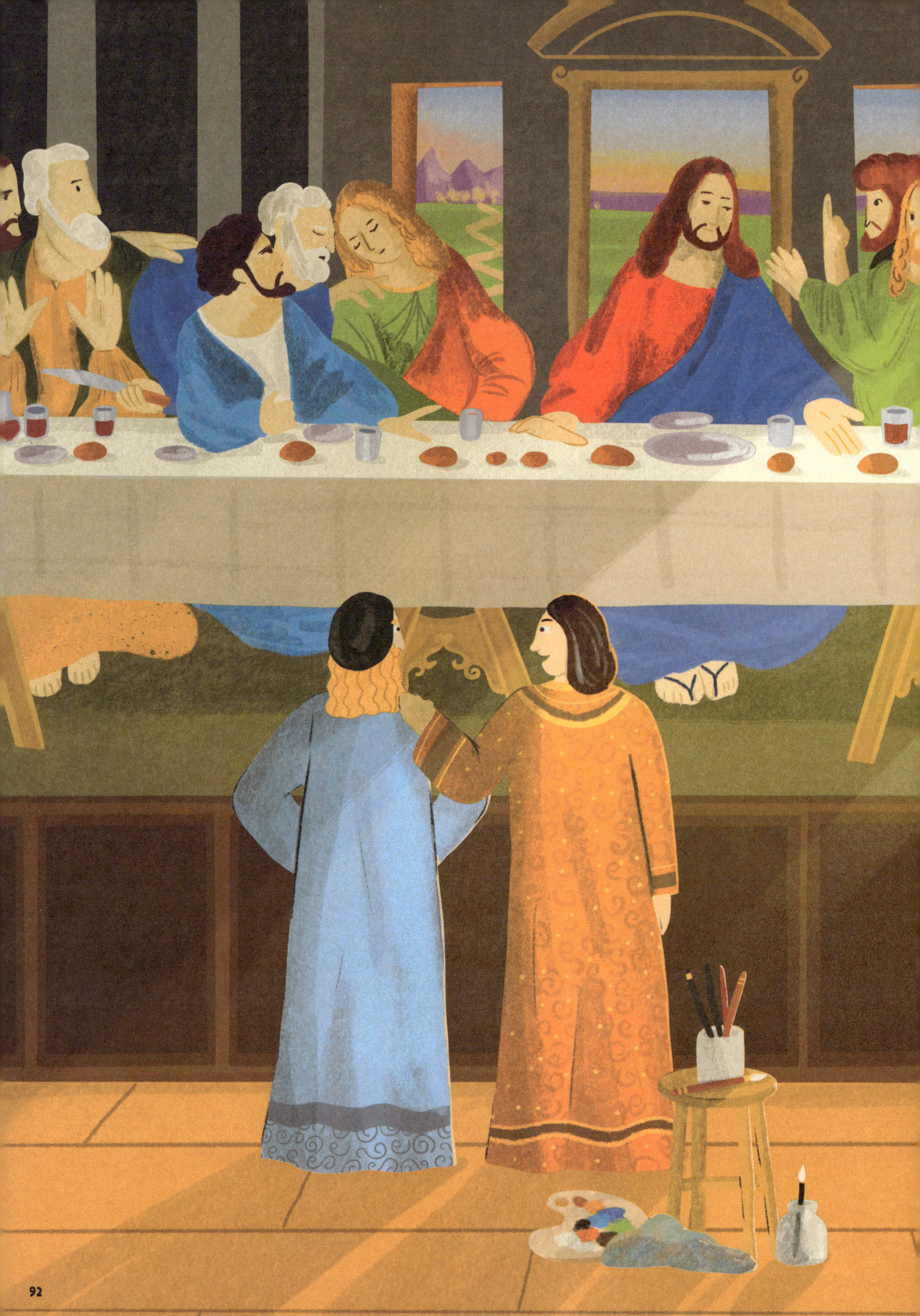

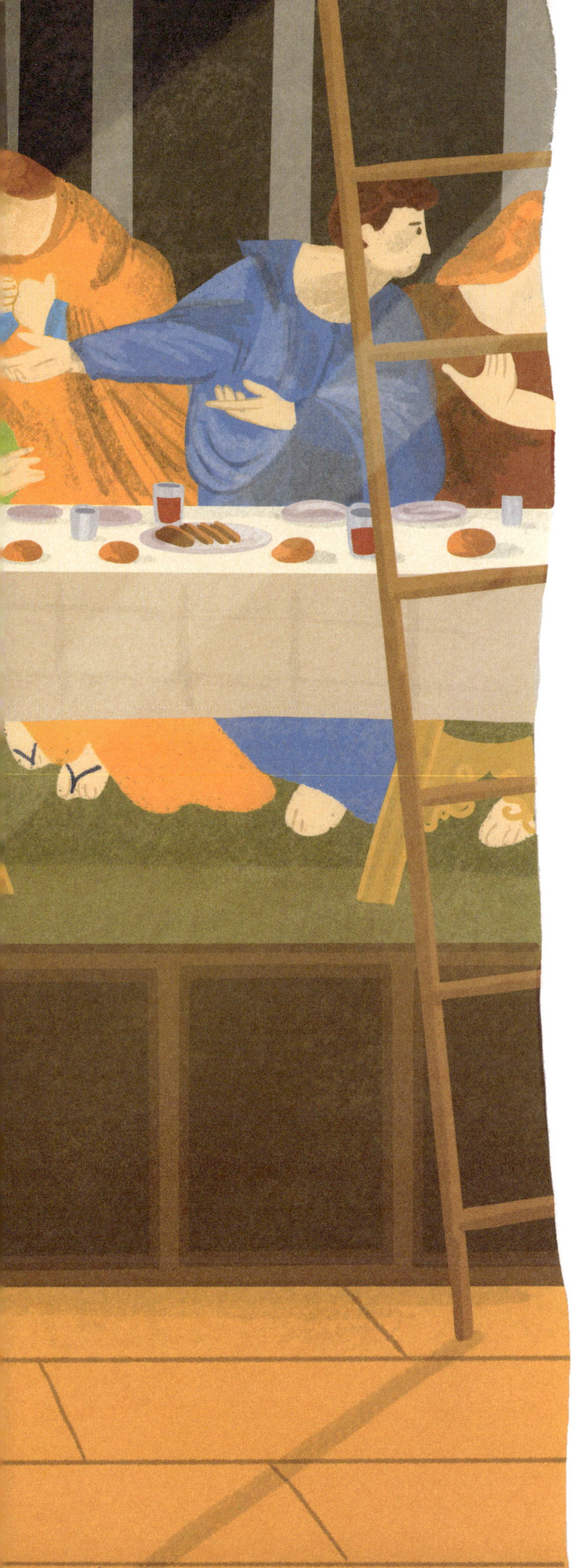

When Leonardo finally finished *The Last Supper*, Ludovico saw that he was right to have asked Leonardo to paint it. Many art experts consider it one of the greatest paintings in history.

It shows a long table with Jesus Christ sitting in the middle. There are twelve of his followers sitting with him, six on either side.

Each one seems to have their own thoughts and feelings. This had become a big part of Leonardo's genius. He had mastered the art of showing human emotions in his work.

He did this through details such as the expression on a person's face or the movement of their hands.

But there was a problem with *The Last Supper*. A very big one . . .

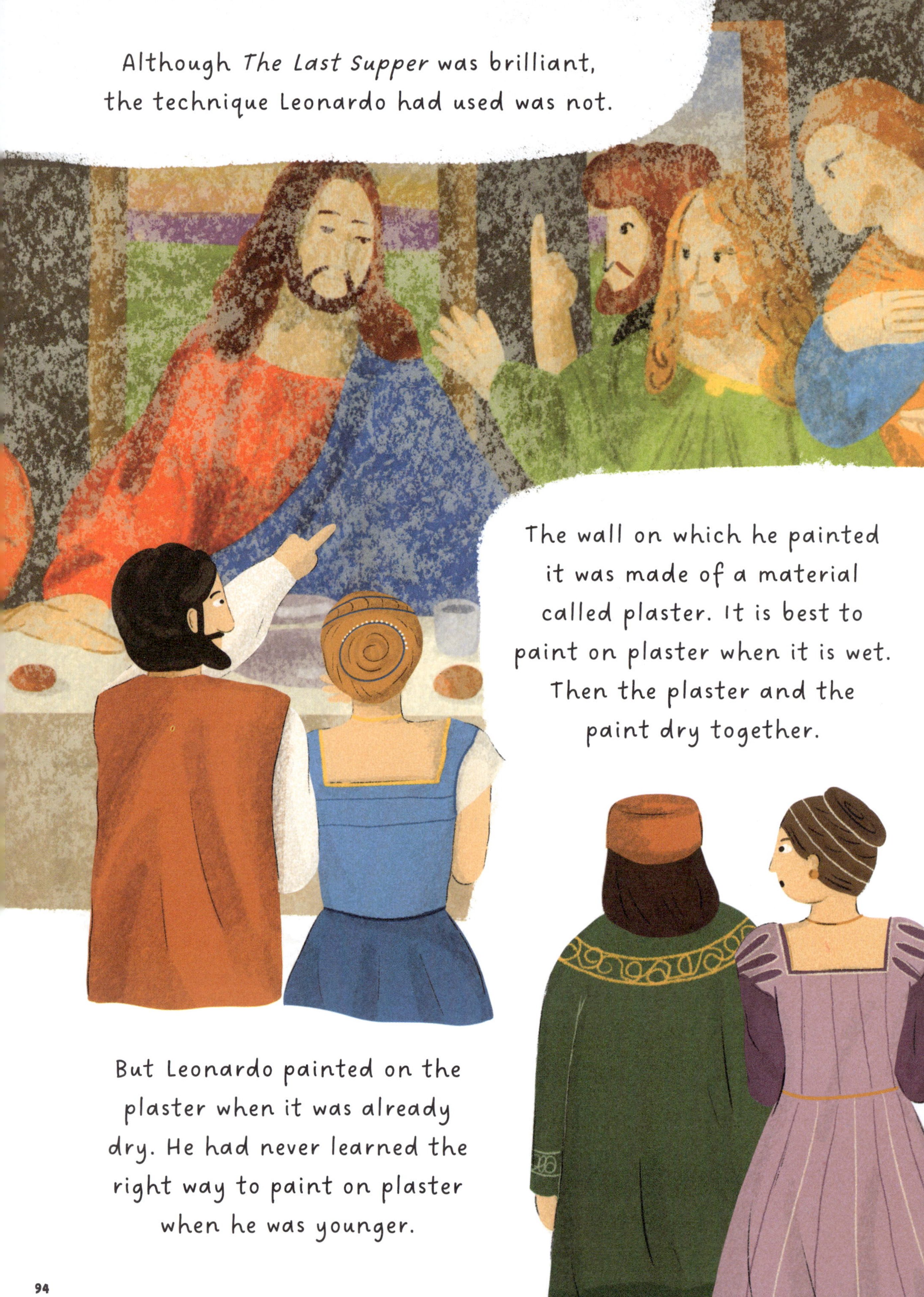

Although *The Last Supper* was brilliant, the technique Leonardo had used was not.

The wall on which he painted it was made of a material called plaster. It is best to paint on plaster when it is wet. Then the plaster and the paint dry together.

But Leonardo painted on the plaster when it was already dry. He had never learned the right way to paint on plaster when he was younger.

Also, he experimented with different types of paints. These paints did not stick to the plaster very well.

The Last Supper began to flake away.

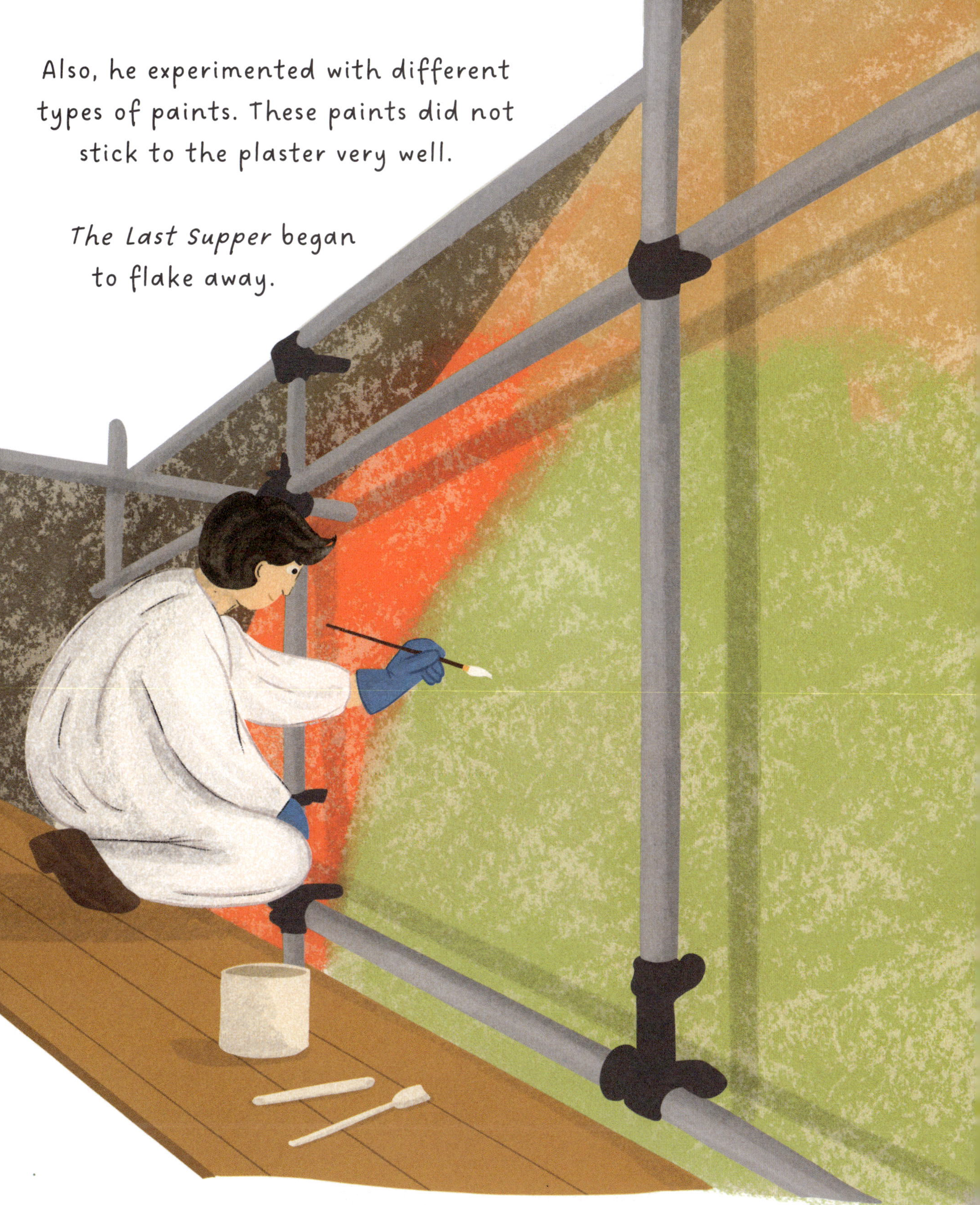

It has been fixed through the years, but most of Leonardo's original paint is gone.

Painting a FRESCO

Painting on plaster is called fresco painting. A good fresco painting is created in different steps.

In one of the most common methods, known as **buon fresco**, the base layers are made of **plaster**. Plaster starts out like a paste, made mostly from water, sand, and cement. The artist spreads out one to two layers of plaster and lets it dry.

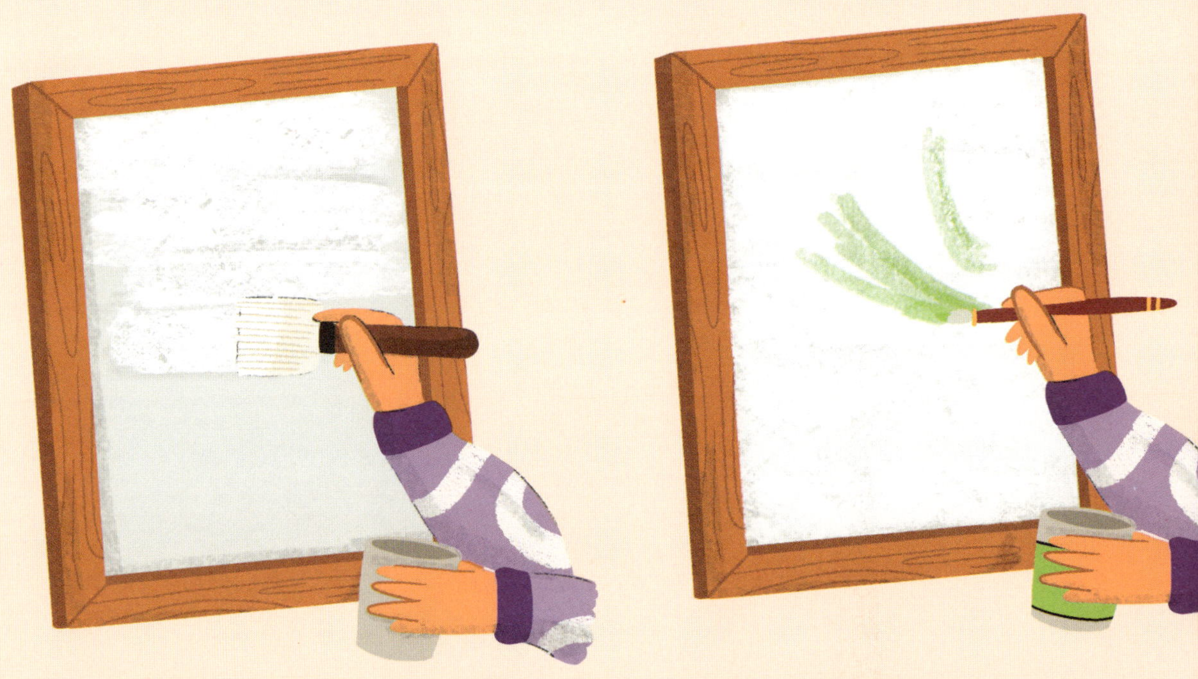

Once the first layers dry and harden, another layer of plaster is added on top. The artist must **paint** on this layer while it is still wet.

The best paint to use is a dry, colored **powder** mixed with water.

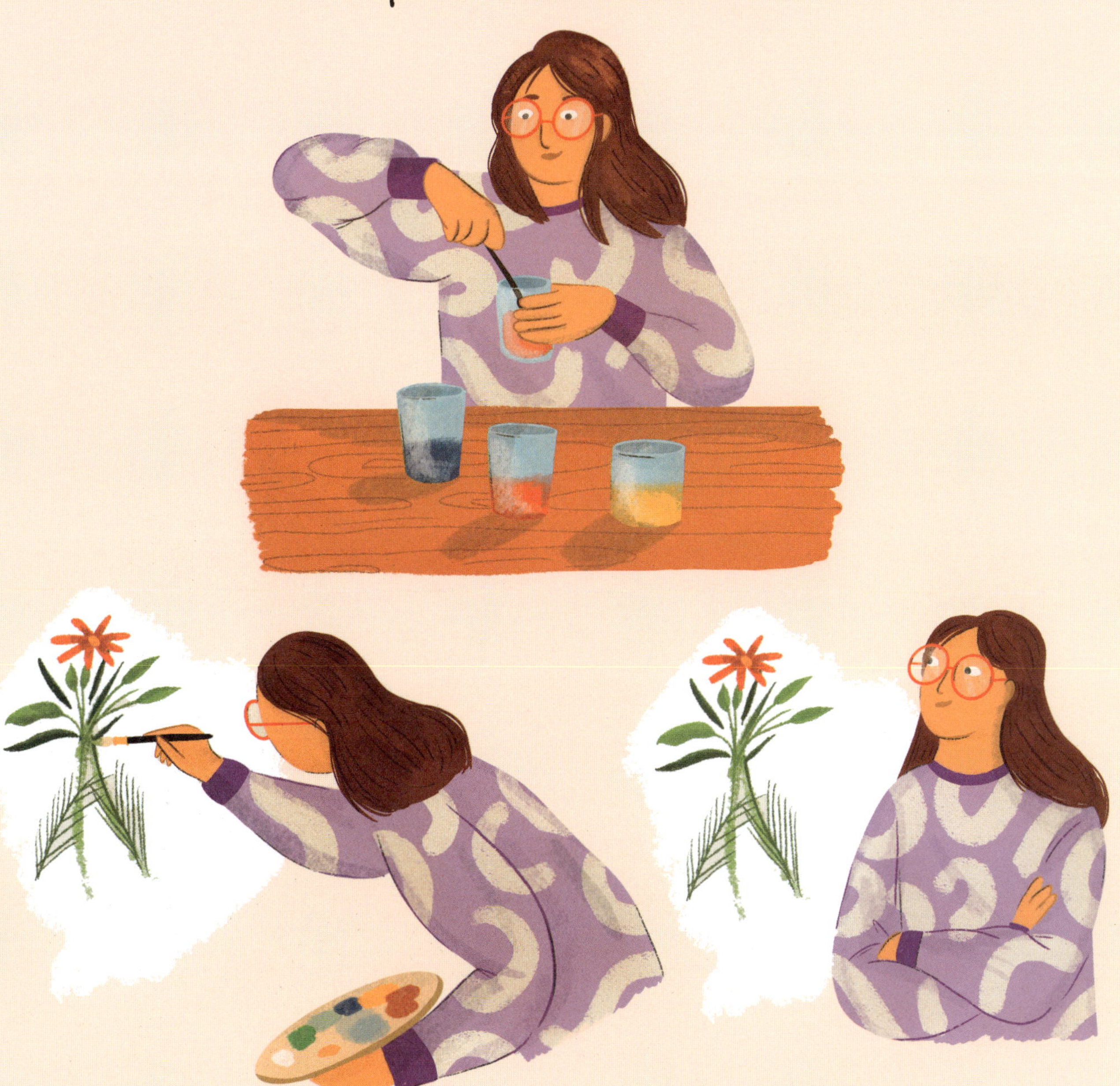

The artist will often spread out just enough wet plaster to paint on it in a single day. Then it **dries overnight**, and the artist starts the next day with more wet plaster.

THE FAMOUS SMILE

Leonardo's Masterpiece

In the early 1500s, Leonardo was asked to paint a portrait of a young woman. This portrait would become the world's most famous painting.

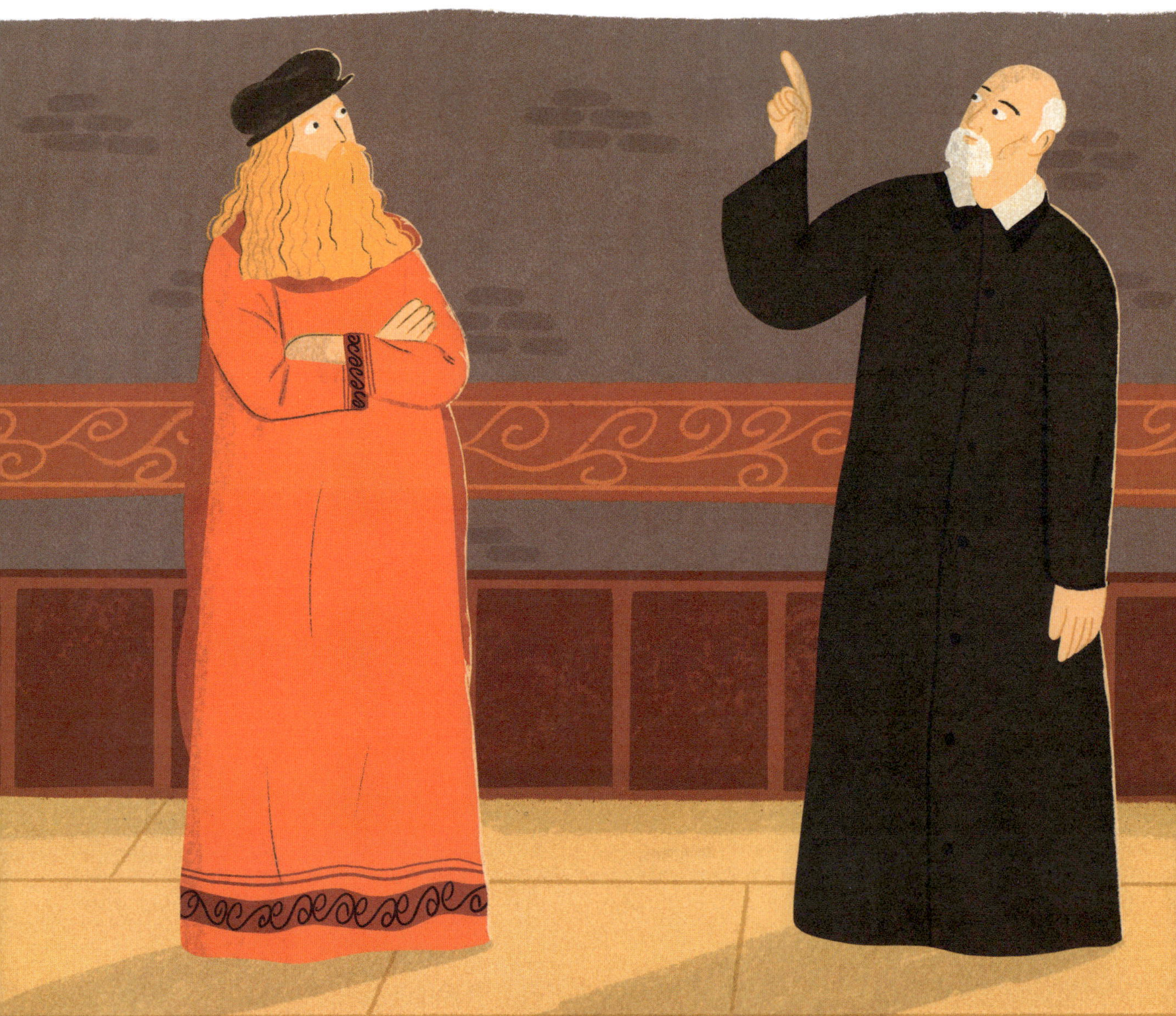

Leonardo had painted a few portraits before. This one would be for Francesco del Giocondo. He lived in Florence and was a wealthy merchant.

Francesco made most of his money selling different types of cloth, mostly silk. He had recently bought a new home and had gotten married for the second time.

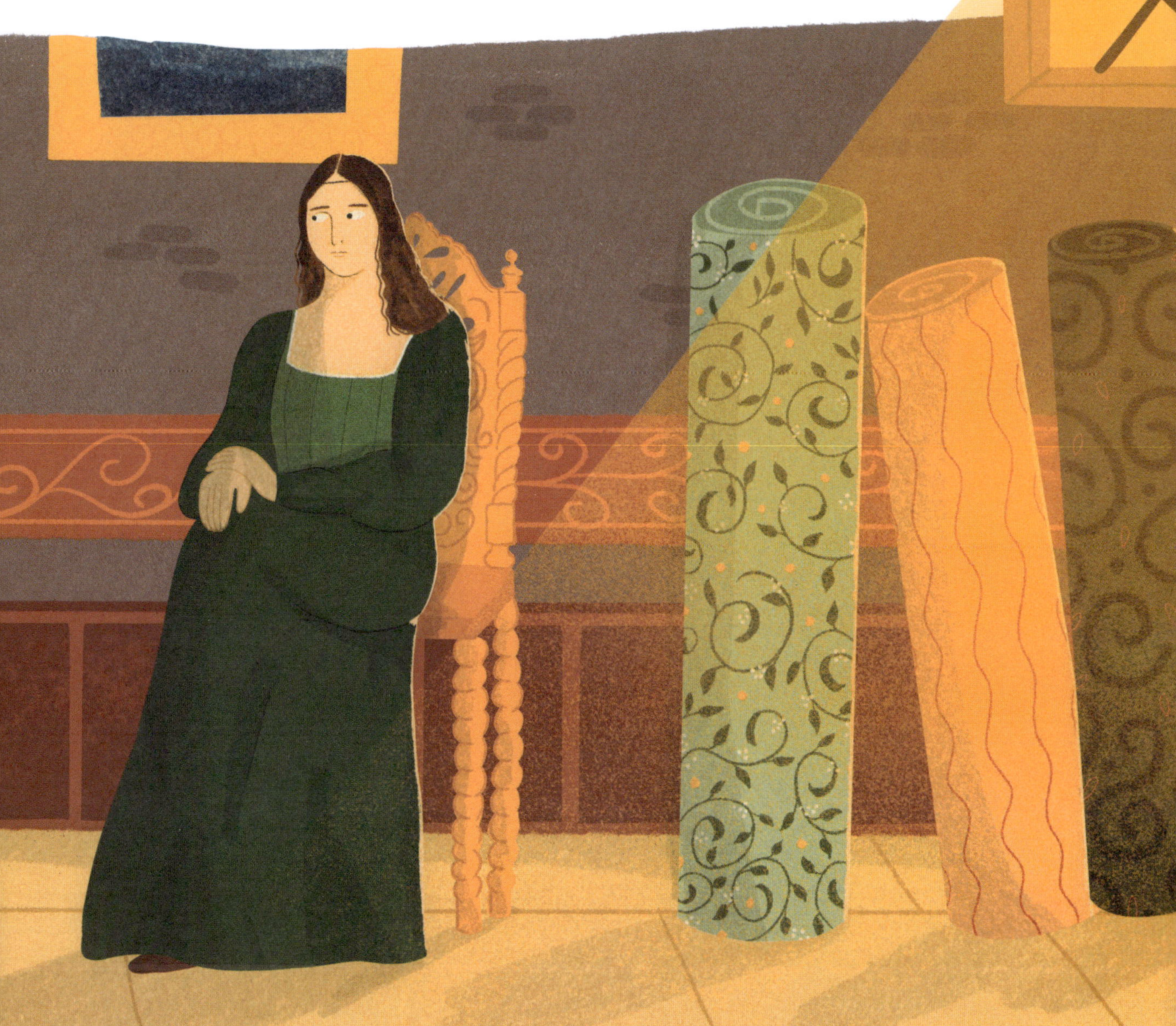

The name of his second wife was Lisa. Francesco wanted to hang the portrait of Lisa in his new house.

By the early 1500s, Leonardo wasn't doing much painting. His interests had moved to scientific studies, such as zoology and human anatomy.

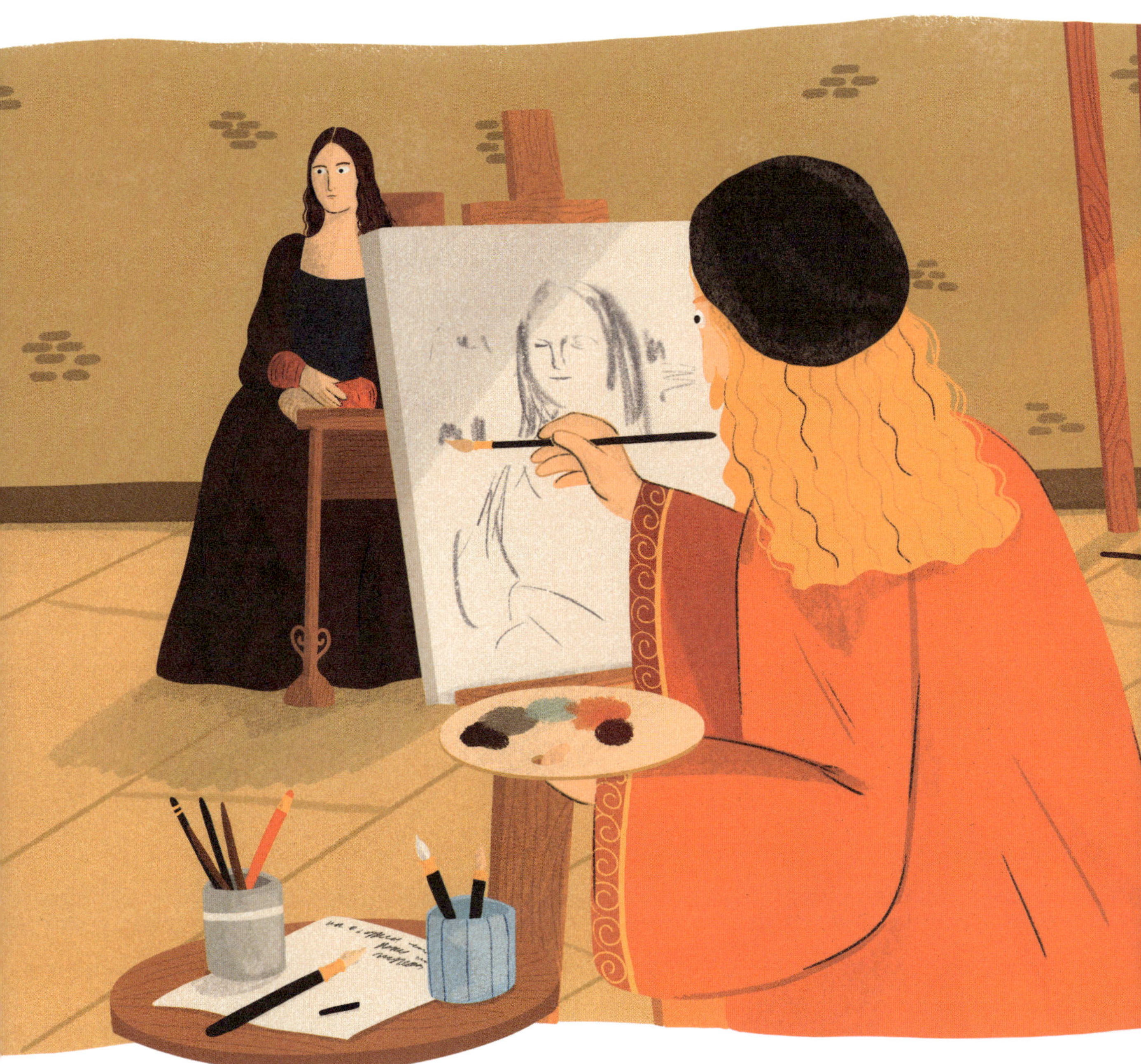

Leonardo had become famous for his artwork throughout Italy, and he finally had a little money in the bank. But it wouldn't be enough to last the rest of his life.

Leonardo's father, Piero, wanted to help. Piero knew Francesco del Giocondo well, so he encouraged Leonardo to do the painting.

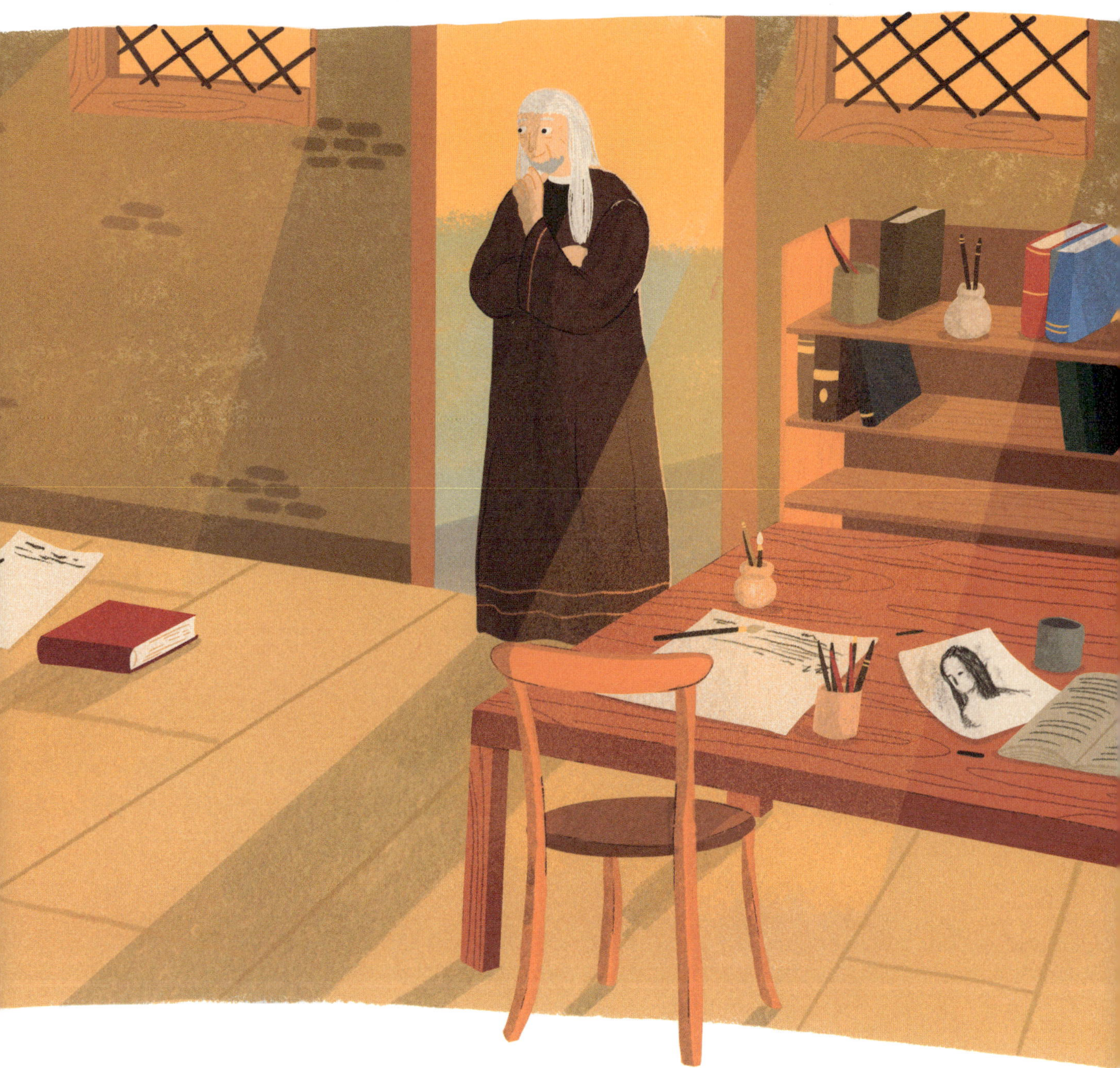

Leonardo accepted the job and started working on the portrait in 1503.

Leonardo liked that Lisa wasn't a religious figure or someone famous. And she had a natural beauty that seemed perfect for a portrait.

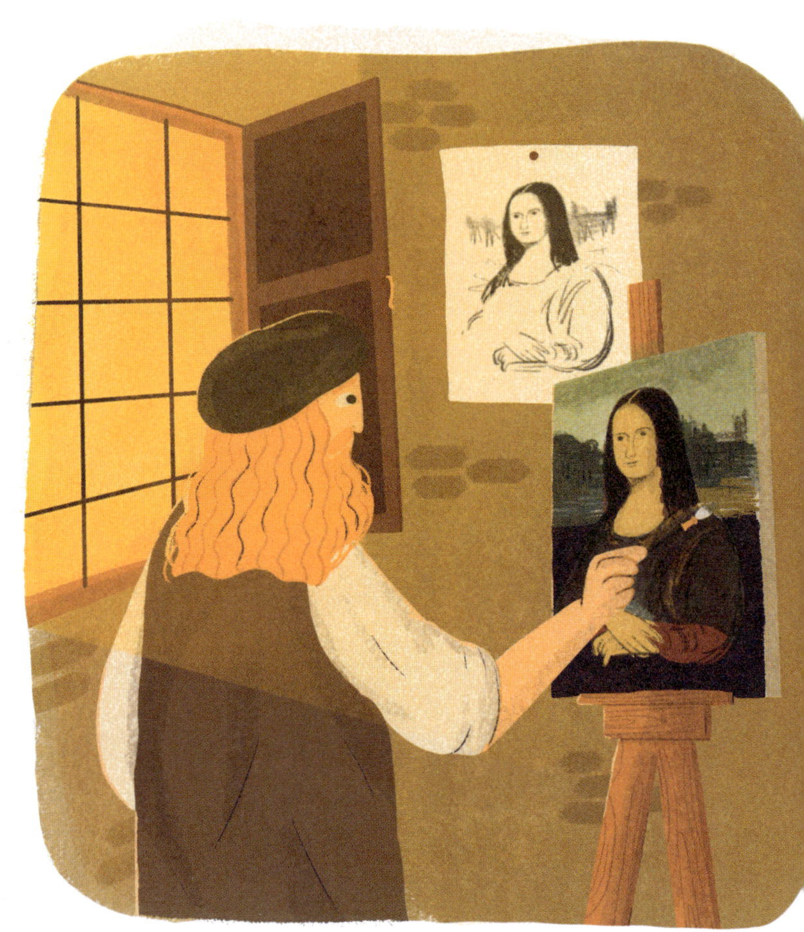

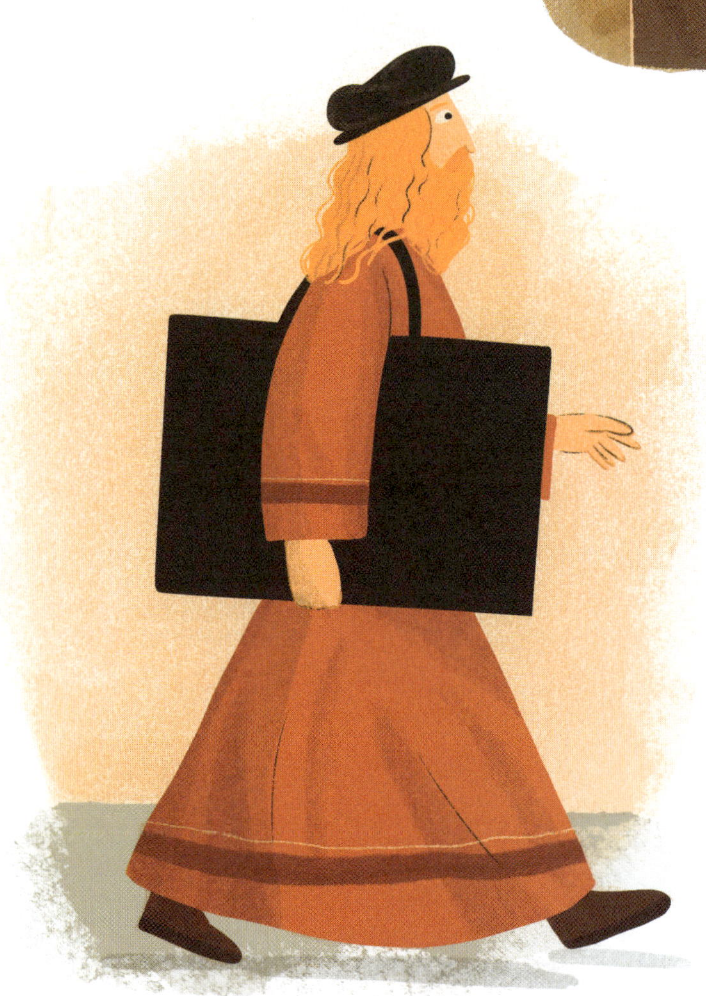

Leonardo created his paintings slowly, but he *really* took his time with this one. He brought it with him whenever he moved from one city to another.

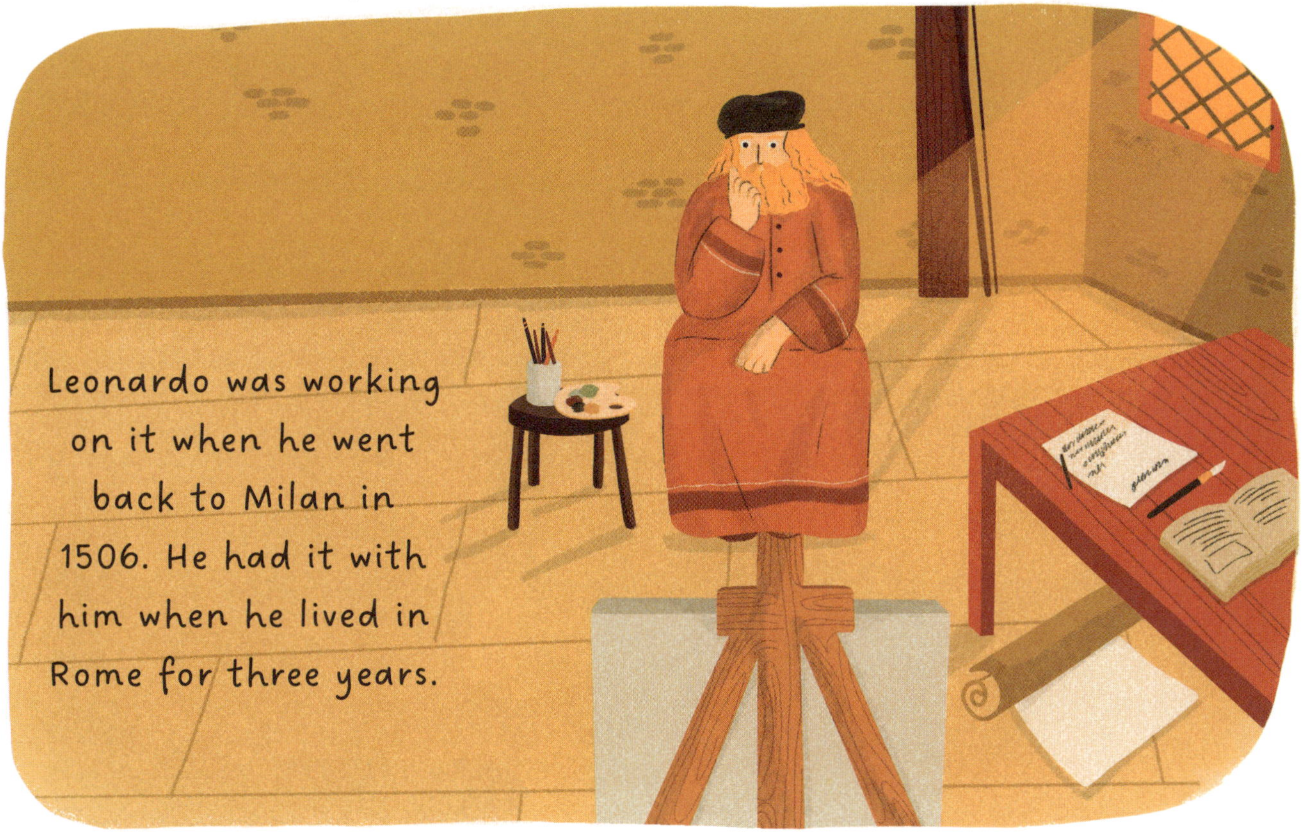

Leonardo was working on it when he went back to Milan in 1506. He had it with him when he lived in Rome for three years.

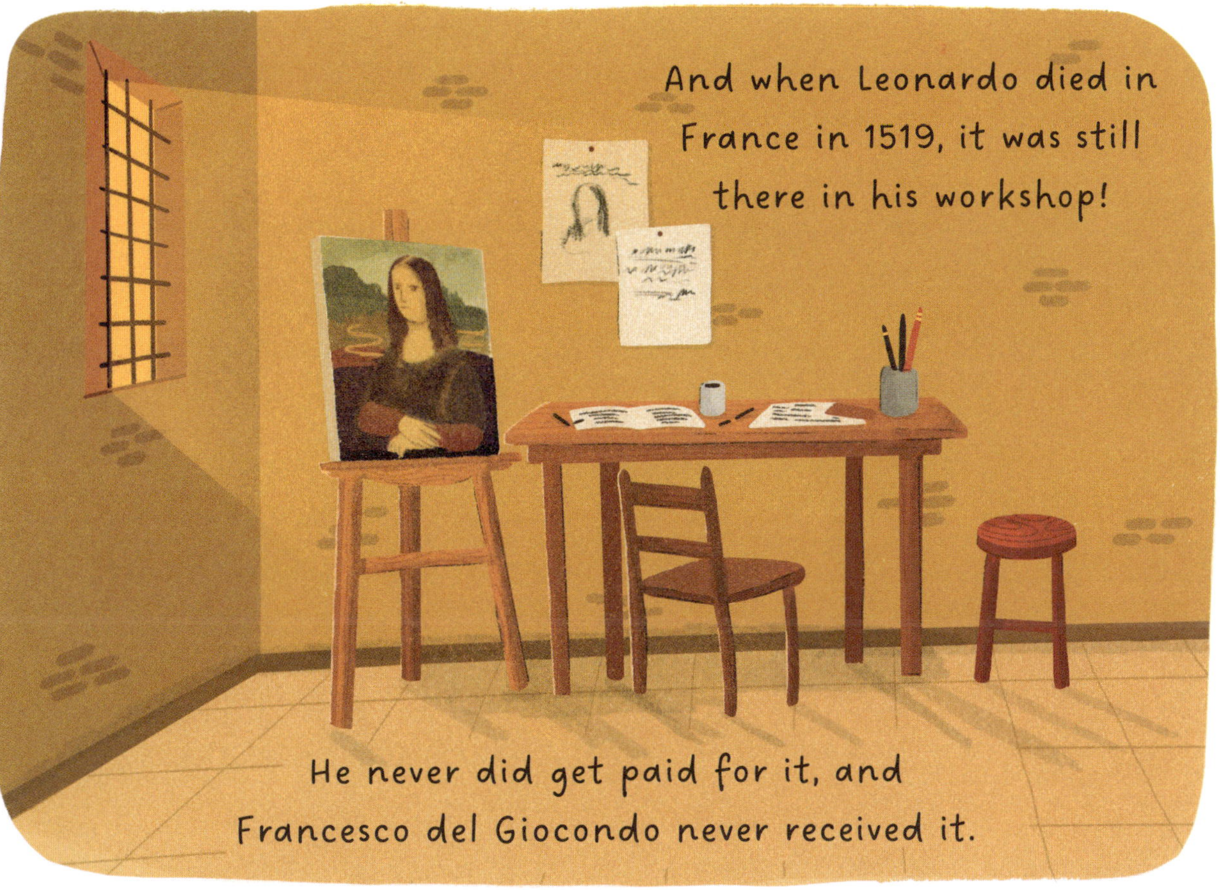

And when Leonardo died in France in 1519, it was still there in his workshop!

He never did get paid for it, and Francesco del Giocondo never received it.

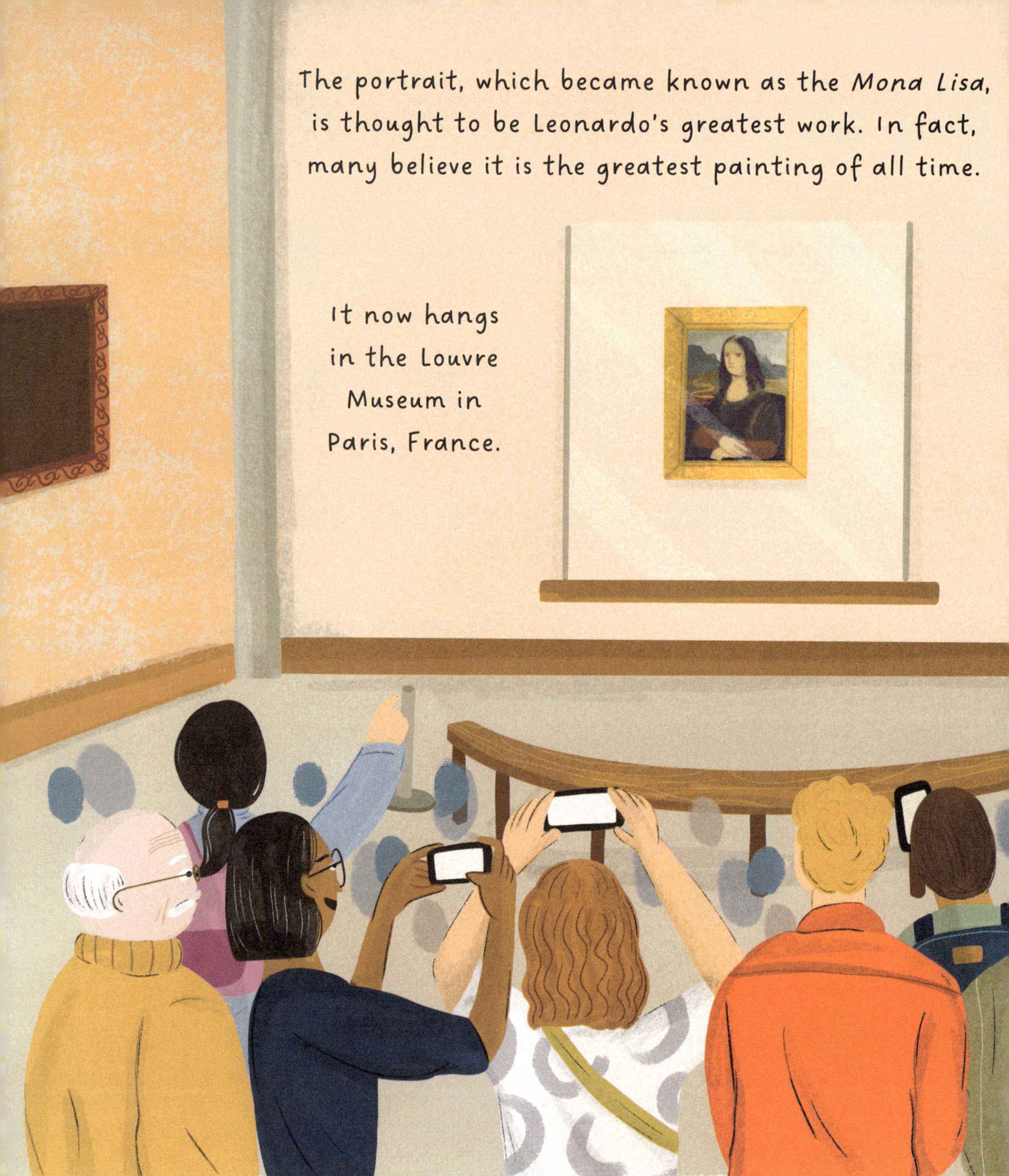

The portrait, which became known as the *Mona Lisa*, is thought to be Leonardo's greatest work. In fact, many believe it is the greatest painting of all time.

It now hangs in the Louvre Museum in Paris, France.

The original colors of the painting were bright and beautifully balanced.

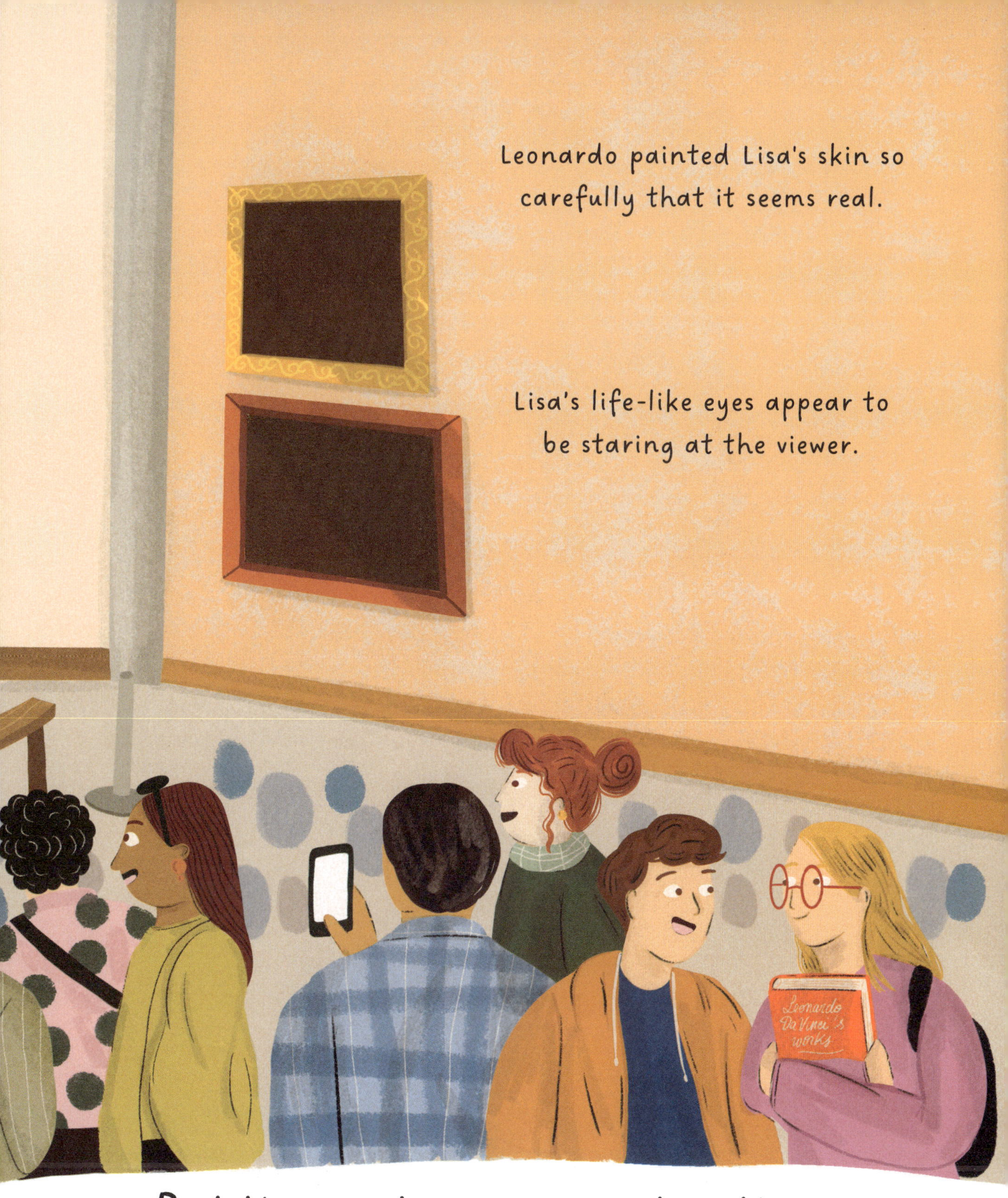

But the most famous part of the *Mona Lisa* is her mysterious smile. People have wondered what Lisa is feeling for centuries.

The True RENAISSANCE MAN

Leonardo's talents covered a broad range of subjects, including painting, sculpting, music, and engineering. His notebooks reflect his varied interests.

Leonardo lived during a time in Europe known as the **Renaissance**. It was an age of higher thinking, with a strong focus on art and education. It suited Leonardo perfectly!

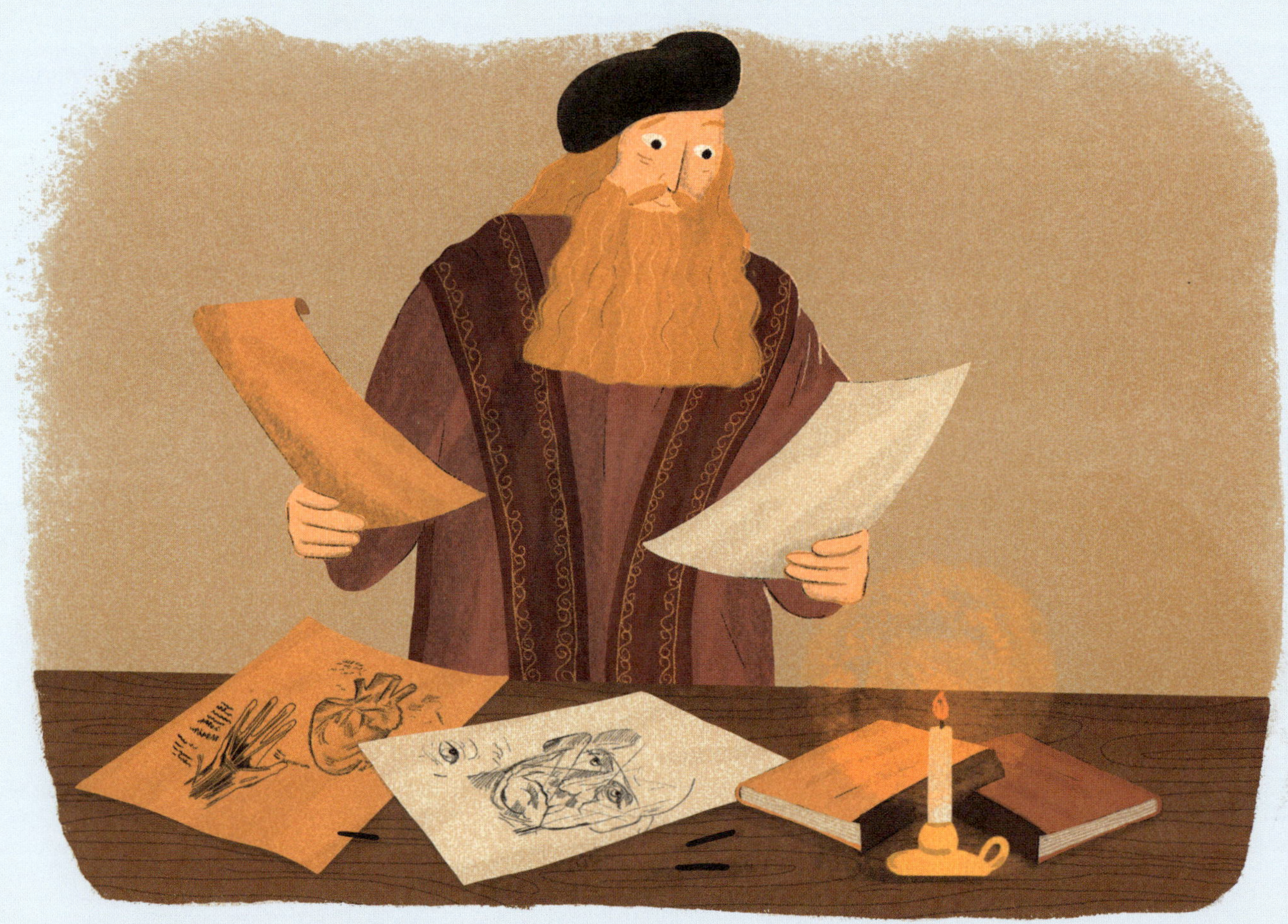

Leonardo also explored different **branches of science**, studying how the human heart functioned, what made water move the way it did, and why birds could fly. He was a true **Renaissance Man** in every way.

Leonardo kept **notebooks** through most of his life. He filled at least 7,000 pages with sketches, drawings, and notes. Experts believe thousands more may have been lost over time.

Leonardo could write well with both his right and left hands. When writing left-handed, he developed the habit of writing from right to left so the ink wouldn't smudge. This became known as a **"mirror script"** because it could be read more easily when held up to a mirror.

His notebooks are still being studied by **historians** today.

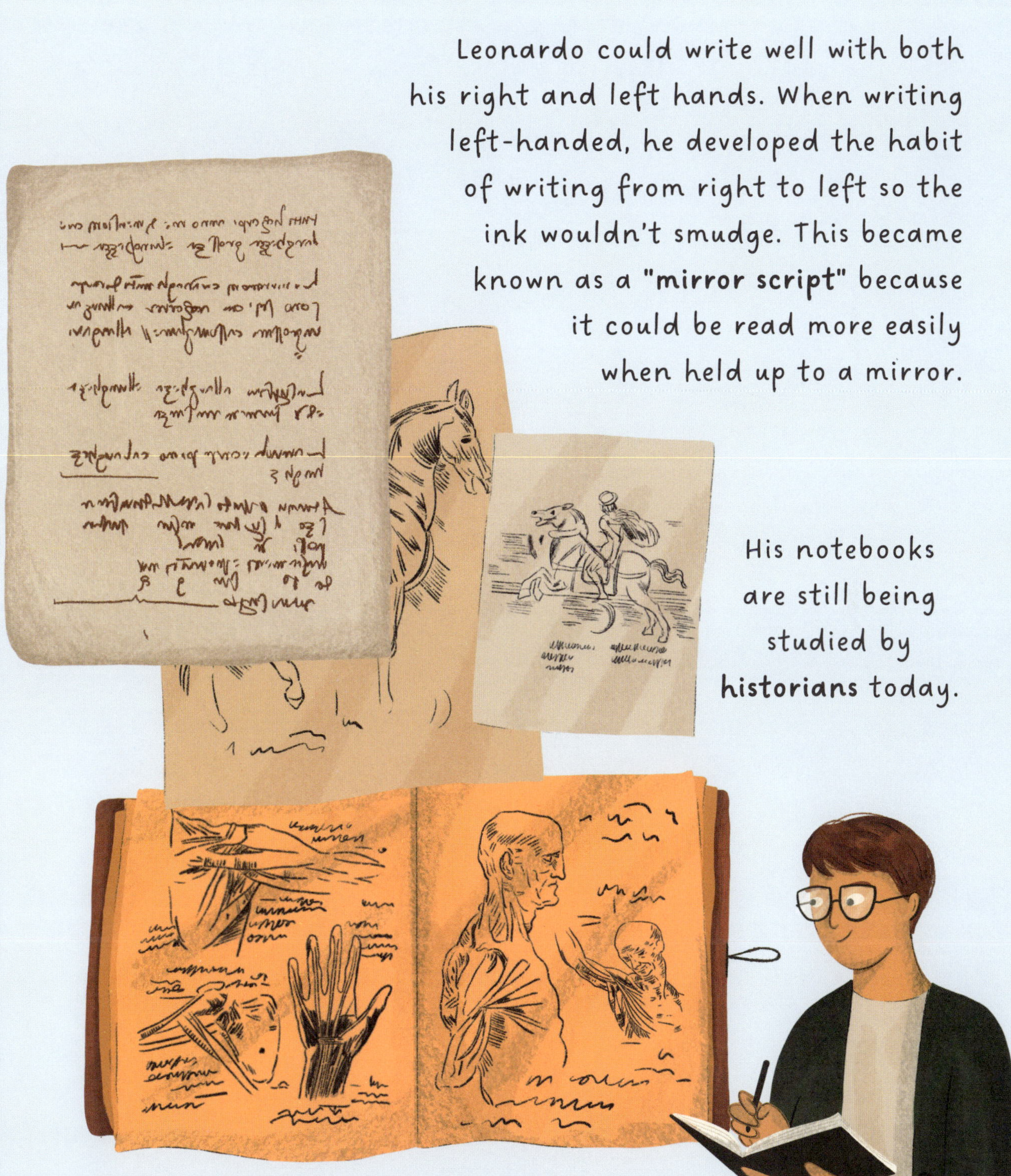

LEONARDO DA VINCI'S JOURNEY TO BECOMING A RENAISSANCE ICON

1452

15 April

Leonardo is **born** in Italy's Tuscan region in or near the town of Vinci.

Leonardo is accepted as an **apprentice** into the workshop of Florentine master Andrea del Verrocchio.

Verrocchio, Leonardo, and others place the **"golden ball"** they created atop the Cathedral of Santa Maria del Fiore.

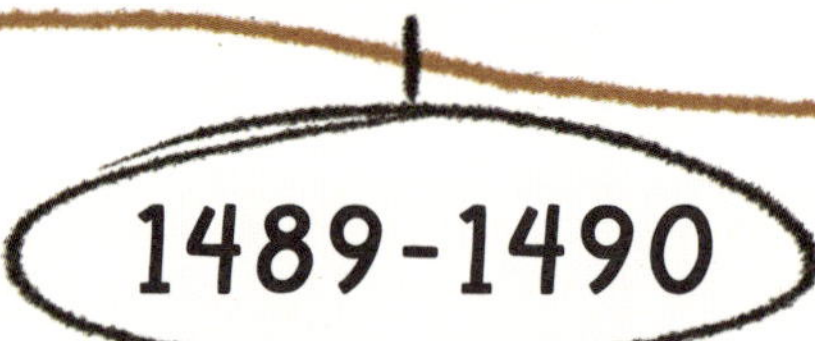

Leonardo begins a deep study of **human anatomy**. This will involve not only observing living people but cutting into dead ones.

During a live performance, Leonardo plays a **stringed instrument** of his own design for the Duke of Milan.

Leonardo begins work on ***The Last Supper***, which he will complete in 1498.

Leonardo develops a **theater stage** that can rotate, making it easier to go from one set to the next during a play.

Leonardo returns to Florence and is welcomed back as a **celebrity**.

1473

Leonardo begins sketching the Arno Valley, possibly the first **landscape drawings** intended as art ever made in Western culture.

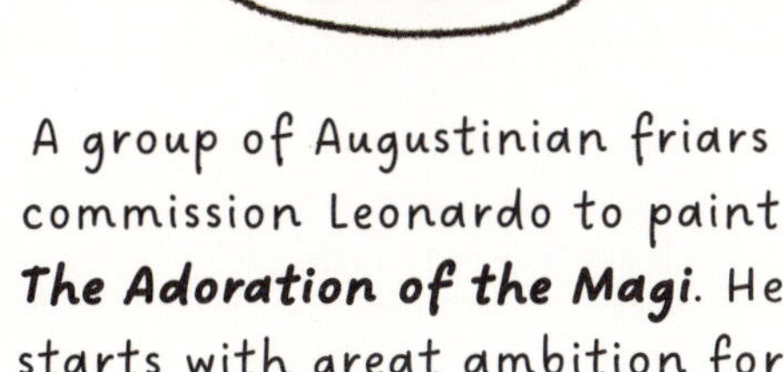

1481

A group of Augustinian friars commission Leonardo to paint ***The Adoration of the Magi***. He starts with great ambition for the work but never completes it.

1482

Leonardo **moves to Milan**. Not long after arriving in Milan, Leonardo writes a letter to the Duke, Ludovico Sforza, describing all sorts of services he can perform.

1487

Leonardo begins making sketches for his **"Ideal City,"** based on the city of Milan.

1503

Leonardo begins work on the ***Mona Lisa***, as commissioned by wealthy silk merchant Francesco del Giocondo.

1519

2 May

Leonardo **dies** at the age of 67, already a legend.

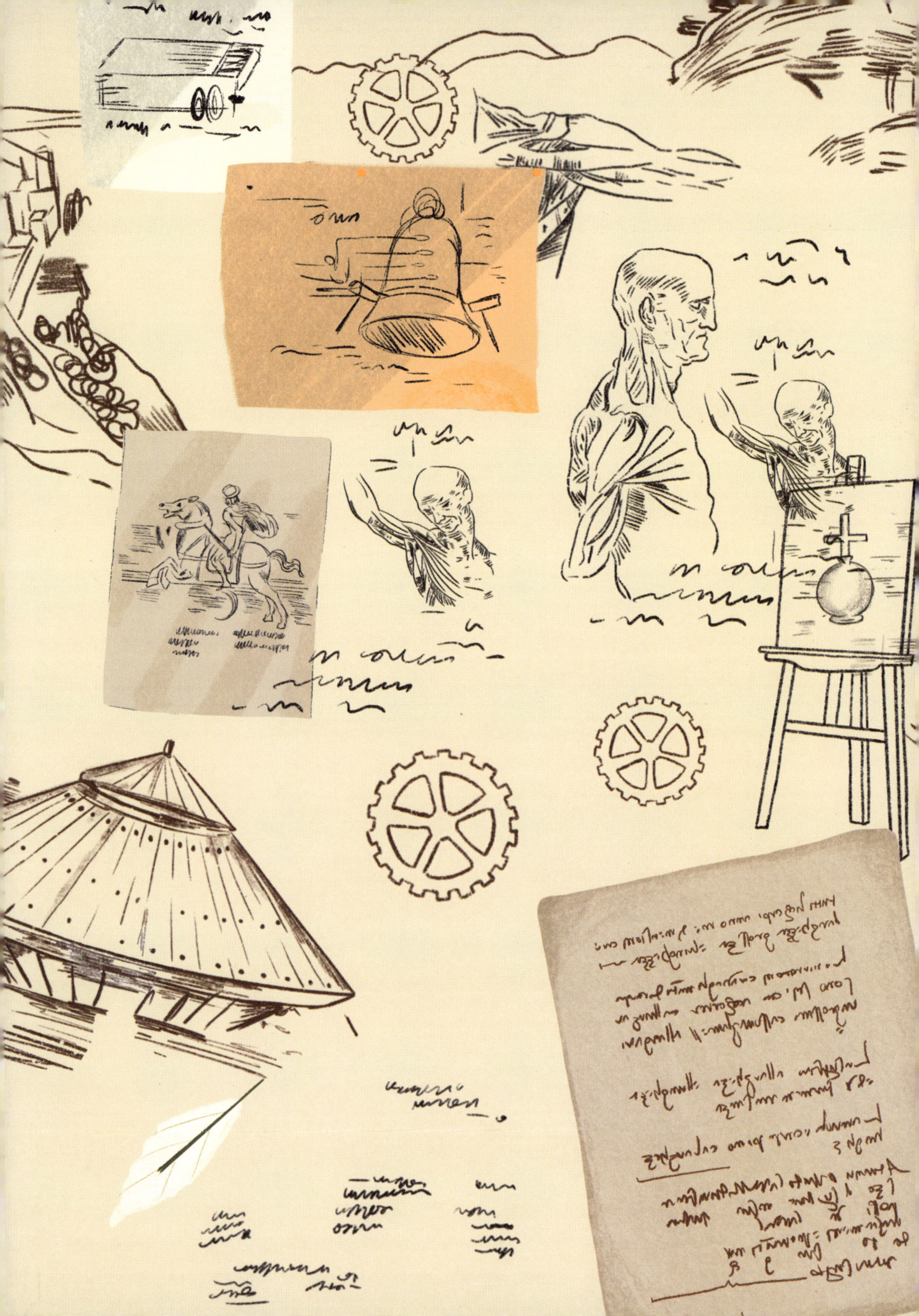